The Future of Library Service: Demographic Aspects and Implications

Edited by
FRANK L. SCHICK

Assistant Director, Library Services Branch
U. S. Office of Education

ILLINOIS CONTRIBUTIONS TO LIBRARIANSHIP NO. 6
UNIVERSITY OF ILLINOIS
GRADUATE SCHOOL OF LIBRARY SCIENCE
URBANA, ILLINOIS
1962

Library of Congress Catalog Card Number: 62-62687
Reprinted from *Library Trends,*
Volume 10, Numbers 1 and 2,
July and October 1961
Published February 1962

Printed by
Pantagraph Printing Company
Bloomington, Illinois

TABLE OF CONTENTS

PART I

PART II

Part I

◇◇

Foreword

THE EXTENDED DISCUSSION needed to develop thoroughly the topic of the demographic aspects of librarianship necessitated using two consecutive issues of *Library Trends*, the July and October numbers of 1961. The potential importance of the subject to the profession and the desire to make the material as easily available as possible has led to the decision by the Publications Board to reprint the two issues in this single combined volume.

In the pages which follow, especially in the material incorporating the statistical projections of the growth and movement of the population of the United States during the next two decades, the reader will find one key to the future of American libraries. Here, too, is an evaluation of the probable effects of those demographic influences insofar as it is possible for a group of thoughtful, imaginative people to peer into the years ahead. Doing this has been for them a stimulating intellectual exercise but one fraught with difficulties hardly anticipated.

The authors of the several articles which follow will disclaim, with vehemence, any imputation that they are soothsayers or prophets. Conscientious and responsible, they have guarded against uninhibited conjecture. Rather, sobered by the tremendous implications to American librarianship of population increase and fluidity, they have tried to think out the possible and probable effects of this expansion and shifting upon libraries of all types in this country. It is hoped that these reflections and prognostications, based upon the informed and expert opinion of competent demographers, will be useful to those responsible for the planning and development of libraries and library services.

One immediate use of these two issues, here reprinted, will be their use as the working papers for an Institute on "The Future of Library Education" to be held in Cleveland, April 25–28, 1962, under the auspices of the Library Services Branch of the U.S. Office of Edu-

[6]

cation and The Western Reserve University School of Library Science.

The Publications Board for *Library Trends* wishes to acknowledge with appreciation the financial assistance of the Council on Library Resources and the Grolier Foundation. These grants, secured through the efforts of Dr. Frank L. Schick, made possible two meetings of the contributors and the preparation of many tabulations and charts, many of which are included in this publication.

Harold Lancour

Introduction

FRANK L. SCHICK

THE IDEA TO DIRECT the attention of librarians, educators and all those responsible for library development to problems of the future occurred originally to the writer in 1947. Working on a survey of public library administrative problems,[1] he found that agenda of library trustee board meetings were indicative of future policy changes, in this case the recognition of the significance of audio-visual materials for public library use. Lack of time precluded a follow-up of this type of study.

At the annual conference of the A.B.P.C. in 1956, F. H. Wagman's paper on the future of academic libraries [2] was a reminder that looking ahead demographically could yield useful insights for administrative decisions. The most direct invitation to tackle the problem was supplied by R. M. Hall, former Assistant Commissioner (of Education) for Research, who commented in the fall of 1958 that the statistical work of the Library Services Branch relating to schools and libraries is sound but provides few guidelines for the planning of future needs. This criticism provided the shock of recognition which led to action.

As a result, possible approaches for a broadly-gauged survey were discussed with J. G. Lorenz, Director of the Library Services Branch, who provided every encouragement and assistance to arrange for such a study, which was to cover all major fields of Librarianship. It was agreed that this project be undertaken outside the Library Services Branch to permit the participation of the many skilled specialists who would be assisted by our staff. An approach to the Editor of *Library Trends* revealed his interest, and these issues are the result.

Points of departure for an exploration into the future of libraries were recently made in several instances which seem particularly

[8]

appropriate. The American Library Association prepared for its 1961 Cleveland Conference an exhibit under the title "Libraries in the Sixties, ALA Goals for Action." Three panels here reproduced indicate graphically the gaps between the standards of school, college and university, and public libraries and the present status. J. N. Gardner stated recently that the "1960's should be a great decade for agencies with a special responsibility to facilitate learning outside the formal system, such as libraries, university extension divisons and adult education departments of public schools. The one hazard ahead is that heavy enrollments and straitened finances may lead universities and boards of education to cut the budget of what seems a peripheral activity. This must be avoided. It is no longer peripheral." [3]

Gilbert Highet, while discussing the future of knowledge, looked farther ahead when he wrote:

Three areas of human effort in which we can hope for massive progress during the next century, and in which progress will most surely benefit humanity, are literacy, land use, and public health. Of these, the one in which most progress is possible is surely literacy.

Together with that, we may hope for the steady expansion of libraries throughout the world. No library is useless. The smallest local collection of books may contain unique treasures or inspire a genius. Every library is an assertion of man's durable trust in intelligence as a protection against irrationalism, force, time, and death. A town or church or school without an adequate collection of books is only half alive. Indeed, libraries are far more necessary now than benefactors like Carnegie ever imagined, because, in the constantly growing flood of useless and distracting appeals to our surface attention—rapidly written magazine articles, flimsy and fragmentary newspapers, and torrents of talk, talk, talk pouring from the radio—they provide a place to rest, be quiet, step off the moving platform of the Moment, and think.[4]

Libraries, while basically in agreement with this statement, would not have it left unsaid that, their concept of library service reaches now beyond books towards the records of human thought and imagination, toward all the manifestations of man's unconquerable mind, regardless of their format, be it a book, pamphlet, disc or film. Libraries are not merely a silent refuge from the noise abroad, but in themselves throbbing creations of our civilization, ready to accept youth and the aged to share with them enduring values and temporary fancy.

[9]

SCHOOL LIBRARIES
fill basic educational needs

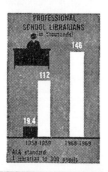

PROFESSIONAL SCHOOL LIBRARIANS
(in thousands)

146
112
19.4

1958-1959   1968-1969

ALA standard:
1 librarian to 300 pupils

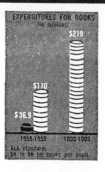

EXPENDITURES FOR BOOKS
(in millions)

$219
$170
$36.9

1958-1959   1968-1969

ALA standard:
$4 to $6 for books per pupil

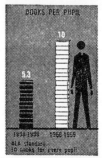

BOOKS PER PUPIL

10
5.3

1958-1959   1968-1959

ALA standard:
10 books for every pupil

■ ACTUAL   ☐ RECOMMENDED

COLLEGE and UNIVERSITY LIBRARIES
workshops of the academic world

4-YEAR INSTITUTIONS

PRIVATE   PUBLIC

below standard 60%   33%

ALA standard: minimum of 50,000 volumes

below standard 57%   21%

ALA standard: minimum of 3 professional librarians

below standard 62%   69%

ALA standard: minimum of 5% expenditure ratio

2-YEAR INSTITUTIONS

PRIVATE   PUBLIC

below standard 90%   84%

ALA standard: minimum of 20,000 volumes

below standard 78%   71%

ALA standard: minimum of 2 professional librarians

below standard 68%   58%

ALA standard: minimum of 5% expenditure ratio

PUBLIC LIBRARIES
for lifelong learning

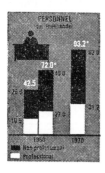

PERSONNEL
(in thousands)

93.2*
72.0*
42.5
62.0
45.8
27.0
26.0
10.0
31.2

1960   1970

■ Non-professional
☐ Professional

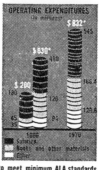

OPERATING EXPENDITURES
(in millions)

$832*
545
$630*
410
166.4
$260
190
126
120.6
94

1960   1970

■ Salaries
☐ Books and other materials
☐ Other

*to meet minimum ALA standards

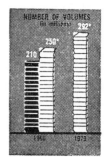

NUMBER OF VOLUMES
(in millions)

292*
250*
210

1960   1970

An entirely different aspect of future development of libraries deals with the automation of information storage and retrieval and the science of miniaturization. J. G. Kemeny recently estimated that a "book page would occupy about one square millimeter." "Thus," he explains, "more than 645 pages could be stored on a square inch [of tape]." [5]

As envisaged by this mathematician, library materials on tape would permit random access. "Instead of using a traditional card catalog," he forecasts, "a scholar would find the volume or article he sought by using something equivalent to a telephone dial system." [6] Such a central library would be linked to other libraries by a communications cable. This forecast would indicate that individual libraries are destined to continue to play their role and to succeed through their proven talent for combining adherence to values of the past with adaptation to new technological developments.

The "Century 21" Exhibit to be held during 1962 in Seattle, Washington, plans to include a "Library 21," which would display these concepts through appropriate equipment and technologies adaptable to library purposes by demonstrating typical library resources and services which can best be handled centrally because smaller satellite libraries would lack sufficient staff, resources or funds. "Library 21" will stress the value of interlibrary communication and cooperation and will attempt to integrate machines into an environment of books and will display new equipment, imaginative ideas and advanced library programs for individual services. As now envisaged, it would show the library as the community's information center by providing an active environment for adult and self education, research and recreation.

The general theme of the two issues of *Library Trends* dealing with the "Future of Library Service: Demographic Aspects and Implications" has been approached in three stages: Philip M. Hauser and Martin Taitel's lead article and supporting materials, forming the bases for further elaboration by subject specialists; the group of articles by specialists; and finally a summary by David H. Clift and Germaine Krettek, the last reflecting the point of view of the American Library Association.

Where libraries are to proceed from here to render services which a dynamic society is most likely to require, expect, and demand is given with detailed emphasis in the following papers. It is hoped that they will serve as significant guideposts for challenging opportunities and their solutions.

References

1. Schick, F. L.: Board-Librarian Relationships in American Public Libraries. *Library Quarterly,* 19:201-207, July 1949.

2. Wagman, F. H.: College Library Market. *Publishers' Weekly,* 171:28-30, June 17, 1957.

3. Gardner, J. W.: U.S. President's Commission on National Goals. *Goals for Americans; Programs for Action in the Sixties* . . . Englewood Cliffs, N.J., Prentice Hall, 1960, p. 95.

4. Highet, Gilbert: *Man's Unconquerable Mind.* New York, Columbia University Press, 1954, p. 47.

5. Schmeck, H. M., Jr.: Librarian of 2,000 May Be Computer. *New York Times,* March 28, 1961, p. 41.

6. *Ibid.*

Population Trends—Prologue to Library Development

PHILIP M. HAUSER

AND

MARTIN TAITEL

LIBRARIES SERVE PEOPLE. Facts and expectations about the people to be served are basic ingredients in the decision-making process of those whose tasks are to design and operate libraries. Relevant knowledge does not guarantee good decisions, but does increase the chances of attaining goals.

Included in the relevant facts and expectations are numbers of persons, their geographical distribution and their attributes. In this article, only a small part of the information about people relevant to major decisions concerning libraries will be presented. The presentation will be directed toward the broad overall picture in the United States. It should be recognized, however, that most or at least a very large proportion of decisions are made for local situations which vary widely.

Also it should be noted that the authors have drawn primarily upon the publications of the U.S. Bureau of the Census. The article was prepared before any final data were available and is, therefore, based upon preliminary data, except as otherwise noted.

Until the beginning of World War II, the long-time trend of the total population of the United States had been consistent growth *but at a declining rate*. The population doubled five times between 1790 and 1950, and the time for a doubling was 25 years between 1790 and 1865 (three doublings); 35 years between 1865 and 1900; 50 years between 1900 and 1950. During the depression of the thirties, the

Mr. Hauser is Chairman and Professor, Department of Sociology, and Director, Population Research and Training Center, University of Chicago. Mr. Taitel is Statistician, Population Research and Training Center, and Research Associate, Graduate School of Business, University of Chicago.

birth rate and the population growth rate reached new lows. Widely accepted population projections during the 1930's presented 165 million or thereabouts as the maximum population to be reached by the century's end and to be followed, perhaps, by smaller numbers shortly thereafter.[1] This is in comparison with 133 million in 1940; 63 million in 1890; 32 million in 1860; and 17 million in 1840.

But the projections of the thirties have already been contradicted. In the forties and fifties, there was an upsurge in marriage and fertility rates, neither anticipated with regard to magnitude or to duration. In consequence, the population of the United States passed the 165 million mark in 1955 and is over 180 million today.

Already considerable research has been done to uncover "explanations" and "causality"; much more will be done in the future. Here we may note that World War II and developments since then, such as intense international tensions and unprecedented levels of national output, present an environment vastly different from that of the thirties. With this changing of circumstances, the people of the United States have moved vigorously in the direction of expanding their numbers. The vigor of expansion has already been and may be further tempered by an enlightened appreciation of the inevitable consequences—too many people for too little earth. Yet, in looking forward, it seems clear that population growth rates during the next few decades can best be gauged in terms of the fifties rather than the thirties. In short, the pace of population growth can be expected to be substantial.

Geographic Distribution and Change. The final census count of the number of inhabitants of the United States as of April 1, 1960, was 179.3 million. That figure represents a population of 28 million or 18.5 per cent above the comparable 1950 figure of 151.3 million for the 50 states and the District of Columbia. Both counts exclude members of the Armed Forces and their dependents living abroad, crews of American vessels at sea or in foreign ports, and American citizens living in foreign countries.

Table I shows the states ranked by 1960 population. New York, continuing as our largest state, had a population of 16.8 million in 1960. At the other extreme was Alaska with a population of fewer than one-quarter million, a fact which means that New York had 74 times as many inhabitants as Alaska.

Over 40 per cent of our population lives in our six largest states, New York, California, Pennsylvania, Illinois, Ohio and Texas, each with over 9 million persons. Only 10.1 per cent of our population resides in the 20 states and the District of Columbia, each of which has fewer than 1.8 million inhabitants.

The 28 million gain in total population was not evenly distributed throughout the country (Table II). More than 60 per cent of the increase in numbers was accounted for by eight states, each of which gained more than 1 million persons during the nineteen fifties. California alone gained over 5 million; Florida over 2 million; Texas, New York and Ohio, over 1.7 million each; and Michigan, Illinois and New Jersey, between 1 and 1.5 million persons each.

During the decade, despite the population boom for the nation as a whole, Arkansas, Mississippi, West Virginia and the District of Columbia actually registered declines. For Arkansas and Mississippi, the losses of the fifties were continuations of the losses which occurred during the forties. By contrast, the two other states, which lost population in the forties, North Dakota and Oklahoma, reversed the pattern and showed some population increases during the fifties.

The range of state growth rates was substantial, and this range is partially portrayed in Chart I. Florida was the striking leader with a 78.7 per cent increase in population. In the ranking of states by size, it jumped from 20th to 10th position between 1950 and 1960. At the other extreme was a 7.2 per cent *decline* for West Virginia. Half the states, however, were concentrated in a relatively narrow range from 8.5 to 28.5 per cent.

A complex of factors lies behind the differences in growth of the individual states. Migration provided the primary surface explanation of the differences for some individual states, most especially those with extreme rates of change. And behind migration were more basic economic, social and even political factors. Thus, California and Florida, combining desirable climates with economic advantages, have drawn people to them in large numbers. By contrast, West Virginia, Arkansas and Mississippi, with economic growth or social problems, have lost people, on balance, to other states. In addition to migration are the intrastate explanations, such as differences in birth, death and marriage rates. These, like migration, rest upon more basic factors, such as racial and ethnic composition, urbanization, educational level, income level, and age composition, which differ widely among the states. For example, in Alaska, relatively youthful in both biologic and economic terms, there was a relatively high crude birth rate of 37 per thousand and a relatively low crude death rate of 6 per thousand

[15]

in 1959; by contrast, in much more mature Maine, the corresponding figures were 24 and 12, respectively.

The unevenness of population change during the fifties is dramatically shown by the proportions for the various states of the counties which lost population (Table III). These data show the extent to which migration occurred within the nation. According to the 1960 Census, there were 3,107 counties. Despite the very large population increase of 18.5 per cent for the entire nation, 1,578, or 51 per cent, of these counties actually lost population during the fifties as revealed by preliminary Census tabulations. Some counties in every state, except Connecticut and Delaware (both with substantial population increases), lost population. Even in Florida, Nevada and Arizona, states with the largest rates of population increase, almost 20 per cent of the counties registered population declines. In California, where population increased by over 5.1 million persons, 7 out of 58 counties lost population during the decade.

The state-by-state proportions of counties with population declines reflect the exodus of people from rural, especially farm and distressed areas, which took place during the fifties. It is safe to draw this conclusion despite the fact that, at this writing, detailed statistics from the 1960 Census on the farm population and on the economic characteristics of the people of the United States are not yet available. An enumeration of the states in which 50 per cent or more of the counties lost population indicates, almost without exception, that each state in the list was either (a) predominantly a rural or farm area in 1950; (b) if it had a large industrial or non-farm population, it also had large expanses of farm and rural territory; or (c) it contained economically distressed areas. On the other hand, an enumeration of the states in which less than 30 per cent of the counties lost population shows that, for the most part, they are highly industrialized or urbanized areas with comparative economic advantages. This group includes 8 of the 10 states in which, in 1950, more than 70 per cent of the population was classified as urban.

In Table IV, a projection of the total population of the United States for 1980 is shown as 246 million. This projection is based on the assumption that the fertility level of the United States will be at the 1949-51 level from 1965-70 to 1980, after a decline from the postwar high level of 1955-57. It assumes further that death rates will continue to decline moderately, that net immigration will average about 300,000 per year, and that no catastrophic events, such as war, will occur. This projection is conservative since it assumes that the postwar birth rate boom will decline during the current decade.

A population of 246 million in 1980 would represent an increase after 1960 of 66 million persons, an increase of 37 per cent. Though such a growth rate would be only slightly below that for the fifties, it would mean a greater increase in number, year by year, than occurred during the fifties. The Bureau of the Census projections of population for 1980 range from a low of 231 million to a high of 273 million. To match population increase alone, libraries must be prepared to expand from a minimum of around 30 per cent to a maximum of over 50 per cent.

The ranges of possibilities about the projections for geographic divisions, shown in Table IV, are percentagewise significantly greater than those for the United States as a whole. The range of assumptions necessary to cover future possibilities is wide in comparison with that for the nation as a whole. For example, rough estimates of net migration between geographic divisions during eight years of the fifties include figures ranging from 10 to 20 per cent of total population.[2] Net migration within the United States as a whole, of course, is zero. Also, the possible effect of changes in death rates is limited for the United States as a whole; but for, say, the East South Central states, it may be possible for changes to alter substantially the course of population growth. Caution in using the figures is obviously advisable.

The projections in Tables IV and V and Chart II are based on the general underlying assumption that past trends in growth factors and growth patterns will continue. One consequence of this assumption is that the projections show population increases for every division. The differences in growth rates among the geographic divisions between 1960 and 1980 are projected as large. At one extreme is the East South Central Division for which an increase of only 8 per cent is projected. At the other extreme is the Pacific Division for which a 62 per cent increase in population is projected.

About 26 million or 39 per cent of the total projected population increase of 66 million will be accounted for by the Middle Atlantic and East North Central Divisions. The projection is that they will continue to have 39 per cent of the population and will remain the most populous. Highly industrialized and urbanized, further developments in those directions are anticipated. The two next most populous divisions, the South Atlantic and the Pacific, account for another 38 per cent of the projected increase; their projected proportion of the total population in 1980 is almost 30 per cent, compared with 26 per cent in 1960. These divisions include not only areas with rather special climatic advantages but also some which have demonstrated large industrial potentials. Should they continue to register markedly higher growth rates than the present most populous divisions, they would become the most populous parts of the nation within a half-century.

Very mature New England, the agricultural West North Central Division, and the two divisions of the deep South account for only 8 million or 12 per cent of the projected total increase. According to the projections, they will account for only 19 per cent of the population in 1980 by contrast with 22 per cent in 1960. Finally, the Mountain states, even with a projected expansion of almost 4 million persons or over 55 per cent, are computed to remain the smallest of the divisions with about 10.6 million persons in 1980.

Metropolitan Population. Throughout its history, the population of the United States has become increasingly concentrated in urban places; and during the course of this century in metropolitan areas. In 1790, when the first Census was taken, there were only 24 urban places in this country. They contained only 5 per cent of the nation's population. Only two of them had more than 25,000 persons. By 1950, there were over 4,700 places in urban territory. They included almost 97 million persons or about 64 per cent of the total population. The comparable figures for 1960 are 125 million persons, almost 70 per cent of the total population.

Even more dramatic than urban growth has been the metropolitan explosion during this century. In 1900, areas which would have been classified as metropolitan under later federal definitions numbered about 50 and contained fewer than 26 million persons, about one-third of the nation's population. In 1950, about 56 per cent of the population, almost 85 million persons, lived in 168 Standard Metropolitan Areas while by 1960, 63 per cent of the population, or almost 113 million persons, lived in 212 Standard Metropolitan Statistical Areas.[3] (Final data.)

The population has become increasingly concentrated in urban and metropolitan areas as a result of basic forces which determine the distribution of population: technological, economic, social and political. People have crowded into urban and metropolitan areas to form efficient producer and consumer units.

For the 1960 Census, the Federal Government (through the Division of Statistical Standards of the Bureau of the Budget) changed the term and definition used for the areas called metropolitan. The 1950 designation "Standard Metropolitan Area" was replaced by the 1960 designation "Standard Metropolitan Statistical Area" (abbreviated here to SMSA) in 1960. The change emphasized that, for statistical and analytical purposes, areas are more or less arbitrarily delineated as metropolitan. For 1960 an SMSA was defined as one or more central cities of 50,000 or more persons, the balance of the county or counties containing such a city or cities, and such contiguous counties as, by certain criteria, are "essentially metropolitan in character and are socially and economically integrated with the central city." (This is essentially the same as the definition used for the 1950 Census.) Despite the arbitrary character of the definition, the SMSA data are closer representations of the actual realities of our grouping of economic activities and population than are statistics relating to cities alone.

There is a difference between change in the number of persons in a specified class (e.g., living in a metropolitan area) and change in the number of persons living in a specified set of areas (e.g., SMSA's). The long-term data in Table VI relate to the former type of change as best it can be gleaned from estimates and data based on changing definitions; the data for 1950 and 1960 obtained from the preliminary Census SMSA reports and presented in Tables VII to XI, inclusive, relate to the latter, i.e., to areas classified as SMSA's in 1960. Both kinds of comparisons provide insight into the nature and significance of the population changes in the United States in the fifties. Differences between the two kinds of changes may be illustrated by the statement that between 1950 and 1960, there was an increase in the population classified as living in metropolitan areas of 28.4 million; at the same time there was only a 23.6 million increase in the population living in areas classified as SMSA's in 1960.[4] In this case, the figures differ, mainly because 30 or more areas classified as SMSA's in 1960 would not have been so classified in 1950; hence, the 1950 population of these areas is excluded in the "same class" comparison and included in the "same area" comparison, while the 1960 population of those areas is included in both comparisons.

Preliminary 1960 Census data for population growth in and outside SMSA's by region during the fifties are shown in Table VII and Chart III. For the United States as a whole, SMSA population grew explosively by contrast with growth outside SMSA's—25.3 per cent as against 6.5 per cent. Within this structure, there were marked regional differences. In the Northeast the division of population between metropolitan and nonmetropolitan changed only slightly during the fifties. Growth rates were about the same in and outside SMSA's. New entrants to the SMSA category and annexations were of minor importance.

What was true for the Northeast, however, does not apply elsewhere. The most striking change in the division of population between metropolitan residents and others occurred in the South. There, about 16 areas crossed the SMSA definitional line between 1950 and 1960. When the Census results are modified to take account of this change, there appears to have been a decline of around 800,000 persons in the nonmetropolitan population. Thus, in the South, metropolitan population growth exceeded the total growth of about 7.3 million as a result of a net shift from nonmetropolitan to metropolitan residence. All this growth speaks of the very greatly increased importance to the South of industrial and service activities, as well as the importance of climatic advantages. The shift emphasizes also the sharp relative decline in the importance of agriculture and related activities in the South. Even so, the South remains the least metropolitanized region, with the nonmetropolitan category still containing over half the South's population.

Essentially the same development occurred in the West where about 10 new areas qualified as SMSA's after 1950. Taking account of this development indicates that the nonmetropolitan population remained about the same. As in the South, the West's increase in population of around 7.5 million was of a metropolitan character.

For the North Central region, the development was intermediate between the Northeast and the South and West. There was only a small increase, roughly 900,000 persons, or 4 per cent, in the nonmetropolitan population by contrast with the total increase for the region of about 6.8 million. Undoubtedly, this small increase reflects the continued exodus of rural and farm population with the increased mechanization and productivity of agriculture and is indicative of the rise in importance of industry and service trades in the region.

The following chart summarizing preliminary and approximate percentages of metropolitan population highlights the regional differences in population composition and changes during the fifties.

There was relatively little difference between growth rates for the fifties among the various sizes of SMSA's as size is determined by

Region	1950	1960
Total U.S.	57.2	62.8
Northeast	78.6	78.8
North Central	57.1	60.0
South	38.4	48.0
West	62.4	71.7

the 1960 population. Except for the 500,000 to 1,000,000 class, with a rate of 34.5 per cent, all fell within the narrow range of 22.1 to 25.3 per cent (Table VIII).

Total population increases were concentrated in a few areas. The five largest SMSA's—New York, Chicago, Los Angeles, Philadelphia and Detroit—contributed 5.7 million to the overall 22.5 million increase in population for the areas classified as SMSA's in 1960; the 19 SMSA's in the 1,000,000 to 3,000,000 size class, another 5.7 million. At the other extreme, the 23 smallest SMSA's (population of under 100,000 in 1960) contributed about 350,000. Thus, if growth patterns remain the same, there will be a small number of very large increases in numbers and a large number of very small increases among the SMSA's.

The following is what the 1960 Census indicates as a possible range in magnitude of problems of expansion for varying sizes of SMSA's:

1960 SMSA's		Average increase per SMSA
Size Class	Number	1950 to 1960
3,000,000 or more	5	1,139,727
1,000,000 to 3,000,000	19	299,030
500,000 to 1,000,000	28	169,808
250,000 to 500,000	48	67,082
100,000 to 250,000	88	32,204
Under 100,000	23	15,439

A similar pattern may well occur in the seventies and eighties.

Table IX shows, for 1960, the number of SMSA's in each size class and the per cent of total SMSA population in the areas in each size class. A large proportion of the SMSA population is concentrated in a relatively small number of areas; e.g., 55 per cent in 24 SMSA's of 1,000,000 or more persons. And a very small proportion of the SMSA population resided within a very large number of the smallest SMSA's,

15 per cent in 111 SMSA's. Phenomena of this character have, of course, been well known to demographers and others for many years.

At this time comparable data for 1950 are not available. The limited analysis now possible does show that the distribution of metropolitan population among the size groups changed somewhat during the fifties. Our 5 largest SMSA's in 1950 as well as 1960 suffered a small decline in relative importance within the SMSA family, even though their relative importance as a group within the United States increased during the fifties; they grew more rapidly than the rest of the United States combined, but not quite as rapidly as did the total metropolitan population. Unlike the very largest SMSA size class, the second largest size group, 1,000,000 to 3,000,000, increased sharply in relative importance during the fifties, largely through the addition to the group of 9 areas; the proportion of total metropolitan population in that size group increased from 18.7 to 26.4 per cent. For the individual classes in the broad "Under 1,000,000" category, detailed analysis is not readily accomplished. Yet it is clear that, while some of them may have increased in importance within the SMSA family, as a broad category they have declined in the sense of containing a smaller percentage of metropolitan population in 1960 than in 1950.

The overall SMSA picture during the fifties is one of very great population increase, in terms of absolute numbers, in terms of per cent change, and in terms of the proportion of the total population accounted for. Within the overall picture, the variation among individual SMSA's was very wide. This is shown by Table X in which the 211 areas designated as SMSA's, as of the 1960 Census date, are classified by per cent change between 1950 and 1960. The most striking feature of the distribution is the fact that 9 SMSA's *actually lost population*. At the other extreme are the 6 SMSA's which more than doubled their populations during the decade, four being newcomers to the metropolitan community. Leaving aside the high growth rates among these new entrants to the metropolitan class, the overall range of variation was from a decline of 12 per cent to an increase of over 123 per cent.

Despite the very wide range, SMSA population growth rates were concentrated about the national SMSA rate. Thus, just about half the SMSA's, 107 of 211, grew at rates between 15 and 35 per cent, and just about two-thirds, 140 of 211, at rates between 10 and 40 per cent. The modal, or the most frequent, percentage increase was somewhat greater than 20 per cent. This is smaller than the overall 25.3 per cent increase for SMSA's, since the weight of the rapidly growing areas is less in determining a modal rate than in determining an overall rate. In the future, something like this pattern of variation may be expected.

Under favorable economic, social and climatic conditions, growth rates of more than 50 per cent in a decade may be expected to occur in the future as they have in the past. In the fifties, there were 30 SMSA's with such rates; they are listed in Table XI. Only one, Wichita, Kansas, fell outside the South and West; and 18 were in three states, California, Texas and Florida. Finally, it may be noted that 14 of the 30 would not have qualified as SMSA's in 1950, indicating that in the future, as in the past, opportunities for smaller communities to expand rapidly to metropolitan status may well be expected to occur.

Under unfavorable conditions—denudation of natural resources, and loss of comparative economic and social advantages—population stagnation and even decline may be expected. In the fifties, this apparently occurred in at least 20 SMSA's, nine with an actual loss of population and 12 with increases of less than 5 per cent, as shown in Table XII. None is in the West. The 10 in the South represent one extreme of widely varying conditions, of virtually an economic and social upheaval. Those in the Northeast and North Central regions appear to reflect a variety of underlying conditions—declining agriculture, exhaustion of natural resources, defeat in economic struggles.

Between 1900 and 1920, the ratio between central-city and suburban populations for metropolitan areas remained almost constant, about one-third in the suburbs and two-thirds in the central cities (Table VI). Since 1920, since there has been wide use of 20th-century transportation and communication technology, suburbia has outpaced central city. In 1950, well over two-fifths of the metropolitan population was in suburbia; in 1960, nearly half. Suburbia increases of 19 million between 1950 and 1960 represent at least 70 per cent of the total change in metropolitan population.

The decade of the fifties was critical in the relation between central–city and suburban population growth. It may well be described as the decade of suburban boom and central–city bust. The population of the suburban areas (as of 1960) of the United States—i.e., the population outside central cities, but within the SMSA's—increased by 48 per cent. By contrast, the population of the central–city areas (as of 1960) increased by only 9 per cent (Table VII). (Final data show increases of 10.7 and 48.6 per cent for central cities and outside central cities, respectively.) For many individual areas, of course, the difference was much greater.

The 1960 Census was the first of our Decennial Censuses to show population losses in a large number of cities. Eleven of the twelve largest cities in 1950 registered population declines. During the decade, of the 256 central cities in the 211 SMSA's, 73 lost while 183 gained population.

Such population losses do not necessarily imply economic decline or stagnation in a city or area. They may reflect an interchange of place of residence and place of work within an expanding metropolitan community. This interchange is indicated by the many cases where total SMSA population increased although, for one or more central cities, population declined, including four of the five largest areas: New York, Chicago, Philadelphia and Detroit.

The data already presented understate the population decline or stagnation in the inner cores of SMSA's. They do not show population increases accounted for by annexations. Final census data [5] show 4.9 million or over 86 per cent of the central–city population increase was from annexations. Thus, the inner cores of the metropolitan areas tended to grow very slowly or not at all because they were already filled.

The patterns of population growth were accompanied by changes in patterns of land use and in the character of communities or neighborhoods within SMSA's. Students of the city have documented growth patterns which indicate that our metropolitan areas grew outward from one or more centers of origin. Although characterized by both vertical and horizontal growth, the latter was the dominant form of development. The newer areas were always those farthest from centers of origin and embodied the new advances in technology. Our metropolitan areas tended to develop definite spatial patterns in terms of the age and the modernity of their residential structures.

Differences in physical facilities tended to produce a parallel socio-economic stratification of the urban and metropolitan population. Persons of the lowest income, educational, and occupational status, usually the newcomers to the urban environment, tended to occupy the less desirable residences toward the center of the city. Persons of higher income, education and social status tended to locate toward the peripheries of the metropolis. Agencies and institutions of all sorts tended to reflect, and are attuned to, the characteristics of the people contained in the areas in which they are located.

As our metropolitan plant has aged, the early patterns of rapid growth have been paralleled by equally remarkable obsolescence and decay. Just as cities grew community by community, not structure by structure, so have the cities decayed, characterized by areas of substandard housing and by slums which have become a national disgrace. Federal, state and local programs for urban renewal have tended to consolidate efforts of slum clearance, rehabilitation and conservation. The start has been to rebuild the slum areas one community at a time. Populations of inner-zone areas are, under these programs, being uprooted and dispersed to various sections of the metropolitan areas. Inner zones are being rebuilt or rehabilitated so as to attract higher as well as lower social and income groups. All this added to new developments in suburbia presages basic changes in the physical structure of our metropolitan areas, and in the manner in which they are used.

The fundamental forces at work may be expected to continue to operate over the next couple of decades with the expectation of further growth of urban and metropolitan populations. They will account for greater proportions of the total in 1970 than in 1960 and in 1980 than in 1970. Projections to 1980 for metropolitan areas, based upon a continuation of past trends, are shown in Table VI. They show an increase of about 58 million in the metropolitan population between 1960 and 1980. Such an increase would represent about 88 per cent of the projected increase of 66 million in total population, and would result in close to 70 per cent of the population being in metropolitan areas in 1980.

Suburbs have been growing more rapidly than central cities because of the impact of 20th-century technology and the relatively fixed boundaries of central cities. While technology was developing, the boundaries of central cities remained relatively fixed despite annexations. On the average, the central city in the United States has been filled since the 1920's. Since central cities became filled within their relatively fixed boundaries, continued growth could take place only in suburbia, beyond the borders of the city.

The forces accounting for the differential in the growth of suburbs and central cities may be expected to continue operating during the next decade or two. Of the projected increase of 58 million in the population of metropolitan areas between 1960 and 1980, about 45

[25]

million is projected for absorption by suburbia (Table VI). By 1980, of some 170 million people in metropolitan areas, close to 100 million may well be in suburbs, only around 70 million in central cities.

The spatial patterning of the physical residential plant of our metropolitan areas, with its correlative socio-economic stratification of the population, is likely to be drastically modified. It is possible that, while the obsolescent inner areas are replaced or renovated, decay will occur in the suburban rings. With increased intervention and urban renewal programs, it is likely that the physical and socio-economic character of a community in the future will depend less upon the historical accident of its origin and more upon the will of organized population groups as manifest in their planning and development activities.

It is also possible that in the decades to come an emergent pattern of residence within the metropolitan area may become the modal one. There is increasing evidence that, in accordance with the family cycle, the family is tending toward a corresponding use of the metropolitan area. As children come, their families tend to move to the outlying suburban area in order to place them in surroundings of green lawns and open spaces. As the last youngster departs for college or gets married to start his own family, the parents show a tendency to move back to a rebuilt or renovated inner zone of the metropolitan area.

City and Country Population. While SMSA's are defined to obtain as close a representation of the actual realities of our larger population agglomerations as possible, urban territory is defined largely upon the basis of the existence of a charter granted by a state legislature for a relatively small area with 2,500 or more persons. (This applies even though the definition was modified in 1950 to include urban-fringes around cities of 50,000 or more and unincorporated places of 2,500 or more.) Most of the inhabitants of SMSA's are also in urban territory. But substantial numbers reside in places of fewer than 50,000 which are within urban territory but outside SMSA's. In addition, some population in rural territory lies within SMSA's. Hence, though the overlap is large, each basis of assembling data provides some information about population which the other does not.

Data such as are shown in Table XIII are of limited value for shedding light upon the size and structure of metropolitan areas or for purposes of counting people by the extent to which they participate in "urbanism as a way of life." However, Table XIII does show that urban places accounted for all of the expansion of total population of the United States between 1950 and 1960, and, in addition, absorbed, on balance, some rural population. This was a continuation and an acceleration of the long-term trend of urbanization which brought the urban population to almost 70 per cent of the total.

Until 1950, our rural population increased decade by decade, but, in general, at a declining rate. During the fifties, rural population actually declined; all of the overall population increase of 28 million and the 400,000 decline in rural territory was absorbed in urban territory. Just as important as the absence of population growth in rural territory during the fifties was the shift of population from rural-farm to rural-nonfarm areas. Except for the depression thirties, the rural-farm population has been declining since 1910 when the first rural-farm Census count was made. In the forties and fifties the decline was sharp. Farm population as defined in earlier censuses decreased from about 30 million in 1940 to about 25 million in 1950, and then to about 20 million in 1960.

On the basis of the changed definition of "farm population" introduced in 1960, the count of the farm population was only 16 million.[6] Despite the change in definition, it is probably correct to say that the farm population of 32 million in 1910 decreased to 16 million in 1960. This conclusion is justified because the persons residing on "farms" without actually producing farm products, a group excluded from the 1960 definition, increased greatly between 1910 and 1960. Within rural territory there has been a major decline of persons living on farms who are directly dependent upon agricultural production for their livelihood. To some extent the decline in farm population may be the result of the development of "town" residence and "farm" work. In the main, however, the decline in rural-farm population reflects the increased mechanization and productivity of American agriculture. Acreage under cultivation throughout the entire period of decline of farm population has changed little, whereas productivity per acre has continued to increase greatly.

It may also be noted that during the fifties the distribution of rural population among "places" and "open territory" changed hardly at all. Furthermore, the number of places showed a net decline of little significance. Undoubtedly, some places moved from the rural to the urban classification during the fifties, while new places were born in rural territory.

In urban territory, by contrast, the number of cities climbing the size ladder during the fifties was far and above the number necessary to offset the downhill slides of some cities. Old places expanded into higher size classes, new places were formed, and there were some new arrivals from rural territory. The total number of places with 2,500 or more inhabitants increased from 4,300 in 1950 to 5,400 in 1960. Except for the largest size class, cities of 1,000,000 or more inhabitants, every size class showed an increase in the number of places. Cities of 50,000 or more, each of metropolitan size, increased in number from 233 to 333. The net upward movement was facilitated by the long-used American procedure of expansion and annexation. The extent to which this growth occurred is illustrated by California, where 188 of the 253 incorporated places of 2,500 or more inhabitants in 1950 annexed territory during the decade.

The relative importance of the various size groups within urban territory changed during the decade. It was the cities of intermediate size, populations between 10,000 and 100,000, which increased in relative importance. They contained less than 31 per cent of the urban population in 1950, but more than 37 per cent in 1960. Most of this growth was at the expense of our larger cities, particularly those with populations of 1,000,000 or more. In large part, this change reflects the rapid growth of suburbs, i.e., of places really metropolitan in character by virtue of contiguity with large cities, while the larger cities, the central cities, were growing slowly, if at all. Finally, it may be noted, the smaller places, with populations of fewer than 10,000, and "other urban" territory also declined slightly in importance during the decade.

In relation to the total population of the United States, it was the intermediate-size cities which increased in relative importance. They contained less than 20 per cent of the total population in 1950, but almost 26 per cent in 1960, and accounted for all the net increase in relative importance of urban territory. The larger cities declined slightly, and the smaller cities increased slightly in relative importance during the decade.

By 1980, between 75 and 80 per cent of our population may live in urban territory, which would place about 10 million more persons in urban territory in 1980 than are in the entire United States today. This figure contrasts with about 64 per cent in 1950 and almost 70 per cent in 1960. Even so, it leaves room for a modest increase in rural population within the projected total increase.

Farm population may be expected to decline further in view of mechanization developments and productivity increases. By 1980, the farm population may include no more than 12 million persons [7] as compared with 16 million in 1960.

Government Structure. In dealing with community services, the urban population approach, based on cities and legal entities, is more appropriate than the SMSA population approach. Such services tend to be organized, financed and administered by individual government units rather than on an SMSA-wide basis. The mere number of governmental units is staggering—over 100,000. About half of these are school districts, and another 15,000 are special districts. Municipalities number about 17 or 18 thousand, being approximately the same places for which data are shown in Table XIII. Data from the 1957 Census of Governments [8] are as follows:

Governmental Unit	Number
Local governments except school districts	51,887
County	3,050
Municipality	17,215
Township	17,198
Special district	14,424
School districts	50,454
Other public school systems	2,489

The disparity between the legal entities (cities) and the population entities (SMSA's) poses problems for public agencies concerned with providing services to metropolitan populations. To serve well at low cost, an agency must make full use of the economies of large-scale operation, but a large number of small purchasing units, the relatively small governmental units, act with monopsonistic effect to limit agency size and the provision of integrated and unified services. This is true not only in rural, farm and small-town areas, but also within our large metropolitan areas.

With the continuation of extensive urbanization and metropolitanization during the next few decades will come increased recognition that our 20th-century technological, economic and demographic units have governmental structures of 18th- and 19th-century origin and design. Already there is a discernible trend toward changes in local government units to meet area-wide problems more adequately. Increasing numbers of elections have been held to consolidate city and county governments; in increasing numbers, special units have been created to deal with specific functions such as sanitation, drainage, water supply, and port facilities. It is certain that in the next decade or two, area-wide planning and functional governmental units will emerge at an accelerated pace.

Age Structure. Perhaps the most important single characteristic of a person is age. Activities of individuals change with the stage of the human life cycle, from infancy to retirement and eventual death. Each stage generates its own distinctive activities and demands.

In 1800, the "average" American was only 16 years old; in 1950, he was over 30. As late as the third quarter of the 19th century, over 40 per cent of the population was under 15 years of age and only 4 per cent, 60 years of age or more. Such an age structure is much like that of the underdeveloped areas of the world today. By 1950, however, the proportion of persons under 15 had declined to 27 per cent, and those 60 and over had increased to 12 per cent. Thus, by 1950, the United States had become "aged" on the basis of the United Nations classification of nations by age.

Age changes of such magnitude and depth have significantly affected the character of American society. Tables XIV and XV and Chart IV include the age distributions for the United States at the beginning and end of the fifties. The usual Census presentation by 5-year intervals has been modified (by interpolation, when necessary, in the absence of detailed data) to show separately the various school-age groups. Perhaps the most striking feature of the data is found in the decreased median age of the population. From the moment of birth a person can only age. But a population may, over time, either age or grow younger. The explosive birth rates of the fifties decreased the median age for the first time in the history of the United States, from 30.2 years in 1950 to 29.5 years in 1960.

Even more significant than this decline in median age is the great variation in the per cent of change during the decade among the specific age groups. Thus, the number 10 and 11 years of age increased by over 50 per cent during the decade. At the other extreme, the number of persons in the 20 to 30 year interval *actually decreased;* the 20 to 24 year olds decreased in number by 12 per cent during the decade.

These large differences between the growth rates of age groups were largely the result of fluctuations in birth rates. For example, the baby crop of the depression thirties, when birth rates were at all-time lows, generated the 20 to 29 year olds of 1960; the baby crop of the prosperous twenties, when birth rates were much higher, generated the 20 to 29 year olds of 1950. The effect of the decline of birth rates was great enough to result in a decline in the number of 20 to 29 year olds between 1950 and 1960, despite the larger child-bearing population and despite the lower mortality rates in the depression thirties. By contrast, the effect of the postwar rise in birth rates was sufficient to result in the "under 15" population expanding most rapidly during the decade.

With regard to those persons 30 years of age and over, the declining birth rates of much earlier decades were, of course, important. But the counter-directional effects of the long-term mortality decline and the prior increase of the child-bearing population were sufficient to maintain growth at a rate close to the overall 18.5 per cent increase during the fifties. In the case of the senior citizens, those 65 years of age and over, the increase in numbers was almost 35 per cent during the decade. Thus, although the population of the United States grew younger during the decade, as measured by median age, it also grew older as measured by the increase in the proportion of persons 65 years of age and over. This continuation of the "aging" trend over the decades brought the number of senior citizens to more than 9 per cent of the total in 1960.

The decade of the fifties was, in a unique way, the decade of the elementary school child. The number of youngsters 5 to 13 years of age increased by 45 per cent, as contrasted with less than 9 per cent during the forties. To a lesser extent, it was also a decade for the high school group, which increased by 35 per cent. Curiously enough, it was also a boom decade for our senior citizen group so that both ends of our age structure increased more rapidly than the intermediate sector. Those 18 to 65 years of age, who include almost all of the working population of the country, increased by only 7 per cent. As already noted, the young adult group actually declined in numbers.

The projected rates of growth and expansions in numbers vary widely among the age groups. Between 1960 and 1980, the population 65 years of age and over will increase by some 8 million persons or by close to 50 per cent. Since everyone who will be 65 years of age or over by 1980 has already been born, this projection can be accepted as quite accurate; uncertainty of birth rates is not a factor, and uncertainty of mortality and migration is of minor importance.

[31]

Increases for those 65 years of age and over will be at varying rates among various localities. Elderly persons have been migrating to places in the West and South with special climatic conditions, for example, to Florida, California and Arizona. This movement may be expected to continue during the sixties and seventies. It may also be noted that the senior citizens of 1980 will have attained higher levels of education and will have more leisure than their counterparts of earlier dates.

Like the senior citizens of 1980, those who will be from 30 to 64 years of age in 1980 are already here; thus, the projections for them are quite reliable. The rate of increase for the group 30 to 64 years of age, however, will be much smaller, only about 20 per cent. This percentage represents an increase of about 15 million, somewhat short of twice that for our senior citizens. This broad group is composed almost entirely of active members of the labor force and persons well along in the course of marriage and parenthood.

A really explosive expansion in number will occur for the group 18 to 29 years of age. The increase will be 80 per cent. In terms of numbers, it is an increase of over 21 million persons, close to one-third of the projected 66 million overall increase in population. This group includes college students, new entrants to the labor force, newlyweds and young parents.

The major unknown factor for the group 14 to 17 years of age, the high school age group, is, of course, the birth rate during the years 1962 to 1966. The projections in Tables XIV and XV assume some decline from the 1955-57 highs and in that sense are conservative. Current birth rates are already below the highs of a few years ago, but they may rise again, especially should high levels of economic activity return and international tension lessen. On the other hand, the decline in birth rates could be greater than that assumed. On the conservative basis of projection used here, a 45 per cent increase, or about 5 million persons, is a reliable projection from 1960 to 1980.

Projections for persons 5 to 13 years of age, the elementary school group, are less reliable than those given for other age groups. The major uncertainty is birth rates during the years 1966 to 1975, for which the projections assume birth rates equal to those in the 1949-51 period. Between 1960 and 1980, an increase of 10 million or about 31 per cent may be expected in the group 5 to 13 years of age. Such an increase during the two decades would be about the same as the increase for the single decade of the fifties when the elementary schools felt the full impact of the postwar baby boom. The major part of this difference arises because the underlying birth rates assumed for the projections are considerably below those during the 1946–1955 period of the postwar baby boom.

Enrollment in Schools. School enrollment depends on the number of persons in the various school-age groups and on their enrollment rates. As the American income level has increased, greater educational opportunities have been offered to and accepted by our younger citizens.

At least since 1910, when such data were first included in the censuses, school enrollment rates have increased, and most strikingly so in the fifties. Even as early as 1910, about 86 per cent of the youngsters 7 to 13 years of age were enrolled in school; by 1950, about 95 per cent and, by 1960, almost every one of them was enrolled (99.5 per cent). Between 1910 and 1950, the rate for youngsters 5 and 6 years of age changed only from 35 to 39 per cent, but in the fifties the rate swelled to roughly 80 per cent. Between 1910 and 1950, enrollment rates for teenagers 14 to 17 years of age rose from 60 to 84 per cent and then continued to increase to roughly 90 per cent in 1960. Thus, in the mass-education ages of 5 to 17 years, almost 97 per cent are enrolled in schools. For the ages of 18 years and above, enrollment rates are much lower, reflecting the fact that college and post-graduate education is obtained by relatively few. But, for these age groups also, there was a sharp increase in enrollment rates in the fifties, which extended earlier advances.

The most visible consequence of the changing age structure during the fifties was the tremendous pressure on kindergarten and elementary school facilities (Tables XVI, XVII and XVIII). The grade schools of the United States were inundated by the tidal wave of postwar babies who reached school-entrance age and filled the schools in the fifties. Enrollment in kindergartens and elementary schools increased by 11 million children or by well over 50 per cent. This rise was somewhat more than the 45 per cent increase for youngsters 5 to 13 years of age, the difference representing in large part the increase in enrollment rates during the decade.

During the sixties and seventies, the pressure on the grade schools will be much less, but it will not disappear. Between 1960 and 1980, enrollment may increase by over 9 million or by 29 per cent. But this is a 29 per cent increase over two decades by contrast with more than 50 per cent over one, the fifties.

During the fifties, high school enrollment increased by about 54 per cent, roughly by about the same rate as that for the grade schools. But while the pressure on grade schools will decline in the sixties, that on high schools will continue unabated. The projected increase in enrollment is 5 million or about 48 per cent. Relief will come in the seventies, however, when the projected increase is only a few per cent, about 1 million students.

An explosive increase in enrollment is projected to occur in our colleges and professional schools during the sixties. Following on the heels of a 61 per cent increase in the fifties, the sixties will bring an increase of about 120 per cent, or of 4.2 million students, to raise total college and professional school enrollment to 7.8 million persons. A further increase of 4.1 million in the seventies is projected to bring the enrollment in 1980 to about 12 million persons, 235 per cent above the 1960 figure. Only in part does this rise result from the projected 81 per cent increase in the college age group. In crude terms, the only ones available, about three-fourths of the explosive increase in college and professional education will be the result of much greater rates of enrollment of the college age groups in institutions of higher education.

In overall summary, school enrollment in 1980 is projected as more than 70 million persons. This would be about 24 million more than in 1960, representing an increase of about 52 per cent which was about the same as the increase in the one decade of the fifties.

Other Characteristics of the Population. In 1940, the first year for which census data on years of schooling were collected, the "average" person 25 years of age and over in the United States had completed little more than an elementary school education with 8.6 years of school (Table XIX). By 1950, median years of schooling had risen to 9.3 and, by 1960, to about 11 years. With a continuation of recent trends in educational improvement, a significant milestone will have been passed in the educational advance of the nation during the sixties. Projections indicate that by 1970 the "average" American 25 years of age and over may have achieved a high school education; median years of schooling will have risen further to 12.3 years. That those 25 to 29 years of age may have attained an even higher level presages even higher educational attainment levels after 1980 (Table XXIII).

Part of the rising of our educational level has been the reduction of the proportion of persons with little or no schooling. In 1940, about

13.6 per cent of the population 25 years of age and over had fewer than 5 years of schooling, a level below that of functional illiteracy. In 1950, 11.1 per cent were still in the group. By 1960, however, the proportion of functionally illiterate had declined to about 8 per cent. Should the trend continue, the proportion will decline further to less than 6 per cent in 1970 and less than 4 per cent in 1980 (Tables XX to XXIII).

With the effects of the rise in educational level added to the effects of increases in population, the numbers of high school and college graduates expanded rapidly (Table XXIV). Since the expectations are for both factors to continue to rise, further increases in the numbers of such graduates are projected for the sixties and seventies.

The number of high school graduates increased during the fifties by more than 13 million, from 38.3 to 51.6 million, or 35 per cent. The number at the beginning of the decade was equal to 37 per cent of the population 18 years of age and over, of those at or above the age at which completion of our mass-education high school programs is typically scheduled. In 1960, the percentage was 45. Sometime during the sixties high school graduates will pass a number equal to 50 per cent of the population 18 years of age and over. And, by 1980, the number will equal close to 60 per cent of the population 18 years of age and over. Between 1960 and 1980, a 40 to 45 million increase in the number of high school graduates is projected to bring the total to around 95 million, an increase of 80 to 85 per cent.

The college graduate group expanded during the fifties at about the same rate as the high school graduate group, from about 6 to about 8.1 million. But during the sixties and seventies, the rate for the college graduate group will be higher. By 1980, the number of college graduates may approach 15 million, close to 85 per cent above the 1960 figure. This figure would equal over 10 per cent of the number of persons in the population 22 years of age and over, i.e., the number at or above the typical age of completion of a college education.

Despite heavy immigration, the foreign-born white population of the United States never exceeded 15 per cent of the total. The maximum of 14.5 per cent occurred in 1890 and again in 1910. The proportion has been declining ever since. Such a decline was assured by our immigration exclusion acts of the 1920's and the reenactment of restricted immigration provisions by the Immigration and Nationality Act of 1952. With a continuation of these policies in the decades ahead, the proportion of foreign-born will continue to decline.

The population projections presented here assume net immigration of about 300,000 per year. If restrictions hold immigration to this level, the number of foreign-born will remain about the same, about 10.8 million in 1980 by contrast with an estimate of 10.4 million in 1960 (Table XXV). However, since the native population will be growing very rapidly, the proportion of foreign-born will shrink considerably. By 1980, only about 4 per cent of the population will be foreign-born by contrast with about 6 per cent in 1960.

As the foreign-born have declined in relative importance and numbers during recent decades, the nonwhite population, approximately 95 per cent Negro, has not. From 10.2 per cent of the total in 1930, the nonwhite population gradually increased to 11.4 per cent in 1960. A further gradual increase may be expected so that, by 1980, the nonwhite population may approach 13 per cent of the total. These relatively small gains in the proportion of nonwhite obscures the great difference between white and nonwhite rates of growth. During the fifties, the nonwhite growth rate was 26.7 per cent; the white, 17.5 per cent. Continuation of present trends means a 53.5 per cent growth of the nonwhite population between 1960 and 1980 by contrast with a 34.9 per cent growth of the white population.

Along with the recent explosive growth of the nonwhite population, there have been massive and important changes in the location of that population. On facet of this growth has been the migratory flow of the Negroes from the South to the remainder of the country. This trend, started during World War I, has continued ever since, except for substantial diminution during the depression thirties. About 89 per cent of the Negroes were in the South in 1910; by 1950, only about two-thirds were in the South; and by 1960, less than 60 per cent. This decline may be expected to continue; and, by 1980, it is possible that as many Negroes may be in the North and West as in the South.

A second facet has been the increasing urbanization and metropolitanization of Negroes in the South as well as elsewhere. In 1910, before the flow of Negroes to the North and to urban places began, only 27 per cent lived in urban places as defined by the Census (places of 2,500 inhabitants or more). By 1950, over 90 per cent of the Negroes in the North and the West and about 48 per cent of those in the South lived in cities. Census data available as of this writing do not fully reveal the changes during the fifties. They do show that in 1960, almost 39 per cent of the Negroes resided in the 25 SMSA's which include our 25 largest cities.

A third facet has been the settling of the Negro in the central cities of SMSA's rather than the suburbs. Complete data are not available for 1960, but for the 25 SMSA's containing the 25 largest cities, central-city Negro population numbered 84 per cent of all Negroes in those SMSA's. As the Negroes moved into the inner-zones, the whites moved outward. Among the changes was an increase in population density. The Negro population concentrated in a relatively few areas. This distribution is indicated by Table XXVI. Thus, 4.9 of the 18.8 million Negroes in 1960 resided in 10 SMSA's in the North and West. Another 2 million resided in 8 SMSA's in the South. At the same time, each of 21 states had fewer than 50,000 Negroes.

Along with expansion and relocation, Negroes have been traveling and will continue to travel the road of acculturation, a change from a primitive folk culture in the economically underdeveloped rural South to urbanism and metropolitanism as a way of life. One index of the difficulties along the way is the level of educational attainment. As recently as 1950, median years of schooling for the Negro 25 years of age and over in the rural South were 4.8 years, that is, less than 5th grade of a Southern rural education. As recently as 1950, then, the "average" Negro in the rural South was functionally illiterate. For such a person to reach the current educational level of the urban white population would require about 6 *additional* years of schooling.

There is evidence that in some respects the pathway followed by the immigrant groups in acquiring a place to live and economic and social status in the community is being followed by the Negro. The limited evidence that is available indicates that the Negro is climbing the social and economic ladder as measured by education, occupation and income. The evidence also indicates that he is moving outward from the inner zones of the city, which constituted his port of entry and, in fact, is beginning to knock at the door of the suburb. The most important respect in which Negro accommodation to his new environment differs from that of the immigrant is to be seen thus far in the continuation of the pattern of segregated residence. Although the time span involved is still a brief one, the evidence indicates increased rather than decreased segregation of the Negro within the cities.

The impact of the expansion, relocation and acculturation of the Negro population has been and will continue to be a major one. It cannot be predicted with accuracy, but will certainly be much greater than increases in numbers alone might indicate.

One consequence of the rapid technological change which started with the industrial revolution and which is still going on is a change in the occupational structure of the working population. This in turn leads to changes in the activities and demands of the population, because occupation influences activities and demands. The data in Table XXVII indicate the very marked changes which occurred during the fifties and which reflect the underlying technological development. The major features of the table are the following:

1. Despite the 12 per cent increase in total employment, farmers and farm managers declined in number by almost 37 per cent. This decline is indicative of the movement from farm to city already discussed.

2. Professional, technical and kindred workers increased by almost two-thirds. This increase speaks of (a) the increased demand occasioned by rising income levels for consumers' services such as those of doctors, dentists, lawyers and the like; and (b) the rising professionalism inherent in productive activities which require engineers, accountants, corporation lawyers, labor lawyers, television operators, airplane pilots, research physicists, and so on in relatively greater numbers than ever before.

3. Farther down the occupational scale, the shift from blue-collar to white-collar occupations continued as shown by an increase of over 28 per cent for clerical and kindred workers in comparison with only 4 per cent for laborers outside the farm and mine.

4. Finally, the 32 per cent increase in service workers speaks of the shift of consumption demands from those for tangible products to those for services, the production of which requires, among others, waiters, cooks, ushers, bartenders, manicurists, hospital attendants.

Reliable projections of the occupational structure are not feasible. Further changes in the direction, though not necessarily of the magnitude, of those of the fifties may be expected, if for no reasons other than those arising out of bringing production techniques and consumer demands up-to-date. Beyond this, technological advances, which to a greater or lesser extent will make the "new" of today the "old" of tomorrow, are uncertain in extent and effect. One indication of a slower tempo in the near future than in the recent past is the projection by Yale Brozen that the number of research and development employees in industry will increase by only 50 per cent in the sixties compared with a quadrupling in the fifties.[9]

Important changes took place during World War II and in the postwar period in the labor force participation of women. In 1940, women made up 24.4 per cent of the labor force. By 1950, women were 28.7 per cent of the labor force; by 1960, almost one-third. It is possible that by 1980 women will make up between 35 and 40 per cent of the nation's workers. A significant aspect of the changes, past and prospective, is the increased work activity of married women living with husbands. By 1980, it may be that between 40 and 45 per cent of all married women 14 years of age and over will be in the labor force.

Summary

The projections utilize conservative assumptions about the future. The critical one is the birth rate. If it should not decline during the sixties, and then remain at the lower level, the total population of the United States may well be over 260 million by 1980 and close to 400 million by the end of the century.

Differences in growth rates will change the distribution of population among the geographic divisions and regions. The West, the South Atlantic Division and the East North Central Division will increase in relative importance.

All or almost all of the increase in population between 1960 and 1980 will be in urban territory, most of it in metropolitan areas. This increase will leave between 75 and 80 per cent of our population in urban territory and almost 70 per cent in metropolitan areas. Within metropolitan areas, close to 60 per cent of the population will be in suburbs.

Expansion of population will not be uniform among SMSA's, cities or counties. In fact, very wide variation may be expected within each type of smaller area.

College and university enrollment in 1980 is projected to be between 3 and 3½ times the 1960 figure. Elsewhere, enrollment will expand at less than the rates of the fifties. High school enrollment, however, will expand much more rapidly than the population as a whole.

Marked shifts in the composition of our population may be expected to continue. Perhaps the most significant is the changing age structure. In terms of average age, the population will be younger in 1980 than in 1960, but the underlying long-term increase in the proportion 65 years of age and over will continue. The most striking development during the sixties and seventies will be the increase of 80 per cent in persons 18 to 29 years of age.

Educational attainment levels will continue to rise so that, by 1980, the "average" adult 25 years of age and over will have received more than a high school education. By 1980, close to 60 per cent of the persons 18 years of age and over will be high school graduates; 10 per cent of those 22 years of age and over, college graduates.

Assuming continuation of recent net immigration, by 1980 the foreign-born population will number only 4 per cent of the total, and will have declined substantially in relative importance. By contrast, our nonwhite population, mostly Negro, growing more rapidly than the white population, will increase in importance and may well approach 13 per cent of the total by 1980. Negroes will continue to migrate to the North and the West and will become more and more urbanized and metropolitanized.

Changes in the occupational structure may not be as marked as in the past few decades. However, trends in the direction of increasing proportions of professional and technical, white-collar and service-trade workers may be expected to continue.

General References

Hauser, P. M.: Community Developments and Their Effect on Library Planning. *Library Quarterly*, 27:255-266, October 1957.

Hauser, P.M.: *Population Perspectives*. New Brunswick, N.J., Rutgers University Press, 1960.

References

1. Whelpton, P. K.: *Forecasts of the Population of the United States, 1945 to 1975*. Washington, D.C., U.S. Government Printing Office, 1947, p. 41.

2. Bogue, D. J.: *The Population of the United States*. Glencoe, Ill., The Free Press, 1959, p. 397.

3. U.S. Bureau of the Census: *1960 Census of Population*. "Supplementary Reports," PC(S1)-1 (April 10, 1961).

4. *Ibid.*

5. *Ibid.*

6. U.S. Bureau of the Census and Agricultural Marketing Service: *Farm Population*. Series Census-AMS (P-27), No. 28 (April 17, 1961) and No. 29 (April 18, 1961).

7. Bogue, *op. cit.*, p. 785.

8. U.S. Bureau of the Census: *Statistical Abstract of the United States: 1960*. 81st ed., Washington, D.C., 1960, p. 401.

9. University of Chicago Ninth Annual Management Conference, March 1, 1961.

CHART I

Per Cent Change in Population, by State, 1950–1960

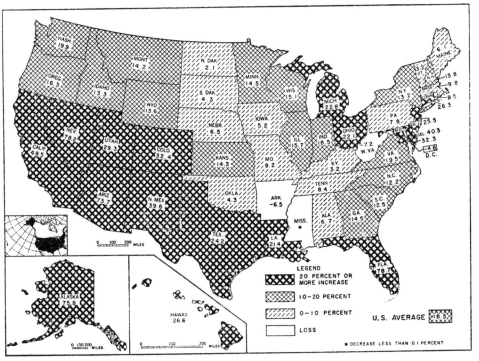

Source: U.S. Bureau of the Census: *1960 Census of Population.*
"Advance Reports," PC(A1)-1, p. 6 (November 15, 1960).

CHART II
Population, by Geographic Divisions, 1950–1980

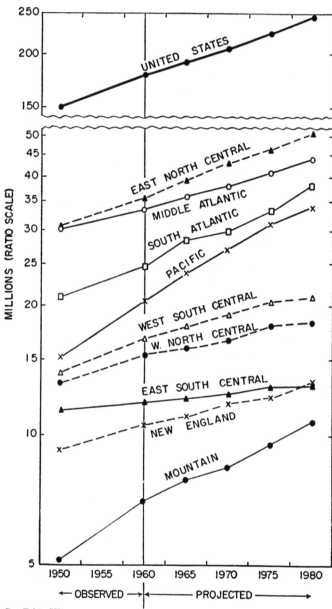

Source: See Table IV.

CHART III

Population Growth In and Outside SMSA's, by Regions, 1950–1960

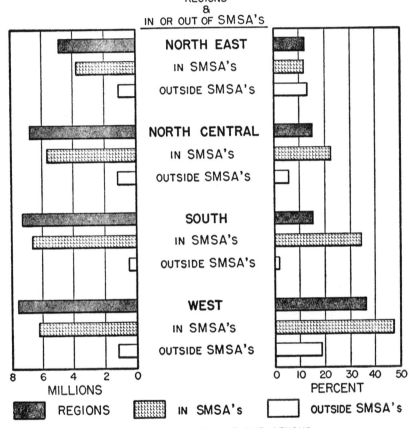

REGIONS
&
IN OR OUT OF SMSA'S

NORTH EAST
IN SMSA'S
OUTSIDE SMSA'S

NORTH CENTRAL
IN SMSA'S
OUTSIDE SMSA'S

SOUTH
IN SMSA'S
OUTSIDE SMSA'S

WEST
IN SMSA'S
OUTSIDE SMSA'S

8 6 4 2 0
MILLIONS

0 10 20 30 40 50
PERCENT

REGIONS   IN SMSA'S   OUTSIDE SMSA's

SOURCE: U.S. BUREAU OF THE CENSUS

CHART IV

Population by Age, 1950–1980

(Age in Years)

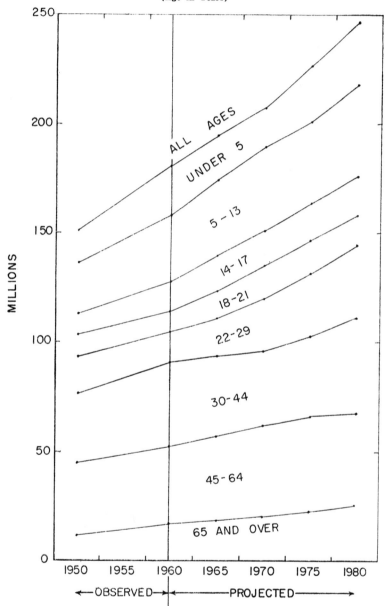

TABLE I
Rank of States According to Population: 1960

Rank	State	Population	Rank	State	Population
1	New York........	16,782,304	26	South Carolina....	2,382,594
2	California........	15,717,204	27	Oklahoma........	2,328,284
3	Pennsylvania.....	11,319,366	28	Kansas...........	2,178,611
4	Illinois..........	10,081,158	29	Mississippi.......	2,178,141
5	Ohio.............	9,706,397	30	West Virginia.....	1,860,421
6	Texas............	9,579,677	31	Arkansas.........	1,786,272
7	Michigan.........	7,823,194	32	Oregon..........	1,768,687
8	New Jersey.......	6,066,782	33	Colorado.........	1,753,947
9	Massachusetts....	5,148,578	34	Nebraska.........	1,411,330
10	Florida..........	4,951,560	35	Arizona..........	1,302,161
11	Indiana..........	4,662,498	36	Maine...........	969,265
12	North Carolina...	4,556,155	37	New Mexico......	951,023
13	Missouri.........	4,319,813	38	Utah............	890,627
14	Virginia.........	3,966,949	39	Rhode Island.....	859,488
15	Wisconsin........	3,951,777	40	Dist. of Col......	763,956
16	Georgia..........	3,943,116	41	South Dakota.....	680,514
17	Tennessee........	3,567,089	42	Montana.........	674,767
18	Minnesota........	3,413,864	43	Idaho...........	667,191
19	Alabama.........	3,266,740	44	Hawaii..........	632,772
20	Louisiana........	3,257,022	45	North Dakota....	632,446
21	Maryland........	3,100,689	46	New Hampshire...	606,921
22	Kentucky........	3,038,156	47	Delaware........	446,292
23	Washington.......	2,853,214	48	Vermont........	389,881
24	Iowa............	2,757,537	49	Wyoming........	330,066
25	Connecticut......	2,535,234	50	Nevada..........	285,278
			51	Alaska..........	226,167

Source: U. S. Bureau of the Census: *1960 Census of Population.* "Advance Reports," PC(A1)-1, Table 4 (November 15, 1960).

TABLE II

Population of the United States, by Regions, Divisions, and States: 1960 and 1950

(Minus sign (−) denotes decrease)

Area	Population		Increase, 1950 to 1960	
	1960	1950	Number	Per Cent
United States.............	179,323,175	151,325,798	27,997,377	18.5
REGIONS:				
Northeast.................	44,677,819	39,477,986	5,199,833	13.2
North Central.............	51,619,139	44,460,762	7,158,377	16.1
South....................	54,973,113	47,197,088	7,776,025	16.5
West....................	28,053,104	20,189,962	7,863,142	38.9
DIVISIONS:				
New England.............	10,509,367	9,314,453	1,194,914	12.8
Middle Atlantic...........	34,168,452	30,163,533	4,004,919	13.3
East North Central.........	36,225,024	30,399,368	5,825,656	19.2
West North Central........	15,394,115	14,061,394	1,332,721	9.5
South Atlantic.............	25,971,732	21,182,335	4,789,397	22.6
East South Central........	12,050,126	11,477,181	572,945	5.0
West South Central........	16,951,255	14,537,572	2,413,683	16.6
Mountain.................	6,855,060	5,074,998	1,780,062	35.1
Pacific...................	21,198,044	15,114,964	6,083,080	40.2
NEW ENGLAND:				
Maine....................	969,265	913,774	55,491	6.1
New Hampshire............	606,921	533,242	73,679	13.8
Vermont.................	389,881	377,747	12,134	3.2
Massachusetts.............	5,148,578	4,690,514	458,064	9.8
Rhode Island.............	859,488	791,896	67,592	8.5
Connecticut..............	2,535,234	2,007,280	527,954	26.3
MIDDLE ATLANTIC:				
New York................	16,782,304	14,830,192	1,952,112	13.2
New Jersey...............	6,066,782	4,835,329	1,231,453	25.5
Pennsylvania..............	11,319,366	10,498,012	821,354	7.8
EAST NORTH CENTRAL:				
Ohio.....................	9,706,397	7,946,627	1,759,770	22.1
Indiana..................	4,662,498	3,934,224	728,274	18.5
Illinois..................	10,081,158	8,712,176	1,368,982	15.7
Michigan.................	7,823,194	6,371,766	1,451,428	22.8
Wisconsin................	3,951,777	3,434,575	517,202	15.1
WEST NORTH CENTRAL:				
Minnesota................	3,413,864	2,982,483	431,381	14.5
Iowa....................	2,757,537	2,621,073	136,464	5.2
Missouri.................	4,319,813	3,954,653	365,160	9.2
North Dakota.............	632,446	619,636	12,810	2.1

(Table II, continued.)

Area	Population		Increase, 1950 to 1960	
	1960	1950	Number	Per Cent
WEST NORTH CENTRAL—CON.				
South Dakota.............	680,514	652,740	27,774	4.3
Nebraska.................	1,411,330	1,325,510	85,820	6.5
Kansas..................	2,178,611	1,905,299	273,312	14.3
SOUTH ATLANTIC:				
Delaware.................	446,292	318,085	128,207	40.3
Maryland.................	3,100,689	2,343,001	757,688	32.3
District of Columbia........	763,956	802,178	−38,222	−4.8
Virginia..................	3,966,949	3,318,680	648,269	19.5
West Virginia.............	1,860,421	2,005,552	−145,131	−7.2
North Carolina............	4,556,155	4,061,929	494,226	12.2
South Carolina............	2,382,594	2,117,027	265,567	12.5
Georgia..................	3,943,116	3,444,578	498,538	14.5
Florida..................	4,951,560	2,771,305	2,180,255	78.7
EAST SOUTH CENTRAL:				
Kentucky.................	3,038,156	2,944,806	93,350	3.2
Tennessee................	3,567,089	3,291,718	275,371	8.4
Alabama.................	3,266,740	3,061,743	204,997	6.7
Mississippi...............	2,178,141	2,178,914	−773	(¹)
WEST SOUTH CENTRAL:				
Arkansas.................	1,786,272	1,909,511	−123,239	−6.5
Louisiana................	3,257,022	2,683,516	573,506	21.4
Oklahoma................	2,328,284	2,233,351	94,933	4.3
Texas...................	9,579,677	7,711,194	1,868,483	24.2
MOUNTAIN:				
Montana..................	674,767	591,024	83,743	14.2
Idaho....................	667,191	588,637	78,554	13.3
Wyoming.................	330,066	290,529	39,537	13.6
Colorado.................	1,753,947	1,325,089	428,858	32.4
New Mexico..............	951,023	681,187	269,836	39.6
Arizona..................	1,302,161	749,587	552,574	73.7
Utah....................	890,627	688,862	201,765	29.3
Nevada..................	285,278	160,083	125,195	78.2
PACIFIC:				
Washington...............	2,853,214	2,378,963	474,251	19.9
Oregon..................	1,768,687	1,521,341	247,346	16.3
California................	15,717,204	10,586,223	5,130,981	48.5
Alaska...................	226,167	128,643	97,524	75.8
Hawaii..................	632,772	499,794	132,978	26.6

SOURCE: U. S. Bureau of the Census: *1960 Census of Population.* "Advance Reports," PC(A1)-1, Table 2 (November 15, 1960).

¹ Less than 0.1 per cent.

TABLE III

Counties With Population Decreases Between 1950 and 1960, by Regions, Divisions, and States

Region, Division and State	Total Counties	Counties with Population Decrease 1950 to 1960 (preliminary)	
		Number	Per Cent
Total United States...............	3,107	1,578	50.8
REGIONS:			
Northeast.........................	217	55	25.3
North Central....................	1,055	549	52.0
South............................	1,419	818	57.6
West.............................	416	156	37.5
DIVISIONS:			
New England.....................	67	18	26.9
Middle Atlantic..................	150	37	24.7
East North Central...............	436	136	31.2
West North Central...............	619	413	66.7
South Atlantic....................	585	268	45.8
East South Central...............	364	252	69.2
West South Central...............	470	298	63.4
Mountain........................	278	124	44.6
Pacific...........................	138	32	23.2
NEW ENGLAND:			
Maine............................	16	7	43.7
New Hampshire...................	10	1	10.0
Vermont.........................	14	8	57.1
Massachusetts....................	14	1	7.1
Rhode Island.....................	5	1	20.0
Connecticut......................	8	0	0.0
MIDDLE ATLANTIC:			
New York........................	62	10	16.1
New Jersey.......................	21	1	4.8
Pennsylvania.....................	67	26	38.8
EAST NORTH CENTRAL:			
Ohio.............................	88	10	11.4
Indiana..........................	92	19	20.7
Illinois...........................	102	51	50.0
Michigan.........................	83	17	20.5
Wisconsin........................	71	39	54.9
WEST NORTH CENTRAL:			
Minnesota.......................	87	39	44.8
Iowa.............................	99	61	61.6
Missouri.........................	115	85	73.9
North Dakota....................	53	41	77.4

(Table III, continued.)

Region, Division and State	Total Counties	Counties with Population Decrease 1950 to 1960 (preliminary)	
		Number	Per Cent
WEST NORTH CENTRAL—CON.			
South Dakota....................	67	44	65.7
Nebraska........................	93	72	77.4
Kansas..........................	105	71	67.6
SOUTH ATLANTIC:			
Delaware........................	3	0	0.0
Maryland........................	24	4	16.7
District of Columbia..............	1	1	100.0
Virginia [1].....................	130	50	38.5
West Virginia....................	55	43	78.2
North Carolina..................	100	39	39.0
South Carolina..................	46	21	45.7
Georgia.........................	159	97	61.0
Florida.........................	67	13	19.4
EAST SOUTH CENTRAL:			
Kentucky........................	120	86	71.7
Tennessee.......................	95	59	62.1
Alabama.........................	67	46	68.7
Mississippi......................	82	61	74.4
WEST SOUTH CENTRAL:			
Arkansas........................	75	69	92.0
Louisiana.......................	64	20	31.2
Oklahoma.......................	77	65	84.4
Texas...........................	254	144	56.7
MOUNTAIN:			
Montana........................	56	25	44.6
Idaho...........................	44	19	43.2
Wyoming........................	23	9	39.1
Colorado........................	63	36	57.1
New Mexico.....................	32	16	50.0
Arizona.........................	14	2	14.3
Utah............................	29	13	44.8
Nevada.........................	17	4	23.5
PACIFIC:			
Washington......................	39	14	35.9
Oregon..........................	36	7	19.4
California........................	58	7	12.1
Alaska..........................	([2])		
Hawaii..........................	5	4	80.0

SOURCE: U. S. Bureau of the Census: *1960 Census of Population.* "Preliminary Reports," PC (P1)-2 to 52, Table 1.

[1] Counties and independent cities.

[2] Not available.

TABLE IV

Population of the United States, by Geographic Divisions, Observed and Projected: 1950 to 1980

(In thousands. Excludes members of the Armed Forces overseas; includes Alaska and Hawaii.)

Geographic Division	Observed			Projected		
	1950	1960	1965	1970	1975	1980
United States.....	151,326	179,323	193,786	208,372	225,764	245,664
NORTHEAST:						
New England.....	‹9,314	10,509	11,031	11,604	12,281	13,051
Middle Atlantic....	30,164	34,168	36,502	38,791	41,604	44,776
NORTH CENTRAL:						
East North Central	30,399	36,225	39,687	43,141	47,118	51,702
West North Central	14,061	15,394	16,165	16,880	17,745	18,372
SOUTH:						
South Atlantic.....	21,182	25,972	28,167	30,355	33,584	38,150
East South Central	11,477	12,050	12,245	12,443	12,742	12,991
West South Central	14,538	16,951	18,034	19,119	20,301	21,585
WEST:						
Mountain........	5,075	6,855	7,727	8,604	9,574	10,642
Pacific............	15,115	21,198	24,228	27,035	30,815	34,395

SOURCES: Observations—U. S. Bureau of the Census: *1960 Census of Population.* "Advance Reports," PC (A1)-1, Table 2 (November 15, 1960). Projections—Based upon U. S. Bureau of the Census: *Current Population Reports,* Series P-25, No. 187, Table 1 (November 10, 1958) and Series P-25, No. 160, Table 1 (August 9, 1957). See Methodological notes.

METHODOLOGICAL NOTES: (1) For the U. S. totals, the Census projections (Series III in the P-25, No. 187 bulletin) assume fertility would decline from the 1955-57 level to the 1949-51 level by 1965-70 and would remain constant thereafter. Adjustments were made (a) to include Alaska and Hawaii, for which projections were derived from graphic extrapolations and (b) to exclude members of the Armed Forces overseas, for whom projections were based upon the assumption of increases proportionate with population. The census projections assume some lowering of mortality rates and net immigration of 300,000 per year—roughly the 1951-56 average.

(2) For the geographic divisions, the Census projections (Series 1 in the P-25, No. 160 bulletin) through 1970 were extrapolated graphically through 1980. Small adjustment factors were then applied to obtain agreement between the U. S. totals and totals of the divisions.

TABLE V

Population of the United States, Selected Per Cent Distributions and Per Cent Changes, by Geographic Divisions: 1950 to 1980

Geographic Division	Per Cent Increase		Per Cent of Total		
	1950–60	1960–80	1950	1960	1980
United States.........	18.5	37.0	100.0	100.0	100.0
NORTHEAST:					
New England.........	12.8	24.2	6.2	5.9	5.3
Middle Atlantic.......	13.3	31.0	19.9	19.1	18.3
NORTH CENTRAL:					
East North Central....	19.2	42.7	20.1	20.2	21.0
West North Central....	9.5	19.3	9.3	8.6	7.5
SOUTH:					
South Atlantic.........	22.6	46.9	14.0	14.4	15.5
East South Central....	5.0	7.8	7.6	6.7	5.3
West South Central....	16.6	27.3	9.6	9.5	8.8
WEST:					
Mountain.............	35.1	55.2	3.4	3.8	4.3
Pacific...............	40.2	62.2	9.9	11.8	14.0

SOURCES: See Table IV.

TABLE VI

Metropolitan Population of the United States, Estimates and Projections: 1900 to 1980

Year	Number of Areas	Population Number in Millions	Population Per Cent of U. S. Population	Population Per Cent in Suburban rings
Principal Standard Metropolitan Areas [1]				
1900	52	24.1	31.7	33.5
1910	71	34.5	37.5	33.7
1920	94	46.1	43.7	33.8
1930	115	61.0	49.8	36.1
1940	125	67.0	51.1	38.1
1950	147	84.3	56.0	42.4
Standard Metropolitan Areas				
1950	168	84.5	56.1	41.5
Standard Metropolitan Statistical Areas [2]				
1960	212	111.7	62.8	48.7
Projections				
1970	—	137	66	54
1980	—	170	69	58

SOURCES: Principal SMSA's—Bogue, D. J.: *Population Growth in Standard Metropolitan Areas: 1900-1950.* Washington, D. C., U. S. Government Printing Office, December, 1953, pp. 11, 13, and 28.

SMSA's—U. S. Bureau of the Census: *Census of Population: 1950,* Vol. I, pp. 1-3 and 1-69.

SMSA's—U. S. Bureau of the Census: *1960 Census of Population.* "Preliminary Reports," PC (P3)-4, pp. 2 and 19 (October 1960).

PROJECTIONS—Based upon Tables IV, VII and VIII, and upon R. P. Cuzzort: "The Size and Distribution of Standard Metropolitan Areas in 1975." In D. J. Bogue (ed.): *Applications of Demography: The Population Situation in the U. S. in 1975.* Oxford, Ohio, Miami University, 1957, pp. 63-64.

[1] Estimates based upon SMSA's boundaries in 1950 which included a total population of 100,000 or more and a central city with 50,000 or more inhabitants.

[2] Preliminary

TABLE VII

Population Growth In and Outside Standard Metropolitan Statistical
Areas, for the United States, by Regions: 1960 and 1950

(Minus sign (−) denotes decrease)

Region and Metropolitan or Nonmetropolitan Residence	1960 (preliminary)	1950	Increase, 1950 to 1960	
			Number	Per Cent
United States.........	177,874,042	151,325,798	26,548,244	17.5
In SMSA's..............	111,590,163	89,083,989	22,506,174	25.3
Central cities..........	57,173,526	52,243,901	4,929,625	9.4
Outside central cities...	54,416,637	36,840,088	17,576,549	47.7
Outside SMSA's.........	66,283,879	62,241,809	4,042,070	6.5
Northeast...........	44,358,717	39,477,986	4,880,731	12.4
In SMSA's..............	34,791,810	31,034,255	3,757,555	12.1
Central cities..........	17,001,902	17,754,012	−752,110	−4.2
Outside central cities...	17,789,908	13,280,243	4,509,665	34.0
Outside SMSA's.........	9,566,907	8,443,731	1,123,176	13.3
North Central.......	51,308,369	44,460,762	6,847,607	15.4
In SMSA's..............	30,768,320	25,074,674	5,693,646	22.7
Central cities..........	16,378,154	15,836,656	541,498	3.4
Outside central cities...	14,390,166	9,238,018	5,152,148	55.8
Outside SMSA's.........	20,540,049	19,386,088	1,153,961	6.0
South..............	54,463,053	47,197,088	7,265,965	15.4
In SMSA's..............	26,140,978	19,417,751	6,723,227	34.6
Central cities..........	14,828,847	11,720,837	3,108,010	26.5
Outside central cities...	11,312,131	7,696,914	3,615,217	47.0
Outside SMSA's.........	28,322,075	27,779,337	542,738	2.0
West..............	27,743,903	20,189,962	7,553,941	37.4
In SMSA's..............	19,889,055	13,557,309	6,331,746	46.7
Central cities..........	8,964,623	6,932,396	2,032,227	29.3
Outside central cities...	10,924,432	6,624,913	4,299,519	64.9
Outside SMSA's.........	7,854,848	6,632,653	1,222,195	18.4

SOURCE: U. S. Bureau of the Census: *1960 Census of Population.* "Preliminary Reports," PC (P3)–4, Table A (October 1960).

[53]

TABLE VIII

Population of Standard Metropolitan Statistical Areas by Components and by Size of Standard Metropolitan Statistical Areas, for the United States: 1960 and 1950

(Minus sign (−) denotes decrease)

Size and component parts of SMSA	1960 (preliminary)	1950	Increase, 1950 to 1960 Number	Increase, 1950 to 1960 Per Cent
All Sizes				
In SMSA's..............	111,590,163	89,083,989	22,506,174	25.3
Central cities..........	57,173,526	52,243,901	4,929,625	9.4
Outside central cities...	54,416,637	36,840,088	17,576,549	47.7
3,000,000 or More				
In SMSA's..............	31,487,604	25,788,967	5,698,637	22.1
Central cities..........	17,626,869	17,655,217	−28,348	−0.2
Outside central cities...	13,860,735	8,133,750	5,726,985	70.4
1,000,000 to 3,000,000				
In SMSA's..............	29,539,675	23,858,113	5,681,562	23.8
Central cities..........	12,538,009	12,037,125	500,884	4.2
Outside central cities...	17,001,666	11,820,988	5,180,678	43.8
500,000 to 1,000,000				
In SMSA's..............	18,527,237	13,772,608	4,754,629	34.5
Central cities..........	9,699,611	8,092,551	1,607,060	19.9
Outside central cities...	8,827,626	5,680,057	3,147,569	55.4
250,000 to 500,000				
In SMSA's..............	15,956,686	12,736,769	3,219,917	25.3
Central cities..........	7,818,081	6,788,612	1,029,469	15.2
Outside central cities...	8,138,605	5,948,157	2,190,448	36.8
100,000 to 250,000				
In SMSA's..............	14,380,622	11,546,694	2,833,928	24.5
Central cities..........	8,201,132	6,660,188	1,540,944	23.1
Outside central cities...	6,179,490	4,886,506	1,292,984	26.5
Under 100,000				
In SMSA's..............	1,698,339	1,380,838	317,501	23.0
Central cities..........	1,289,824	1,010,208	279,616	27.7
Outside central cities...	408,515	370,630	37,885	10.2

Source: U. S. Bureau of the Census: *1960 Census of Population.* "Preliminary Reports," PC (P3)–4, Table 2 (October 1960).

TABLE IX

Distribution of Standard Metropolitan Statistical Areas, by Size: 1960

Population Size Class	Number	Per Cent of Total SMSA Population
Total..............................	211	100.0
3,000,000 or more.........................	5	28.1
1,000,000 to 3,000,000....................	19	26.4
500,000 to 1,000,000....................	28	16.6
250,000 to 500,000....................	48	14.3
100,000 to 250,000....................	88	12.9
under 100,000....................	23	1.7

SOURCE: U. S. Bureau of the Census: *1960 Census of Population.* "Preliminary Reports," PC (P3)–4, Tables A and B and p. 19 (October 1960).

TABLE X

Standard Metropolitan Statistical Areas by Per Cent Change in Population 1950–1960

Per Cent Change in Population (preliminary)		Standard Metropolitan Statistical Areas	
		Number	Per Cent
Total U. S.		211	100.0
−15.0..............................	−10.1	1	0.5
−10.0..............................	−5.1	3	1.4
−5.0..............................	−0.1	5	2.4
0	4.9	12	5.7
5.0..............................	9.9	12	5.7
10.0..............................	14.9	17	8.0
15.0..............................	19.9	32	15.1
20.0..............................	24.9	32	15.1
25.0..............................	29.9	25	11.8
30.0..............................	34.9	18	8.5
35.0..............................	39.9	16	7.6
40.0..............................	44.9	5	2.4
45.0..............................	49.9	3	1.4
50.0..............................	54.9	5	2.4
55.0..............................	59.9	3	1.4
60.0..............................	64.9	2	1.0
65.0..............................	69.9	2	1.0
70.0..............................	74.9	2	1.0
75.0..............................	79.9	3	1.4
80.0..............................	84.9	1	0.5
85.0..............................	89.9	3	1.4
90.0..............................	94.9	1	0.5
95.0..............................	99.9	2	1.0
100.0 and over......................		6	2.8

SOURCE: U. S. Bureau of the Census: *1960 Census of Population.* "Preliminary Reports," PC (P3)–4, Table 4 (October 1960).

TABLE XI

Standard Metropolitan Statistical Areas with Population Increases of 50 Per Cent or More Between 1950 and 1960

	Population		
Standard Metropolitan Statistical Area	1960 (preliminary)	1950	Per Cent Increase
Albany, Ga.	74,787	43,617	71.5
Albuquerque, N. Mex.	260,162	145,673	78.6
Amarillo, Texas.	147,621	87,140	69.4
Colorado Springs, Colo.	142,643	74,523	91.4
Denver, Colo.	925,569	612,128	51.2
El Paso, Texas.	311,759	194,968	59.9
Fort Lauderdale - Hollywood, Fla.	329,406	83,933	292.5
Houston, Texas.	1,236,704	806,701	53.3
Huntsville, Ala.	116,612	72,903	60.0
Lake Charles, La.	142,307	89,635	58.8
Les Vegas, Nev.	125,466	48,289	159.8
Lawton, Okla.	89,320	55,165	61.9
Los Angeles - Long Beach, Calif.	6,668,975	4,367,911	52.7
Lubbock, Texas.	153,140	101,048	51.6
Miami, Fla.	921,625	495,084	86.2
Midland, Texas.	67,540	25,785	161.9
Odessa, Texas.	89,542	42,102	112.7
Orlando, Fla.	316,772	141,833	123.3
Pensacola, Fla.	202,140	131,260	54.0
Phoenix, Ariz.	657,688	331,770	98.2
Reno, Nev.	83,700	50,205	66.7
Sacramento, Calif.	500,204	277,140	80.5
San Bernardino - Riverside - Ontario, Calif.	800,865	451,688	77.3
San Diego, Calif.	1,000,856	556,808	79.7
San Jose, Calif.	638,054	290,547	119.6
Santa Barbara, Calif.	167,883	98,220	70.9
Tampa - St. Petersburg, Fla.	759,780	409,143	85.7
Tucson, Ariz.	261,428	141,216	85.1
West Palm Beach, Fla.	224,537	114,688	95.8
Wichita, Kans.	347,406	222,290	56.3

SOURCE: U. S. Bureau of the Census: *1960 Census of Population.* "Preliminary Reports," PC (P3)–4, Table 4 (October 1960).

TABLE XII

Standard Metropolitan Statistical Areas with Population Decreases or with Increases of Less than Five Per Cent Between 1950 and 1960

Region and SMSA	Population		Per Cent Increase
	1960 (preliminary)	1950	
NORTHEAST:			
Altoona, Pa.	136,027	139,514	−2.5
Fall River, Mass. - R. I.	137,420	137,298	0.1
Jersey City, N. J.	607,250	647,437	−6.2
Johnstown, Pa.	279,662	291,354	−4.0
Lawrence - Haverhill, Mass. - N. H.	188,663	182,442	3.4
Lewiston - Auburn, Maine	69,967	68,426	2.3
New Bedford, Mass.	142,257	141,984	0.2
Portland, Maine	119,677	119,942	−0.2
Scranton, Pa.	233,271	257,396	−9.4
Wilkes-Barre - Hazelton, Pa.	345,695	392,241	−11.9
NORTH CENTRAL:			
Evansville, Ind. - Ky.	196,634	191,137	2.9
St. Joseph, Mo.	89,897	96,826	−7.2
Sioux City, Iowa	107,863	103,917	3.8
Terre Haute, Ind.	107,668	105,160	2.4
SOUTH:			
Asheville, N. C.	127,367	124,403	2.4
Charleston, W. Va.	250,284	239,629	4.4
Fort Smith, Ark.	66,454	64,202	3.5
Gadsden, Ala.	96,048	93,892	2.3
Huntington - Ashland, W. Va.- Ky. - Ohio	252,780	245,795	2.8
Texarkana, Texas - Ark.	91,231	94,580	−3.5
Wheeling, W. Va. - Ohio	189,490	196,305	−3.5

SOURCE: U. S. Bureau of the Census: *1960 Census of Population.* "Preliminary Reports," PC (P3)–4, Table 4 (October 1960).

TABLE XIII

Population of the United States in Groups of Places Classified According to Size, 1950 and 1960

(Excludes members of the Armed Forces overseas; includes Alaska and Hawaii.)

Size of Place	1960			1950		
	Number of Places	Population Thousands	Per Cent	Number of Places	Population Thousands	Per Cent
United States...............	—	179,323	100.0	—	151,326	100.0
Urban territory...............	6,041	125,269	69.9	4,764	96,847	64.0
Places of 2,500 or more........	5,445	114,728	64.0	4,307	88,925	58.8
1,000,000 or more...........	5	17,484	9.7	5	17,404	11.5
500,000 to 1,000,000........	16	11,111	6.2	13	9,187	6.1
250,000 to 500,000.........	30	10,766	6.0	23	8,241	5.5
100,000 to 250,000.........	81	11,652	6.5	66	9,727	6.4
50,000 to 100,000.........	201	13,836	7.7	126	8,931	5.9
35,000 to 50,000.........	179	7,454	4.2	118	4,870	3.2
25,000 to 35,000.........	253	7,519	4.2	135	3,965	2.6
10,000 to 25,000.........	1,134	17,568	9.8	779	11,878	7.9
5,000 to 10,000.........	1,394	9,780	5.5	1,184	8,193	5.4
2,500 to 5,000.........	2,152	7,580	4.2	1,858	6,529	4.3
Places under 2,500...........	596	690	0.4	457	578	0.4
Other urban territory...........	—	9,851	5.5	—	7,344	4.8
Rural territory...........	13,749	54,054	30.1	13,851	54,479	36.0
Places of 1,000 to 2,500.......	4,151	6,497	3.6	4,186	6,515	4.3
Places under 1,000...........	9,598	3,894	2.2	9,665	4,037	2.7
Other rural territory...........	—	43,663	24.3	—	43,927	29.0

SOURCES: U. S. Bureau of the Census: *1950 Census of Population*, Vol. 1 and *1960 Census of Population*, "Final Reports," Series PC (1)-1A to 57A and courtesy of the Bureau. Cumulation for state data for 1960 gave rise to slight discrepancies with respect to final U. S. group totals.

TABLE XIV

Population of the United States, by Age: Observed and Projected, 1950 to 1980

(In thousands. Excludes members of the Armed Forces; includes Alaska and Hawaii.)

Age in Years	Observed			Projected		
	1950	1960	1965	1970	1975	1980
All ages........	151,326	179,323	193,786	208,372	225,764	245,664
Under 5.......	16,243	20,322	19,585	20,777	24,132	27,225
5 to 13.......	22,282	32,382	36,158	37,034	38,036	42,498
5 to 9...	13,263	18,692	20,586	20,444	21,637	24,983
10 and 11..	4,541	7,001	7,955	8,276	8,268	9,030
12 and 13..	4,478	6,689	7,617	8,314	8,131	8,485
14 to 17.......	8,443	11,398	14,941	15,797	16,566	16,455
14........	2,148	3,083	3,738	4,055	4,107	4,183
15 to 17...	6,295	8,315	11,203	11,742	12,459	12,272
18 to 21.......	8,888	9,406	11,774	14,637	15,932	16,277
18 and 19..	4,377	4,904	6,030	7,488	8,095	8,132
20 and 21..	4,511	4,502	5,744	7,149	7,837	8,145
22 to 29.......	19,344	17,168	18,870	23,485	28,596	31,562
22 to 24...	7,039	6,299	7,489	9,921	11,203	12,191
25 to 29...	12,305	10,869	11,381	13,564	17,393	19,371
30 to 44.......	33,109	36,030	35,333	34,533	36,436	42,927
30 to 34...	11,572	11,949	11,040	11,551	13,726	17,540
35 to 39...	11,296	12,481	11,900	11,095	11,608	13,771
40 to 44...	10,241	11,600	12,393	11,887	11,102	11,616
45 to 64.......	30,723	36,057	39,402	42,462	44,083	44,067
45 to 49...	9,101	10,879	11,431	12,261	11,779	11,023
50 to 54...	8,296	9,606	10,789	11,142	11,968	11,518
55 to 59...	7,252	8,430	9,385	10,321	10,687	11,501
60 to 64...	6,074	7,142	7,797	8,738	9,649	10,025
65 and over....	12,294	16,560	17,723	19,647	21,983	24,653
Median age....	30.2	29.5	28.1	27.2	27.0	27.1

SOURCES: U. S. Bureau of the Census—projections based upon *Current Population Reports*. Series P-25, No. 187 (November 10, 1958); 1950 data from *1950 Census of Population*, Vol. II, Parts 1, 51 and 52; 1960 data for 5-year cohorts from *1960 Census of Population*. "Advanced Reports," PC (A2)-1, Table 1 (March 31, 1961).

METHODOLOGICAL NOTES: (1) For U. S. totals, see (1) under Methodological Notes in Table IV.

(2) For age groups, the Census projections were adjusted (a) to include Alaska and Hawaii, for which the age distributions were assumed the same as for the total U. S. and (b) to exclude members of the Armed Forces, for whom the age distribution was assumed to remain constant.

(3) Except for 1950, data for intervals other than 5-year were cohorts obtained by interpolation, Newton's formula applied to cumulative age distributions.

[59]

TABLE XV

Population of the United States, Selected Per Cent Distributions and Per Cent Changes, by Age: 1950 to 1980

Age in Years	Per Cent Change		Per Cent of Total		
	1950 to 1960	1960 to 1980	1950	1960	1980
All ages.................	18.5	37.0 '	100.0	100.0	100.0
Under 5.................	25.1	34.0	10.7	11.3	11.1
5 to 13.................	45.3	31.2	14.7	18.0	17.3
5 to 9..............	40.9	33.7	8.7	10.4	10.2
10 and 11............	54.2	29.0	3.0	3.9	3.7
12 and 13............	49.4	27.0	3.0	3.7	3.4
14 to 17.................	35.0	44.4	5.6	6.4	6.7
14.................	43.5	35.7	1.4	1.7	1.7
15 to 17.............	32.1	47.6	4.2	4.7	5.0
18 to 21.................	5.8	73.0	5.9	5.3	6.6
18 and 19............	12.0	65.8	2.9	2.8	3.3
20 and 21............	−2.0	80.9	3.0	2.5	3.3
22 to 29.................	−11.2	83.8	12.8	9:6	12.9
22 to 24.............	−10.5	93.5	4.7	3.5	5.0
25 to 29.............	−11.7	78.2	8.1	6.1	7.9
30 to 44.................	8.8	19.1	21.9	20.1	17.5
30 to 34.............	3.3	46.8	7.7	6.7	7.2
35 to 39.............	10.5	10.3	7.4	7.0	5.6
40 to 44.............	13.3	0.1	6.8	6.4	4.7
45 to 64.................	17.4	22.2	20.3	20.1	17.9
45 to 49.............	19.5	1.3	6.0	6.0	4.4
50 to 54.............	15.8	19.9	5.5	5.4	4.7
55 to 59.............	16.2	36.4	4.8	4.7	4.7
60 to 64.............	17.6	40.4	4.0	4.0	4.1
65 and over.............	34.7	48.9	8.1	9.2	10.0

SOURCES AND METHODS: See Table XIV.

TABLE XVI

Fall School Enrollment in the United States: Estimates and Projections, 1950 to 1980

(In thousands. Civilian noninstitutional population 5 to 34 years of age. Includes kindergarten. Excludes Alaska and Hawaii.[1])

Age in Years	Estimates from Sample Data			Projections			
	1950	1955	1960 [1]	1965	1970	1975	1980
Total, 5 to 34	30,276	37,426	46,259	54,608	58,865	63,843	70,401
5 to 13....	20,716	26,548	32,059	34,645	34,711	36,293	40,749
5 and 6....	`4,061	5,520	6,438	7,346	7,413	7,750	9,096
7 to 13....	16,655	21,028	25,621	27,299	27,298	28,543	31,653
14 to 17....	6,953	7,970	10,242	13,286	15,064	15,782	15,856
18 and 19...	1,190	1,232	1,817	3,028	3,780	4,634	4,899
20 to 24....	959	1,010	1,350	2,228	3,243	4,021	4,730
25 to 29....	358	475	514	1,089	1,650	2,549	3,324
30 to 34......	100	192	278	332	417	564	843

SOURCES: Estimates—U. S. Bureau of the Census: *Current Population Reports.* Series P-20, No. 107 (January 16, 1961).
Projections—Those of D. J. Bogue: *The Population of the United States.* Glencoe, Ill., The Free Press, 1959, p. 777, adjusted to the population projections given in Table XIV.
[1] Data for 1960 include Alaska and Hawaii with an estimated enrollment of roughly 250,000 persons.

TABLE XVII

Fall School Enrollment in the United States, by Level of School: Estimates and Projections, 1950 to 1980

(In thousands. Civilian noninstitutional population 5 to 34 years of age. Excludes Alaska and Hawaii.[1])

Level of School	Estimates from Sample Data			Projections			
	1950	1955	1960 [1]	1965	1970	1975	1980
Total, 5 to 34 years..	30,276	37,426	46,259	54,608	58,865	63,843	70,401
Kindergarten	902	1,628	2,092				
Elementary School (grades 1 to 8)....	20,504	25,458	30,349	35,606	35,905	37,581	41,889
High School (grades 9 to 12)....	6,656	7,961	10,249	13,282	15,155	16,170	16,564
College or Professional School....	2,214	2,379	3,570	5,720	7,805	10,092	11,948

SOURCES: Estimates—U. S. Bureau of the Census: *Current Population Reports.* Series P-20, No. 107 (January 16, 1961).
Projections—Those of D. J. Bogue: *The Population of the United States.* Glencoe, Ill., The Free Press, 1959, p. 778, adjusted to the population projections given in Table XIV.
[1] Data for 1960 include Alaska and Hawaii with an estimated enrollment of roughly 250,000 persons.

TABLE XVIII

Fall School Enrollment in the United States, Selected Per Cent
Changes for Age Groups and School Level Groups: 1950 to 1980

	Per Cent Change	
Age or School Level Group	1950 to 1960	1960 to 1980
Total 5 to 34 years of age................................	52.8	52.2
Level of School:		
Elementary and Kindergarten........................	51.6	29.1
High School..	54.0	61.6
College or Professional................................	61.2	234.7
Age in Years:		
5 to 13..	54.8	27.1
5 and 6...	58.5	41.3
7 to 13..	53.8	23.5
14 to 17..	47.3	54.8
18 and 19..	52.7	169.6
20 to 24..	40.8	250.4
25 to 29..	43.6	546.7
30 to 34..	178.0	203.2

SOURCES: Computed from Tables XVI and XVII.

TABLE XIX

Median Years of School Completed by Persons 25 Years Old and
Over and Persons 25 to 29 Years of Age, for the United States:
Observed, Estimated and Projected, 1940 to 1980

Year	All Persons 25 Years Old and Over	Persons 25 to 29 Years of Age
1940...................................	8.6	10.3
1950...................................	9.3	12.1
1959...................................	11.0	12.3
1970...................................	12.0	12.5
1980...................................	12.3	12.5

SOURCES: U. S. Bureau of the Census: *1950 Census of Population.* Vol. II, Part 1, Table 115, and this article Tables XX–XXIII.

[62]

TABLE XX

Years of School Completed by Persons 25 Years Old and Over, by Age, for the United States: 1950

(In thousands. Excludes members of the Armed Forces overseas and Alaska and Hawaii.)

Age in Years	Total Population	Years of School Completed								Median School Years Completed
		None	Elementary School			High School		College		
			1 to 4	5 to 7	8	1 to 3	4	1 to 3	4 or more	
Total............	88,116	2,271	7,541	14,431	18,370	15,310	18,252	6,474	5,467	9.3
25 to 29......	12,242	103	466	1,163	1,363	2,677	4,276	1,255	939	12.1
30 to 34......	11,517	99	491	1,280	1,642	2,517	3,617	1,014	857	11.6
35 to 44......	21,451	251	1,279	3,213	4,116	4,404	4,855	1,769	1,564	10.3
45 to 54......	17,342	392	1,594	3,277	4,314	2,821	2,683	1,209	1,052	8.8
55 to 64......	13,294	607	1,717	2,788	3,551	1,701	1,593	719	618	8.4
65 and over...	12,270	819	1,994	2,710	3,384	1,190	1,228	508	437	8.2

SOURCE: U. S. Bureau of the Census: *1950 Census of Population*. Vol. II, Part 1, pp. 1-90 and 1-296. Number of persons in 20 per cent sample who reported education adjusted proportionately to sum to complete count for each age group.

TABLE XXI

Years of School Completed by Persons 25 Years Old and Over, by Age, for the United States, Civilian Population, March 1959

(In thousands. The "civilian population" for March 1959 includes 1,059,000 members of the Armed Forces living off post or on post with their families but excludes all other members of the Armed Forces. Excludes Alaska and Hawaii.)

Age in Years	Total Population	None	Elementary School			High School		College		School Years not Reported	Median School Years Completed
			1 to 4	5 to 7	8	1 to 3	4	1 to 3	4 or more		
Total	97,478	2,109	5,707	12,034	16,456	17,520	26,219	7,888	7,734	1,811	11.0
25 to 29	10,939	66	263	683	775	2,120	4,502	1,226	1,201	103	12.3
30 to 34	11,983	110	322	825	1,065	2,621	4,477	1,172	1,279	112	12.2
35 to 44	23,635	208	785	2,132	2,837	4,756	8,425	2,101	2,130	261	12.1
45 to 54	20,354	340	970	2,706	3,982	3,963	4,819	1,614	1,579	381	10.5
55 to 64	15,273	409	1,285	2,610	3,903	2,316	2,436	1,025	891	398	8.8
65 and over	15,294	976	2,082	3,078	3,894	1,744	1,560	750	654	556	8.3

SOURCE: U. S. Bureau of the Census: *Current Population Reports.* Series P-20, No. 99, Table 1 (February 4, 1960). Based upon a sample.

[64]

TABLE XXII

Years of School Completed by Persons 25 Years Old and Over, by Age, for the United States: Projections, 1970

(In thousands. Excludes members of the Armed Forces overseas and Alaska and Hawaii.)

Age in Years	Total Popu- lation	None	Years of School Completed							Median School Years Completed
			Elementary School			High School		College		
			1 to 4	5 to 7	8	1 to 3	4	1 to 3	4 or more	
Total.................	110,033	1,359	5,003	11,404	14,564	21,913	35,427	10,288	10,078	12.0
25 to 29.............	13,640	84	230	417	501	2,758	6,191	1,622	1,837	12.5
30 to 34.............	11,582	80	216	444	534	2,450	5,069	1,325	1,465	12.4
35 to 44.............	22,990	175	533	1,584	2,006	4,890	8,951	2,419	2,433	12.3
45 to 54.............	23,306	174	835	2,297	2,916	4,989	8,090	2,096	1,908	12.1
55 to 64.............	18,966	221	1,122	2,830	3,625	3,899	4,323	1,569	1,377	10.3
65 and over.........	19,549	625	2,067	3,832	4,982	2,927	2,803	1,257	1,058	8.7

Source: U. S. Bureau of the Census: *Current Population Reports.* Series P-20, No. 91, Table 1 (January 12, 1959).
Note: Projections assume improvement in educational attainment indicated by short-term trends.

TABLE XXIII

Years of School Completed by Persons 25 Years Old and Over, by Age, for the United States: Projections, 1980

(In thousands. Excludes members of the Armed Forces overseas and Alaska and Hawaii.)

Age in Years	Total Population	Years of School Completed								Median School Years Completed
		None	Elementary School			High School		College		
			1 to 4	5 to 7	8	1 to 3	4	1 to 3	4 or more	
Total	130,783	1,101	4,062	9,471	11,987	26,194	49,804	13,800	14,367	12.3
25 to 29	19,441	98	265	465	559	3,621	9,126	2,467	2,841	12.5
30 to 34	17,554	98	266	461	554	3,362	8,164	2,178	2,471	12.5
35 to 44	25,400	166	448	865	1,041	5,245	11,346	2,967	3,323	12.4
45 to 54	22,446	171	518	1,545	1,955	4,774	8,756	2,360	2,369	12.3
55 to 64	21,416	159	761	2,103	2,667	4,583	7,475	1,925	1,742	12.1
65 and over	24,526	409	1,804	4,032	5,211	4,609	4,937	1,903	1,621	9.5

SOURCE: U. S. Bureau of the Census: *Current Population Reports.* Series P-20, No. 91, Table 1 (January 12, 1959).

NOTE: Projections assume improvement in educational attainment indicated by short-term trends.

TABLE XXIV

*High School and College Graduates in the United States,
by Sex: 1940 and 1950, and Projections 1960 to 1980*

(Data for 1940 and 1950 for persons not reporting on educational attainment distributed
pro rata; data for 1960 to 1980 based upon low improvement rate in educational attainment.)

	High School Graduates [1]		College Graduates [2]	
Year and Sex	Number (thousands)	Per Cent of Population 18 Years and Over	Number (thousands)	Per Cent of Population 22 Years and Over
BOTH SEXES				
1940...............	25,670	28.1	3,852	4.8
1950...............	38,293	37.1	5,951	6.3
1960...............	51,571	44.7	8,109	7.6
1970...............	70,341	52.2	10,819	9.0
1980...............	95,115	58.9	14,895	10.4
MALE				
1940...............	11,838	25.9	2,258	5.5
1950...............	17,591	34.9	3,369	7.3
1960...............	23,972	42.3	4,820	9.4
1970...............	32,547	49.7	6,537	11.3
1980...............	43,905	56.0	9,213	13.3
FEMALE				
1940...............	13,832	30.2	1,594	3.9
1950...............	20,703	39.1	2,582	5.3
1960...............	27,599	46.6	3,289	6.0
1970...............	37,794	54.5	4,282	6.9
1980...............	51,209	61.6	5,682	7.6

SOURCE: U. S. Bureau of the Census: *Current Population Reports.* Series P-20, No. 91, Table A
(January 12, 1959) with percentages adjusted for differences in base age groups used.
[1] Persons who completed 4 years of high school or beyond.
[2] Persons who completed 4 or more years of college.

TABLE XXV

Population of the United States, by Color and Nativity: Observed and Projected, 1950 to 1980

(Excludes members of the Armed Forces overseas; includes Alaska and Hawaii.)

| | Total | White | | | Nonwhite |
		Total	Native	Foreign-born	
		Number in Thousands			
1950	151,326	135,150	124,976	10,174	16,176
1960	179,323	158,832	148,432	10,400	20,491
1970	208,372	183,367	172,867	10,500	25,005
1980	245,664	214,219	203,469	10,750	31,445
		Per Cent of Total			
1950	100.0	89.3	82.6	6.7	10.7
1960	100.0	88.6	82.8	5.8	11.4
1970	100.0	88.0	83.0	5.0	12.0
1980	100.0	87.2	82.8	4.4	12.8

SOURCES: U. S. Bureau of the Census: *1960 Census of Population.* "Advanced Reports," PC (A2)-1, Table 1 (March 31, 1961), and *1950 Census of Population.* Vol. II, Parts 1, 51 and 52 for 1950 data, and 1960 data except foreign-born.
Bogue, D. J.: *The Population of the United States.* Glencoe, Ill., The Free Press, 1959, p. 771, for number of foreign-born, 1960 to 1980 and for per cent nonwhite, 1970 and 1980; these latter increased by 0.1 per cent in the light of 1960 Census data.
All other figures are from Table IV of this article, or computed from other figures in this table.

[68]

TABLE XXVI

Negro Population of the United States, by Selected Areas: 1960

Area	Number (thousands)
Total U. S.	18,872
10 SMSA's in North and West	4,893
New York, N. Y.	1,228
Chicago, Ill.	890
Philadelphia, Pa.	671
Detroit, Mich.	559
Los Angeles - Long Beach, Calif.	465
St. Louis, Mo. - Ill.	295
Cleveland, Ohio	257
San Francisco - Oakland, Calif.	239
Pittsburgh, Pa.	161
Cincinnati, Ohio - Ky.	128
Other North and West	2,667
8 SMSA's in South	2,037
Washington, D. C., Md. - Va.	487
Baltimore, Md.	379
New Orleans, La.	267
Houston, Texas	246
Atlanta, Ga.	231
Memphis, Tenn.	227
Dallas, Texas	155
San Antonio, Texas	45
Other South	9,275

Source: U. S. Department of Commerce: (Census) *Press Releases.* CB61-11 (March 7, 1961) and CB61-22 (March 26, 1961).

TABLE XXVII

Major Occupation Group of Employed Persons, for the United States: 1950–1960

(In thousands of persons 14 years old and over. 1950 and 1955 data exclude Alaska and Hawaii and, for occupation groups, have not been adjusted to reflect 1957 change in definition of employment and unemployment.)

Major Occupation Group	1950	1955	1960	Per Cent Change 1950 to 1960
Total, adjusted to 1957 definitions	59,748	62,944	66,681	11.6
Total, not adjusted to 1957 definitions	59,652	62,997		
Professional, technical, and kindred workers	4,490	5,792	7,474	66.4
Farmers and farm managers	4,393	3,739	2,780	−36.7
Managers, officials, and proprietors, except farm	6,429	6,450	7,067	9.9
Clerical and kindred workers	7,632	8,367	9,783	28.2
Sales workers	3,822	3,976	4,401	15.1
Craftsmen, foremen, and kindred workers	7,670	8,328	8,560	11.6
Operatives and kindred workers	12,146	12,762	11,986	−1.3
Private household workers	1,883	1,946	2,216	17.7
Service workers, except private household	4,652	5,160	6,133	31.8
Farm laborers and foremen	3,015	2,798	2,615	13.3
Laborers, except farm and mine	3,520	3,681	3,665	4.1

SOURCES: 1950 and 1955—U. S. Bureau of the Census: *Statistical Abstract of the United States: 1960.* pp. 205 and 216 (as obtained from *Current Population Reports,* Series P-50).

1960—U. S. Bureau of Labor Statistics: *Monthly Report on The Labor Force: December 1960.* Table 20.

Part II

EDITOR'S NOTE: In the following pages references to the Hauser-Taitel data and projections direct the reader to *Library Trends*, X:10-67, July 1961. These references now appear also in Part I of this work, pages 13-70. The numbering of the tables remains as in the journal issue; however, the pagination has been changed.

Libraries In The Federal Government

PAUL HOWARD

LIBRARIES IN THE FEDERAL GOVERNMENT are
as many and varied as the multi-faceted activities of the government
itself which, in turn, reflects the wide-ranging interests of the American
people. In size they range from office collections just beginning to
require organization to the gargantuan Library of Congress or the
world-wide public library service of the Army. There is no federal
library system. It is doubtful that a single system can be organized
or would be desirable. F. Mohrhardt, in 1953,[1] described five library
systems in the federal government, one of which served all elements
in its agency, but he did not conclude that any of these systems included all libraries in its agency. Eight years later this writer still
knows of no federal department which has all of its libraries in a single
system.

For these and other reasons the definition of federal library becomes
difficult. It involves such questions as: When does an office collection
become a library? Is an information center a library? Is a film collection a library? If this paper were a comprehensive study, it would
include libraries serving the research needs of federal officials, national
libraries, presidential libraries, public and general purpose libraries
within the federal establishment, and libraries in federal educational
and correctional institutions and in federal hospitals. They have three
common characteristics: financial support, control, and operation by
the federal government. A more comprehensive study will be found
in *Library Trends* for July 1953.[2]

In order to bring this study within manageable bounds, it is necessary to limit it further to two types of federal library: national libraries
and libraries serving the research needs of federal officials. This limi-
tation is done with regret and with the knowledge that the majority
of federal libraries are excluded. The regret is increased by a belief
that in many ways the excluded libraries are working as effectively

Mr. Howard is Librarian of the U.S. Department of the Interior.

[73]

in their areas as the ones under consideration. However, we do believe that the establishments which most generally carry the connotation of "federal library" are the research libraries of the major executive agencies and the Library of Congress.

When one is considering these libraries, it is necessary to consider the structure of the federal government itself because the government looks upon its libraries as service organizations, and they follow the structure of the agencies they serve. The federal government is composed of three branches, the Legislative, the Executive and the Judicial. In many ways these are separate governments which may cooperate but are not coordinated. This situation is the reason for many of the deficiencies in federal library service today. In a similar way, the Executive Branch of the government is not a centralized, coordinated arm. The mission of each agency is prescribed by statute and regulation. The organization of each agency is guided by the needs of its mission, the evolving theories of administration, and the restraining hand of tradition. In this setting federal libraries have grown, not as a result of planned organized thinking, but in answer to specific needs of an individual office, a division, a bureau, or a department. As a result, there is no typical federal library or federal librarian. The type of pattern developed in the federal library service is like the patterns of nature rather than like the patterns of industrial designers.

In the Executive Branch there are more than 250 libraries of the kind we have under consideration. In addition, the military services operate the equivalent of public libraries and school libraries amounting to more library installations than any other public library system or school library system in the country. There are federal library collections in national parks, Indian schools, and veterans' hospitals, so that the totality of libraries in the Executive Branch is greater than 1,500, and the total expenditures exceed $60,000,000 annually. (This figure is an estimate derived by using Civil Service Commission figures on the number of librarians and library assistants in 1959, plus a figure for other employees derived from the unpublished Brookings Institution's Federal Library Survey.)

There are two national libraries in the Executive Branch and the Library of Congress in the Legislative Branch.

The nature of library collections in the federal government has been changing since World War II. The size has been increasing; the proportion of nonbook materials, such as technical reports and microforms, has grown. There is increasing concern over the scope of collections and the interrelation between them. Although there is yet no government-wide machinery established for coordinating collection policies, this seems imminent and will undoubtedly be stimulated by the report of the Federal Library Survey.[3]

Increasing attention has been paid in recent years to the establishment of higher personnel standards for federal librarians. A determined effort has been made by the federal librarians' group to keep the acute shortage of librarians from diluting their professional quality. New job standards have been developed by cooperative effort of professional library organizations and the Civil Service Commission. Efforts have been made to establish a positive educational requirement for entrance into the federal library service and, although this attempt has not been completely successful, entrance requirements have been strengthened and a program is now underway to develop a comprehensive entrance examination to be used in lieu of graduation from a recognized library school. At the same time there is an increasing demand for competence in the technologies with which the library is involved. This need has led to the employment of "technical librarians," subject specialists who attempt to learn library techniques on the job. Although this effort has not been very successful, it does point to a need and toward the sort of solution developed in some industrial firms, such as the Esso Engineering Company, where the summarizing, analysis, evaluation, interpretation, and application of technical literature are done by scientists and engineers, and the collection, organization, control, and retrieval are done by librarians.[4] A third trend in library personnel is to increase the percentage of clerical and subprofessional personnel in relation to professionals. (Information from the Federal Library Survey indicates that the percentage of increase in the number of library assistants is approximately 45 per cent greater than for librarians.)

Library techniques, in common with techniques in other governmental operations, tend to become more routinized and simplified. More records and communications are committed to standard forms than in the past. Procedures are streamlined. Unessential details are omitted, and the continuous pressure of mounting costs is forcing reconsideration of almost every step in acquiring, organizing, and servicing library materials.

Another pressure which affects library operations is the urgency arising from an exploding technology, which has led to the growing importance of technical reports and to a tremendous increase in technical journal publication. It is leading to experimentation with machine retrieval of information. There is deep concern over the scope and coverage of bibliographic tools, and the federal government is greatly involved in the development of machine translating systems.

The federal library appears to be at a critical point in its development. The tremendous outpouring of information through numerous media and in varied forms is forcing a revision of library programs and a reassessment of the library's role in the research function of the federal government. The development of machine technology and the enthusiasm of some of its proponents are urging changes at a faster rate than either the libraries or the machines can accommodate.

A number of federal agencies are studying this problem ranging from early studies and experimentation in the Department of Defense and the Central Intelligence Agency to the recently announced project in the Library of Congress. A list of such projects involving the federal government would be surprisingly long.[5]

A delineation of the status of federal libraries would be incomplete without consideration of their relation to each other and to nonfederal libraries. The Library of Congress, the National Library of Medicine, and the Library of the Department of Agriculture are recognized as great national libraries. In addition to providing great collections of research materials, they provide bibliographic services unmatched by those of any other libraries, they share the wealth of their collections with other libraries through loans, photoduplication, recordings, etc., and they provide leadership and assistance on professional problems. There are very few programs for the advancement of library work in which federal librarians do not participate.

To convey some idea of the extent of the collection sharing, the Library of Congress' Public Relations Office reports the following statistics on its lending to other libraries:

FY 1945 — 155,770
FY 1950 — 183,685
FY 1960 — 202,451
FY 1961 — 202,010

From observing the proportions of interlibrary borrowing between other federal libraries and between them and the Library of Congress, one might reasonably conclude that the total figure on federal interlibrary loan is slightly more than double this amount.

The three libraries mentioned constitute only a part of those federal libraries which work with other libraries. Most federal agencies have libraries which provide service to other libraries and to scholars in appropriate fields. Some of these libraries are outstanding and give more than they receive; others are weak and receive more than they give. There seems to be no barrier between federal and nonfederal as far as libraries are concerned. There are many services which the federal government provides for libraries which are not provided by the federal libraries themselves. The publications shelved in depository libraries, the postal rates, the statistical programs of the Office of Education, and the Library Services Act come to mind as examples. The federal government is deeply involved with libraries and indications are that it will be more so in the future.

The federal government has been in the throes of almost revolutionary changes in its role in the life of the American people. Much of this change is related to and is a result of the surging pressures of an ever-growing population. The frontier is disappearing. The cream of the free land is gone. Our economy has changed from rural domination to metropolitan domination. We are now in the process of political change to accommodate ourselves to the new situation. The role of the federal government seems destined to be one of greater interest in the general welfare of the people, of great social programs and great scientific research. As our population increases, the proportionate volume of our natural resources decreases until the people as a whole, through their government, are forced to devise newer and better ways of exploiting these resources, of getting more and more value from them. We must renew the renewable resources, conserve the nonrenewable, and develop new materials and resources. We must obtain fresh water from the sea, new minerals from research, and develop unknown wealth through science.

Moreover, the pressures of an increasing population are not confined within the boundaries of the United States. The cry for *lebensraum* did not die with Hitler. China moves in Asia with inexorable pressure. Over the world the demands of the starving increase the problems of our federal government. Our defense establishment grows greater and infinitely more complex. We grow more concerned with the mores and problems of strange people. Our prestige and survival depend upon our understanding and our research, upon our laboratories and libraries.

If these are true portents, a dominant function of the federal government will be research on a long-term permanent basis.[6] The pressure of research upon federal libraries is increasingly felt as is illustrated by the number of congressional reference inquiries handled by the Library of Congress, which rose from 64,849 in 1950 to 123,391 in 1960.[7] All research programs require organized, controlled information, but they do not necessarily require information in the form that we have had in the past. It can be that here lies the federal library's great challenge and opportunity. That evolution of the library program in relation to the research program of the federal government will in the long run outweigh the changes arising from changing techniques whether manual, mechanical, or electronic.

If we assume that there is a historical basis for institutional development and growth, we must assume that out of the problems of today the libraries of tomorrow will be shaped.

These problems are not peculiar to federal libraries. They are faced by research libraries everywhere, in industry and in universities. Most of them are not solely library problems, but are problems faced by scientists and scholars and by the learned world in general. They have to do with the organization of knowledge, with encompassing and controlling the great flood of literature which threatens to engulf us. They have to do with the application of pertinent portions of that literature to the solution of particular problems, with the development of programs and techniques for the mastery of information. They may be divided into four groups: problems of relationship, problems of library technology, problems of literature, and problems of administration.

The relations between federal libraries and federal research, between federal research and nonfederal research or federally-subsidized research form some of the basic problems facing the federal libraries. In general, libraries need to define their role in relation to the research programs in which the federal government participates. Policies need to be established to determine when library participation begins, to what extent the library acts independently, and where bibliographic service merges into analysis, evaluation, and synthesis of the literature. Until this range of participation is made clear, it will be impossible to distinguish between the functions of the librarian and the scientist. Until this distinction is made, there will be confusion, lost motion, conflict, instead of teamwork, and we will experience the frustrations which arise when able, well-intentioned specialists attempt to perform expertly outside their special fields. Until this clarification is accomplished, it will be difficult to obtain the full understanding and support from management which will allow the library to do its job well. The problem is emphasized by current development in literary production, data processing, and the development of technical information programs.

A second group of problems involving relationship has to do with the cooperative relations between libraries. In the federal establishment a great deal of cooperation exists, but there are possibilities for so much greater cooperation that if they were realized, it would amount to a revolution in federal library management. The problems of interlibrary cooperation are so inextricably interwoven with other problems facing libraries that before we have finished considering cooperation we will have discussed the others also.

The Library of Congress, the National Library of Medicine, and the Department of Agriculture Library have been able to reach a sort of working agreement which assigns responsibility for building great national collections which are retrospective and comprehensive in the fields of medicine and agriculture. That such agreements have not been reached in other areas is due to a number of factors: few other agencies in the Executive Branch have defined their missions in such a way that they require the establishment and continuing maintenance in perpetuity of great research libraries which are so comprehensive in scope and depth that they can become in effect national libraries. In fact, few agencies in the Executive Branch have been specific in determining the limits of the library service which they need and desire. Without such definitions it becomes extremely difficult to decide upon the areas of cooperation between federal libraries. It becomes almost impossible to assume that the responsibility for collecting completely in any specific field is being fulfilled, other than in medicine or agriculture, and perhaps geology, except as the Library of Congress has assumed that obligation.

The need for defining library missions in terms of scope and coverage is emphasized if one considers the problem of establishing a federal interlibrary storage center or joint bibliographic projects.

It is surprising that with this lack of clear-cut mission the system of interlibrary loans works as well as it does. Other areas of cooperation, such as joint research projects, joint cataloging, and mechanical preparation of library materials, can be developed without this basic definition of the roles of the various libraries, but in many respects they will be hampered because of this lack.

Federal libraries, in common with other research libraries, are confronted with a flood of literature in innumerable forms and various languages. The problems of listing and analyzing this material and of informing the library's clientele of its existence and of making it available to them have not been solved. However, progress is being made. There are indications that libraries are accommodating their organizations to meet this need, but that there is a long way to go in the federal library system. The federal government is becoming increasingly concerned to see that bibliographic tools are adequate to meet the research needs not only of the government itself but also of the nation as a whole.[8] It is concerned to see that gaps in coverage are filled and that unnecessary duplication is avoided, but that the interests of the various disciplines are adequately represented. It is concerned with prompt issuance of these tools and with the maintenance of effective standards of quality and usefulness. It is attempting to devise some program of joint action in this area.

An integral part of these problems is that posed by foreign literature. The purchase of foreign literature in translation wrecks library budgets. The percentage of foreign journals on federal library shelves is increasing at a rapid rate. In addition to the bibliographic problems posed by English language literature, the problem of translating this material is more complicated than substituting English equivalents for foreign words and phrases. Translators must be versed in the science as well as in the language. If machine translation is used, special vocabularies must be established for each scientific discipline, and these must be kept current. The editing of machine translations poses special problems.[9]

Most federal libraries are faced with serious problems of space and equipment. That they are not the only federal institutions so confronted does not lessen the seriousness of their problems. Three characteristics are typical: inadequacy, obsolescence, and improper planning. Often the library bookstock has overflowed the reader space; the furniture and equipment are the residue from countless moves of other offices. The library is located obscurely in quarters planned for other purposes. The federal librarian in library quarters designed for library service is envied by his colleagues. Some library space problems could be solved by judicious weeding of the collections, but this is often difficult because of lack of staff.

At the beginning of this article it was stated that the author knows of no federal department which has brought all of its libraries under a single system. This decentralization of library administration and operations generally follows the pattern of the departments themselves, especially when the functions of a number of bureaus are dissimilar or when there is widespread geographic dispersion. This administrative decentralization makes the application of standards difficult. It also makes the development of an adequate library program and service difficult. These deficiencies are offset by the closeness of the smaller libraries to their constituents. The problem will be to maintain the advantage of decentralization and at the same time to establish a high quality of service throughout the agency.

Problems of procurement plague federal librarians in many ways. Federal procurement regulations are not designed to take full advantage of the operations of the book trade. The requirements which give undue advantage to price over service in the purchase of books, periodicals, and binding, and the procedural restrictions on such procurement are often handicaps in building adequate collections of materials. The lack of communication between libraries often means that full advantage is not taken of new developments in procurement.

Most federal libraries are open to the public for reference use, and many of them make their materials available to the public through interlibrary loan. However, because federal libraries are usually not planned for use by the general public, problems of budget and administration arise. The most seriously affected is the Library of Congress, which sorely needs the space in a third building now being planned. On the reverse side of the coin many federal agencies have stations on college and university campuses and use their libraries freely. Contracts for federally-sponsored research carry provisions for library support of the projects. As the Federal Research Program expands, the problem will undoubtedly be emphasized.

It has been indicated that the federal government spends a minimum of $60,000,000 per year on library service; yet many librarians and research workers feel that a greater proportion of federal funds spent on the provision, the analysis, and the evaluation of literature will redound to the government's benefit. In addition, there is an evident need for fuller comprehension of the optimum role of the library in a research program on the part of management and directors of research. These problems go to the heart of any program for library development.

The status of federal libraries, the trends in federal library operations, and the problems faced by federal libraries have been examined, together with some of the demographic forces playing upon the federal government itself. Now "fire burn, and cauldron bubble." Will this conglomeration give some indication of what will occur in twenty years? Logic would indicate that it will, that change arises from causes, that the future is built upon the past, and that one may discount the possibility of an entirely new kind of library, unrelated to libraries of today, which will in twenty years spring unheralded from the Jovian brow of an unknown library genius. The odds are against such an event. If some genius should conceive a brilliant revolutionary program, entirely different from anything that has gone before, the chances are (human nature and entrenched interests being what they are) that it would be discarded and that the slow processes of evolution would continue. The library of 1980 will be what the forces of history, demography, politics, and science make it.

This is not to say that the federal library in 1980 will be the same as the federal library of today. The demands upon the government will require changed instruments of service. It is likely that the federal establishment will be much larger. When the population of the United States in 1880 was 50 million, federal employment was less than 140,000 (0.28 per cent), when it became 123 million in 1930 federal employment rose to 856,000 (0.7 per cent), and when it became 179 million in 1960 federal employment rose to 5.2 million (2.9 per cent).[10]

In 1980, with an estimated population of 246 million, federal employment is likely to reach more than 7,500,000 (3 per cent). To provide library service and other essential information services for a staff of this size will require at least 50 per cent increase in the size of the library service, if the factor of size is considered alone. The chances are that the increase will be greater.

However, size of federal employment is only one of a number of factors which are likely to affect the size of the federal library service. The nature of the problems with which the federal government will deal will be a more potent factor than the size of the library's clientele. The development of scientific management within the federal establishment will be another potent factor. A third factor will be improvements in library technology and in the whole area of communications, which may change the nature of staff and services provided by libraries and information centers. Technical advances may have more influence upon the nature of library service in 1980 than any other cause.

In addition to its steady growth in size the federal government has

[82]

experienced a change in the nature of services demanded by its citizens. The general welfare provision in the Constitution covers more and more activities. The increasing mobility of the population makes state boundaries less important and the federal government more important. Government services in public health, in economic assistance and development, in exploiting and conserving natural resources, in educational and social fields are growing apace. In 1961 the military is still the great consumer of government funds, and it is likely to be in the foreseeable future. However, the military grows more and more dependent upon research, as do the civilian agencies. Research seems destined to be the most important function of government as far as expenditures of time and money are concerned. It is likely that applied research will dominate but that pure research in the basic sciences will also increase as a governmental activity. The increased research activities will result in increased production of technical reports, documents, and journals. It will also make it incumbent upon the government to be even more active in the support and direction of documentation and bibliographic programs.

Present indications are that advanced systems of bibliographic service will have been developed by 1980. Judging by present demands and problems, it is likely that such systems will provide faster reporting, more detailed indexing, and more comprehensive coverage. It is also likely that such bibliographic services will not be able to cope fully with the insistent demands of scientific research, because the areas of research expand outward like cancer cells, each cell furnishing sustenance for innumerable new cells. The only limits upon research are the limits to man's unbounded imagination. In spite of improved machines, improved techniques and standardization of the product, bibliographic tools are likely to be extremely expensive. Such increased expense is likely to be caused by refinements in the product for which the improved techniques, standardization, and mass production will not wholly compensate. It must then be assumed that in 1980 federal libraries will merely be upon the threshold of newer and greater developments in bibliographic service.

It is likely that by 1980 machines will be available to assist in every library operation. By that time the problems of circulation controls should have been worked out. This should include not only the problem of charging and discharging books but also the problems of automatic circulation of new materials. A daily summary of library receipts, which would be divided into segments and delivered to the desks of appropriate research workers as part of the library service to readers, should be technically feasible, and in high priority research it should be economically possible by then. Use of machines as tools to assist in such operations would require only the refinement and mass production of machines already in existence or in the development stage in 1961.

This possibility suggests that the development of machines for library use will go through a period of experimentation and adaptation, then standardization and mass production. It is likely that because of cost, libraries will be forced to adjust some of their procedures to take advantage of machine time available in central processing units of the agencies.

In the field of communications current developments promise to lead to increased usefulness for libraries. Instantaneous facsimile transmission of library materials is close to reality. Current equipment is capable of transmitting a limited amount at a still prohibitive price, but the possibility of speeding up the scanning devices and reducing the cost is great. There is doubt that the dream of a laboratory worker dialing a code from his desk and receiving a facsimile of the latest research in his field can be realized by 1980, but communication between library centers by this method may be reached.

Automatic translating machines are emerging from the laboratory stage.[9] Automatic indexing is a possibility although there is still doubt that it can be effective without the application of human judgment. The storage and retrieval of technical data and information on machines are realities today, and millions of dollars are being spent by the government on this kind of program, both for experiment and application. By 1980 the use of machine-stored information in special fields should be almost commonplace in the major government libraries or information centers.

By 1980 technologists should have perfected reading devices which will have overcome many of the handicaps to using microforms. It will then be possible to do adequate research in isolated places, to store great libraries in a few rooms.

There is no doubt that duplication methods will have been improved to such an extent that copying library materials will in many cases be preferred to lending. It will be cheaper to present the reader with facsimiles of source materials than to lend him the volumes.

At present there seems to be no indication of the development of a federal library system, although it is likely that much coordination of federal library services and cooperation among libraries will be achieved. Communication between federal libraries will be more formally and efficiently established. Acting together, they will have established standards of service and a reporting service. Research on library techniques and problems will be operated on a planned program, either in the Library of Congress or in a new joint agency established for this purpose. The number of national libraries will have been increased, with pure science and engineering being the most likely prospects for coverage. There will be jointly operated acquisition programs probably with a limited form of cooperative cataloging which, nevertheless, will go beyond that now provided by the Library of Congress. A federal library storage center will be a necessity and will have been organized but will be experiencing problems of communication and policy.

It is evident that there will be a change in the role of the library. There will be an information service staffed by librarians, subject specialists, and technologists. Literature will be collected, organized, analyzed and evaluated according to the needs of the federal agency served.

The individual library will be able to provide pertinent literature upon every topic of value to its clientele and will do so as the literature appears, as well as upon demand. Machine retrieval of literature upon specific topics from individual points of interest will be available as will summaries and evaluations of the literature for specific purposes. Libraries will be equipped with numerous reading machines which may be loaned with the microforms. They will also be able to provide instant cheap copies of library materials or facsimile copies of materials from selected libraries.

Machine coding will be done at great depth while the general library catalog will have fewer analytics but more annotation. Probably a greater portion will be ready-made and purchased from outside sources. With machine searching of literature it will be possible and will be necessary to use a greater portion of the library staff for organizing the literature.

Of necessity the programming of library operations will be included with the programming of research and development. The cost of libraries will force greater attention from management, and use of the library will have become essential in every research program. Library service within an individual federal agency should be more universally available even in remote locations. Although it is not likely that field libraries can be discontinued, it is likely that more service can be directly available to field personnel from the headquarters library, and the improved communications will have great influence in making a more cohesive group.

This review of possible development of the federal library service in the next twenty years indicates that the group of federal librarians should become more cohesive and that they will develop a program of organized research into their own problems. Because federal library problems are in the core area of library problems, federal librarians will have the opportunity of exercising more and more leadership in library work. The federal library program can become more than ever the focal point for development of research library work in the United States.

References

1. Mohrhardt, F.: National Systems. *Library Trends*, 2:44-62, July 1953.

2. Clapp, V. W., and Adams, S., eds.: Current Trends in Libraries of the United States Government. *Library Trends*, 2:3-170, July 1953.

3. Brookings Institution: *Federal Library Survey*. 1959-60 (Preliminary data).

4. U.S. 86th Congress, Second Session: Documentation, Indexing and Retrieval of Scientific Information. *Senate Document No. 113*. Washington, U.S. Government Printing Office, 1960, pp. 203-208.

5. Library of Congress Gets Grant of $10,000 from the Council on Library Resources, Inc., To Study Automation of Information Processes. *U.S. Library of Congress Press Release No. 61-51*. Washington, D.C., April 23, 1961 (Mimeographed).

6. President of the United States: *Scientific Advisory Committee's Annual Report* (First). Washington, D.C., U.S. Government Printing Office, 1961.

7. Information furnished by Library of Congress, Public Relations Office.

8. National Federation of Science Abstracting and Indexing Services: *Proceedings*. 1958.

9. U.S. 86th Congress, Second Session. House Committee on Science and Astronautics: Research on Mechanical Translation. *Hearings before the Special Investigating Subcommittee*. Washington, D.C., U.S. Government Printing Office, 1960.

10. U.S. Bureau of the Census: *Historical Statistics of the United States, Colonial Times to 1957*. Washington, D.C., U.S. Government Printing Office, 1960, pp. 709-711, 736-737.

State Libraries

WALTER T. BRAHM

PUBLIC LIBRARY SERVICE in the United States has historically been the responsibility of local government and continues to remain so at the present writing.[1]

Reading of the organic laws under which individual state library agencies operate leaves no doubt that most of the early ones came into being as institutional libraries to meet the needs of their state governments: governor, legislators, and state officials.[2] For example, a Michigan commission of inquiry proposed some years ago "that the functions of the state library be reduced to the original purpose of providing a library for the use of state officials."[3] All state agencies today serve the legislative, administrative, and judicial officers of their state government, the only library function which can be found among all the states.[4]

Until late in the nineteenth century state governments had little concern for the development of library service other than for their own housekeeping needs. In fact, as late as 1936 the library profession was slow to acknowledge the role which state libraries were beginning to assume in the development of local library service. In a compilation of papers on library trends that same year, the role of state libraries was conspicuous by its absence.[5] As late as 1941 Miles and Martin pointed out that "far from a proportionate share of attention has been devoted to state library problems by the library profession itself. . . . If present trends continue . . . the most extensive development in the library field during the next decades will take place in state library services."[6] The services which the states were giving in 1940 had not yet loomed large enough to penetrate the consciousness of the library world's leaders. However, library leaders were involving the state in plans for library development, centering on the local library as an accomplished fact, with the state agency as an accessory to the fact. In 1935, Joeckel pointed out that no state had made library service

Mr. Brahm is Librarian, State Library of Ohio.

mandatory: "Unwilling or at least not yet ready to issue a positive mandate for universal library service, the states have turned their attention toward the more limited objective of stimulating the interest of local government in the establishment and maintenance of public libraries. In the accomplishment of this purpose, the states have worked through a variety of organizations, usually grouped under the generic name of 'library extension agencies' which are found today in forty-four states." [7]

Such state assistance to libraries was provided through numerous functions of the extension agency: establishment of libraries; grants in aid, or subsidies; advice and assistance; supervision or inspection; and, upon occasion, certification of personnel of public libraries. Perhaps the most successful of these functions was the establishment of libraries. Joeckel credits the number of public libraries in existence in 1935, 6000, largely to the efforts of the extension agencies and points out that perhaps in their zeal they created too many separate units with inadequate financial resources for library service. [8]

In 1935 some ten states were making direct contributions to individual public libraries, seldom exceeding $100 to each library. [9] By 1935 in the area of supervision and regulation only two states, New York and Wisconsin, had established certification for all professional members of library staffs. [10] But beyond certification, the states had not ventured into the field of library supervision and regulation. Rather they sought to accomplish results by advice and persuasion. Joeckel believed that *in no case had any state sought actual management of local library service.* [11]

Some fifteen years later, a survey [12] reported five library functions which were provided by the states with few exceptions. These functions were general library service to public or state officials, extension service, historical and archival service, legislative reference, and law library service. Using the above findings as a basis, in 1956 the National Association of State Libraries [13] attempted to define the role of the state library. Holding that the state library is the focal point of state-wide library services, it enumerated "the generally recognized components of an integrated state library agency":

1. *General library services.* Considered to include reference, research, and loan functions, with an efficient and reliable bibliographic service and interlibrary loan system; the collection, compilation, and publication of significant statistics from all of the libraries in a state;

the dissemination of information regarding regulations and legislation affecting libraries.

2. *Archives.* Considered a direct function of the state library, including responsibility for establishing a records management program and disposing of state records, also advising local governments on the management of their records.

3. *Government publications.* The collection and servicing of state, federal, and local government publications to meet their primary and original purpose, serving their own state officials.

4. *Law, legislative reference, and state history.* The responsibility for developing a law library as a center for legal reference and research to meet its own governmental needs. Legislative reference service; the collection, preservation, and servicing of materials relating to a state, its people and its history.

5. *Special services.* Many library services geared to particular aims of an individual state such as recruitment, placement, certification of library personnel, library services to state mental and correctional institutions, and services to the blind.

6. *Extension.* It is the extension function which has permitted the state library to bridge the gap between its institutional purpose and the local aspect of public library service. This function with its great potential stirred the imagination of state library personnel and the library profession and created considerable controversy between the profession and students of government.

The library extension movement as we know it today began with state legislation affecting rural library development.[14] Such legislation dates back to 1869, when Vermont authorized libraries to contract for services. Connecticut authorized state grants in 1893. However, major legal provisions for extending library service to rural areas and for providing financial aid to make this extension possible are of comparatively recent date.

Less than a decade after the University of Chicago held its Library Trends Institute in 1936, library extension had become important enough for the University to hold a similar institute in 1944 devoted exclusively to this function. Joeckel keynoted its opening with a comment, "In the year 1944, a century after the beginning of the public library movement in this country, the extension of library service to all people is still a great unfinished task of American librarianship. It is perhaps fruitless to debate whether this particular task is greater than any of the others which confront librarians." [15]

Because the amount spent by state libraries for extension in the early history of such work has never been recorded, no comparison with current expenditures can be made. Even recent expenditures,[16] estimated as $5,601,437 for 1955–56, are not necessarily reliable since this figure excludes state grants. In addition, the fact that many states operate extension service as an integrated unit of their total library system makes it difficult to pinpoint the exact costs of this operation.

While grants-in-aid as a form of library extension had been made by only ten states prior to 1935, ten years later, nineteen states and one territory received this support.[17] By 1961, twenty-seven states had programs of financial assistance to public libraries.[18] As an indication of the extent to which state financial assistance has grown in the past twenty-five years, New York appropriated for 1960 approximately $8,000,000, and Massachusetts appropriated $1,768,000 beginning in 1961.[19]

Although public library service has been considered entirely a responsibility of local government, there are notable exceptions. A number of state libraries lend books directly to borrowers by mail. For some twenty-five years Delaware has supplied direct bookmobile service to two of the state's three counties. Maine, New Hampshire, and Vermont have also provided a form of direct service.[20] Massachusetts, New York, Ohio, Michigan, Illinois, and numerous other states operate or have operated regional branches or experiments.[21] Some of these provide direct service to the public in unserved areas; others serve existing library units in the regions.

At mid-century Garceau [23] identified three broad categories of state policy toward the promotion of public library service: traveling libraries and small subsidies to local libraries, large promotional grants to reorganize local library service along county or multi-county lines, and an emerging pattern of regional offices or units of the state agency.

With the passage of the Library Services Act by the Congress in 1956, state libraries assumed the responsibility of administering federal funds for library service and of planning for the development and coordination of public library service within their states. The Act made a state agency which would promote the extension and improvement of library service a necessity in every state wishing to qualify for a grant. Utah, previously without such an agency, established one to take advantage of the federal funds.[22] While the first five years of the Library Services Act have not yet been evaluated, the states followed pretty much these patterns in their use of the funds. Nearly all moved toward strengthening their own agency with additional staff

[90]

and facilities, consolidating services such as processing, and in some cases providing direct or local library service by means of regional branches or special centers.[24]

Because of their strategic position as an arm of state government, the state agencies in 1960 stand as the key libraries controlling the gateway to future library development, an emerging role which has developed within the past thirty years. The importance of such a role in the library world is further emphasized by the recent grant of $45,000 by the Carnegie Corporation for financing a study of the state agencies and for the establishment of standards for such libraries.[25]

An increase in population would necessitate greater activity at all other levels of state government, which in turn would increase the service demands which state personnel would make. In the area of assistance to local libraries an increase in the population is more likely to have a secondary and delayed effect than a direct effect upon state library agencies. Unless an agency is giving direct service, an increase in population will first exert pressure upon local libraries. Until such libraries call for or are willing to accept state assistance the state library is not likely to be greatly affected. Paradoxically, a decrease in population could conceivably throw a greater load upon the state agency by creating marginal and submarginal library service areas.

In the past state library agencies have been concerned with problems of sparsely settled areas. If the population becomes even more concentrated in metropolitan areas, a corresponding shift of interest of state agencies from rural to urban library problems and solutions could be expected. It seems certain that each state agency will have both problems to face—increasing metropolitan population and declining nonurban areas.

Link and Hope[26] report that 94 per cent of all books are read by 50 per cent of the public and conclude: "Many factors induce people to read books but the underlying influence among all these seems to be formal education. The higher the education, the greater the frequency with which books are read."

Hauser and Taitel project the number of high school graduates in 1980 to be 95 million as compared with 70 million in 1970 and 52 million in 1960, an 80-85 per cent increase in twenty years.[27] At the same time the number of college graduates is expected to increase from 8 million in 1960 to 11 million in 1970 and 15 million in 1980, again 80-85 per cent increase.

Projections of the population in 1929 did not predict this reversal or the advent of a war which restored a migration trend. Similarly projections made in 1940 did not envision the population explosion of the 1950-60 decade. Therefore, present projections are subject to a great margin of error when extended for two decades.

Regardless of the direction population takes, responsibility of the state for library service will continue to increase. In whatever areas the population decides to settle, metropolitan or rural, the areas remain component parts of the state. The trend of population will increase the pressure for over-all planning and the coordination of library service units presently maintained by overlapping or intertwined local governments.

1. *State government, including its library agencies, may well anticipate a significant expansion in all of its various functions and agencies.* Modern living even in the event of a stable population and optimum distribution will require more, not less, state government. Nuclear energy, civil defense, transportation, highway safety, health, education, and welfare are creating demands for new or expanded government functions. The inevitable results are more state employees. In a study of the trend of government employment from 1896–1940, Fabricant[28] points out that every federal or state function pushes up government employment more rapidly than the national or state population grows. He also notes that over this forty-five year period "in not a single function of the federal government, the cities, or New York State (or other states of which we have record), was the number of workers actually reduced. In no other sector of the economy would we find every major division expanding." The Council of State Governments[29] reports that legislative action in 1959 was notable for expansion and improvement of state services in line with the growth of the population and public needs. The number of state employees rose from 804,000 in October, 1946, to 1,469,000 in October of 1958. A comparable increase in the next twelve years would bring the number of state employees to over 2 million in 1970, and near 2½ million by 1980. The demands for additional information, research, and library service from state library agencies will be staggering.

An increase in the number of bills introduced for legislative consideration would place a load on the legislative reference, archives, and government publications functions of a state library, to say nothing of the general library services function and the reference and research aspects of its work load. In addition, numerous special library services geared to special aims of individual state agencies probably would be initiated.

2. *Such increase in state government activities and consequent library demands will result in a decentralization of the state's library services.* History would seem to support this contention. The report of the National Association of State Libraries [30] in 1953 showed the high degree of decentralization of state library agencies which already exists. At that time various functions of state library service were provided by 131 different libraries, library agencies, or administrative units in forty-three states. Indeed, decentralization may well continue with the creation of new state departments and agencies which for one reason or another find themselves widely separated because of geography or building location. For this, and other reasons of convenience, many may set up their own departmental libraries, with the result that a further fragmentation of state library services will occur.

Thus services and demands may increase, but the services will be provided by a multiplicity of different state units, in sharp contrast with policies and practices which the state agencies themselves recommend. However, human nature being what it is, combined with the necessity for personal and political compromise in governmental operation, leaves little hope of great strides in centralization of the states' library agencies in the next twenty years.

3. *The state libraries will assume only limited responsibilities for school library service.*

The appointment of a school library supervisor in every state is one of the goals of the school library profession, and the measure by which the state is judged to have accepted its responsibility for such service. Mahar [31] reports that only half of the states have school library supervisors. It is interesting to note that only five of the states established such a position in the last ten years, indicating that progress has been slow in this area since 1950. [32] The passage of federal aid to schools now pending in Congress could reverse this trend rapidly if such funds were to be earmarked or authorized for school libraries. Nevertheless, with few exceptions education is a fiercely guarded local operation and will remain so regardless of federal aid. The school library and librarian are isolated from state direction by local authority, in the form of the superintendent of schools, and by state authority, in the department of education. Lines of force or cooperation cannot be transmitted directly from the state's library agency to the school library but must go up to the state superintendent, across to the local superintendent, and down to the school librarian.

In most states, responsibility for school library service has been considered the province of the state education agency rather than of the state library agency. In only fifteen states does the state library agency have legal responsibility for school libraries and the Council of Chief State School Officers speaking on this point has just recommended that "the full responsibility for state-level services to school libraries should be assumed by state departments of education." [33] The possibility is remote that state libraries could be given or could assume sufficient authority to have any effect upon the direction or coordination of school library service in the future. This does not mean that the state education agency or state library agency will not work closely with individual school libraries and their staffs, but such possible cooperation is not likely to be on any large or uniform scale.

4. *The state will become increasingly more active in the coordination and consolidation of public libraries into larger library units. Conversely, the legal basis of local library service will see little change in the next decades, the rapid development of "systems" and metropolitan areas to the contrary notwithstanding.*

Joeckel points out that it is largely the result of the efforts of extension agencies of state libraries that the number of public library administrative units in the United States reached a total of over 6,000 by 1930.[34] Today the number exceeds 8,000.[35] It is very likely that state libraries will devote a major part of their energy and activities in the next twenty years *attempting* to reverse this trend and to reduce the number of library administrative units. Consolidation of libraries into larger economic units is the goal sought. However, since "consolidation" is not a pleasant word to local librarians and their trustees, but one which stirs adverse public opinion, state efforts undoubtedly will be channeled in the direction of lesser resistance, that of coordinating libraries and their functions. Such coordination is more likely to take place by the mutual agreement (contract) of all concerned. This practice leaves the local administrative unit intact, giving the appearance of willingly subordinating itself to a larger group activity; yet it is still free to pick up its marbles and go home should it not like the way the other boys are playing. A contract is an agreement, good only as long as those who made it are in agreement, whereas under consolidation, in the event of a disagreement, the majority makes the decision and consolidation remains.

There is evidence to show that state libraries have begun to reverse the trend from creation of administrative library units to "consolidation" or reduction of their number. As early as 1947, Ohio [36] prohibited the establishment of new libraries by cities, school districts, or townships. New libraries have to be operated as branches of existing libraries or as branches of a county-wide library system. From a high of 281 public libraries in existence at the time of the passage of the law, by 1959 the number had been reduced to 270. In 1960 the number was further reduced to 265 by the consolidation of a group of six small libraries in Preble County, Ohio. [37] But this is slow progress, averaging one reduction per year.

Other states have devoted a good deal of effort toward the same ends. They have used a variety of methods, most of which have employed the use of contract or other cooperative agreements. The Buffalo, Erie County, New York, federation of libraries is a good example. [38] Some twenty-six independent community libraries in Erie County surrounding the Buffalo Public Library agreed to operate as a library unit, although each library maintained its own administration along with the right to withdraw from the agreement at the sacrifice of some income. This federation, resulting primarily from local initiative, was aided by the New York State Library and served as a pattern for the State Library's later program of aid and organization of libraries in the state.

Activity of state libraries along these lines was greatly stimulated and the trend accelerated with funds provided by the Library Services Act. States used federal money as an incentive for such consolidations and were successful in occasional situations. Where they were unable to accomplish mergers with funds, they used them as an incentive for contract arrangements or cooperative services. Where contract arrangements were unable to effect joint administrative units, state agencies attempted to pull out certain functions, such as book purchasing, cataloging, film circuits, and use federal funds to establish cooperative contracts or agreements for these specific activities. As a result a considerable number of "regional" libraries have come into being in the past five years. The term "regional" covers a variety of sizes and types of organization, but for the most part their

[95]

existence is based upon contractual arrangements. No doubt in the next twenty years additional states will enact enabling legislation authorizing and encouraging regional libraries and library systems, but these too are likely to be on a contract basis.

Since contract arrangements and special service cooperatives are more palatable to local library officials as an alternative to complete consolidation, it seems to this writer that state libraries again are in danger of committing a mistake comparable to that of their predecessors of a generation ago in promoting the establishment of so many small libraries. It will be a mistake difficult to correct later if state librarians devote zeal and enthusiasm to the preservation of local units of library service by hiding them under a blanket of paper contracts and cooperative agreements, instead of promoting true consolidation on a larger unit basis. The latter would remove forever the possibility of returning to their former status, and prepare libraries for the goal of state-wide library service.

5. *In the next twenty years, state libraries will not confine their attention solely to public library organization, but will also become catalytic agents in coordinating and perfecting cooperation between college libraries and between college and public libraries in their states.* They will most surely be called upon to aid in meeting the library needs of the small colleges and in solving the complex problems of library service to large numbers of students who are making heavy demands upon both public libraries and their school libraries.

6. *State libraries will assume the leadership for integrating certain library functions on a state or regional basis, such as reference services, processing, and central storage of books.* A number of state agencies have already taken action in one or more of these areas: California, Colorado, Michigan, Minnesota, Missouri, Nevada, New York, Ohio, and South Dakota. This is a vast area to be explored, and the great vacuum which now exists will surely draw the state agencies into it.

Supporting evidence for conclusions 5 and 6 above is even now available. In November, 1960, a committee [39] on reference and research library resources of New York's State Commissioner of Education recommended that the state establish a State Reference and Research Library Resources Board with a network of five regional reference and research library systems working closely with the state board to assist in the establishment and development of regional cooperative library programs for college and university students and in the development of a cooperative program of library services for the professional and research community. This program aims primarily at libraries serving higher education and research, and attempts in the reference field to coordinate the library services of college and public libraries. In January, 1960, the State Library of Ohio [40] recommended a similar program to facilitate reference and research sources in metropolitan areas through the employment and placement (by the state) of skilled reference workers in these areas to answer research requests from anywhere in the state and to develop the bibliographic potential of the areas. Early in 1961 the Missouri State Library with the aid of federal funds opened a bibliographic center in the Springfield Public Library to speed up delivery of books and reference material to libraries in twenty counties of southwest Missouri. [41]

7. *The next twenty years may see a more definite, although not rapid trend toward the provision of direct service to residents of the state by state agencies.* In some cases the latter may operate library service by means of branches in communities or villages and administer certain functions, such as processing and special reference. The net result of such a trend may eventually, but certainly not in this 1960–80 period, see the demise of local responsibility for library service and in its place a state-wide and perhaps state-operated library system.

Library literature implies that direct provision of library service to residents of the state by the state has never existed and is not likely to. Joeckel [42] points out that the state has never sought actual management over local library service. This statement, made in 1935, was true as far as the intent of the state was concerned, but even then in actual practice some states were giving direct service, either to residents of the state who would come in person to the state library, or my mail. State libraries of Maine, New Hampshire, and Vermont have been operating bookmobiles for many years, a most direct form of service.

There are many factors which point to the inevitable development of state-wide, state-operated library systems, however remote the possibility appears at the moment. Here listed and briefly discussed are the reasons for this belief:

a. *Demographic factors and the nature of man leave no other conclusion.* Big cities will become bigger. Small cities will become big cities. There will be more marriages, more children, more teen-agers, more college graduates, more educated people who will want more culture, which means more interest in books and libraries. Twentieth-century American life has fluidity built-in. People may live in one community, earn their living in another, and send their children to school in a third, on the basis of what is most convenient for them and what they personally prefer. Daily the line between city, suburb, small town, and farm becomes less visible and has still less reason for existence. By 1980, the vast majority of Americans may have little patience with artificial boundary lines that create problems in their daily lives, instead of solving them.

Library patrons are also on the go, and want to use libraries on the basis of their personal convenience and preference. For these reasons library service must be administered on a much larger base than has been conceived up to now. The state is therefore the next logical step. However, it may be too big a step for local library officials to take in ten or twenty years, and the writer can envision an intermediate step as a distinct possibility—a Regional Library Authority. Encompassing a metropolitan area or a large area of the state, locally-collected library taxes would be converted to state-collected taxes and returned to the Regional Authority—a state agency—for the operation of library service in the entire region.

b. *State grants for library service will increase tremendously.* The number of states providing monetary grants in aid has more than doubled in the past twenty-five years. Coming at the very beginning of these next twenty years, the new and large appropriations of New York, Massachusetts, New Jersey, and Kentucky would seem to herald a trend toward great increases in state aid. Since larger systems are more efficient economically, the day must come when each state accepts that logic and asks why it is not applied to its own state funds.

c. *There will be a continuous expansion to ever-larger units.* The library serving a single county has long been the goal of the county library movement. Gretchen Schenk [43] points out that in many ways, especially in many of its problems, the library serving a single county is now the counterpart of the village library presently decried as inadequate; and that this has led librarians to the next development—multi-county or regional library service. Will not the regional library eventually also become such a counterpart? If so, the next logical development may be the state as the unit.

d. *State-wide registration—one library card good anywhere in the state—is a distinct possibility.* Ohio in 1960 began plans for the development of such a system. Massachusetts [44] as a condition of its

[98]

new state aid appropriation required local libraries "to extend privileges to the holders of cards issued by other public libraries in the state on a reciprocal basis." Michigan and Arkansas officials are studying the possibility of a state-wide card.

Such a development is a state-wide operation for that specific function and will have to be administered from a central point which logically would be the state library agency.

e. *Consolidation will be too little and too late.* Writing on the problems of metropolitan library service in 1960, Hamill[45] points out that while tremendous strides have taken place since 1936 in the improvement of transportation and communication, no progress can be reported in the improvement of the metropolitan hodge-podge of separate governmental units including libraries. In fact the situation has grown worse and continues in that direction. Eastlick,[46] working on the same problem, claims that one of the worst gaps in library service occurs in the suburbs of big cities, that state laws include no enabling legislation for a metropolitan library authority, and that legislatures are slow to recognize the need for such legislation and reluctant to adopt it. The standard recommendation to solve the dilemma is that the state provide funds to existing library units leaving them intact or decentralized—in other words increased state aid, as mentioned previously.

f. *Interrelated use of libraries may be a determinant.* It may be true as Eastlick states that one of the worst gaps in library service occurs in the suburbs of big cities; yet urban and metropolitan areas of the nation are glutted with libraries. Libraries are in elementary schools, high schools, colleges; public libraries and branches are in every city and many suburbs; most large businesses, banks, and industries have special libraries. A recent study[47] of libraries in the university area of Cleveland reported the existence of fifty libraries within one mile of Western Reserve University's main library.

There is no lack of libraries, but lack of coordination. The thundering herds of students are just beginning their stampede through the nation's libraries. The student in his quest for library service sees no difference in various types of library units—school, college, or public. If the public makes no distinction in its use of libraries between the various types of library service, inevitably someone must ask the question: Why then are they supported and administered separately? This query suggests the state as the logical agency for the coordination and eventual administration of library service.

g. *State finances are in better shape than local governments'.* The latter face drastic economic problems. Local government debt increased tenfold in the first half of the century and exceeded 25 billion dollars in 1953. State debt, while also rising rapidly, was only 7½ billion. But state revenue increased significantly for that period and now exceeds that of local government.[48]

h. *Federal funds will accelerate the trend to state provision of direct library service.* Existing federal funds are at present expended and administered by the state. Available since 1957, less than five years ago, they have already been used by a number of states to give direct service. In the future, with resistance to consolidation and with overlapping use of libraries by nonlocal residents, the state may find it easier to cross boundary lines and give direct service than to persuade local libraries to consolidate or patrons to restrict themselves to their own community library. For example, Ohio first offered federal funds to local library units to enable them to provide bookmobile service, but the local units did not want the administrative problems which went with the service. Where the service involved more than one county, the question of crossing boundary lines was also involved; so the State Library was requested to establish and operate the service with the localities providing a portion of the funds. The state did not seek this management, but acquired it because of local demand and because it was the only logical road through which library service could be provided.

Hobson, reporting on library service in Vermont, cites such a trend as a problem for the state agency in its efforts to resist it. "One of the great problems is to stimulate the public libraries to improve their services rather than to be satisfied by accepting all of the services offered by the state agency. This is a real problem in small communities where individuals or splinter groups insist upon trying to get their library services directly from the state agency instead of using their local library."[49]

i. *Automation affects all.* Whatever success the application of machines to library processes such as storage and retrieval of information attains, the more will all libraries, small and large, school and public, need to be organized into some type of network if the full use of such automation is to be realized. Here again the state would seem to be the key agency in organizing and perfecting such a system.

8. *State libraries will have regulatory powers over public libraries.* Most state libraries today have little or no control over public li-

braries. Eastlick[50] warns that the state libraries need to be given regulatory powers because of the necessity for closer coordination of public library service. The factors enumerated above—the large number of libraries in some areas, their lack of coordination, the unwillingness of legislatures to establish metropolitan library authorities, increased state aid, the interrelated use of all libraries by the public—are likely to speed up the establishment of some type of state regulation.

9. *State libraries will be the planning center for library service, library legislation, and library standards throughout their respective states.* State libraries have been the center for developing library legislation for many years, but have been slow to enter the field of total library research.

Leigh, in specific reference to this function, pointed out the need for it and predicted it as a future trend: "as state libraries grow larger and more complex, especially as they take on the responsibility for public library development throughout a state, they need to develop consciously and systematically the intelligence function as part of their structure and on-going program."[51] He believed that it would be necessary for the development of an intelligence function which would provide factual and other material as an aid in defining the library's purposes and policies and evaluate its operations. Such planning might range from brief observational staff studies to very specialized research studies.

10. *The state will become the focal point for library service.* The National Association of State Libraries in 1956 defined the role of the state library as the focal point of integrated library service.

The statement may not have been an accomplished fact at the time it was made. The previous predictions made in this article may be subject to errors of human observation and judgment. The curtain of the future is not transparent, but as time inexorably raises it, we shall most certainly find the state library ready to perform in a number of capacities—producer, director, actor, or stagehand, as the occasion may demand.

References

1. Leigh, R. D.: *Public Library in the United States.* New York, Columbia University Press, 1950, p. 110.

2. Foutts, J. C., ed.: *American Library Laws.* 2nd ed. Chicago, American Library Association, 1943.

3. Michigan. Commission of Inquiry into State Governmental Expenses: *Report*. Lansing, 1932, p. 16.

4. Leigh, *op. cit.*, p. 69.

5. Wilson, L. R., ed.: *Library Trends*. Chicago, University of Chicago Press, 1937.

6. Miles, A., and Martin, L.: *Public Administration and the Library*. Chicago, University of Chicago Press, 1941, p. 59.

7. Joeckel, C. B.: *Government of the American Public Library*. Chicago, University of Chicago Press, 1935, p. 49.

8. *Ibid.*, p. 50.

9. Wachtel, Lee: State Provisions for the Support of Municipal Public Libraries. *Library Quarterly*, 3:373-389, Oct., 1933.

10. Joeckel, *op. cit.*, p. 52.

11. *Ibid.*, p. 53.

12. National Association of State Libraries. Committee on Organization of State Library Agencies in the Structure of State Government: *Tentative Report*. Appendix p. 5.

13. National Association of State Libraries: *Role of the State Library*. [Columbus, Ohio, Stoneman Press, 1956].

14. Morin, W. L., and Cohen, N. M.: *State Library Extension Services*. Washington, D.C., U.S. Government Printing Office, 1960, pp. 5-6.

15. Joeckel, C. B., ed.: *Library Extension Problems and Solutions*. Chicago, University of Chicago Press, 1946, p. 9.

16. Morin, *op. cit.*, p. 8.

17. Joeckel, *Library Extension*, p. 198.

18. U.S. Department of Health, Education, and Welfare: *L.S.A. Memorandum No. 53*, June 1961, p. 2.

19. Moloney, F. X.: State Aid for Massachusetts. *Library Journal*, 85:4429-4431, Dec. 15, 1960.

20. Miles, *op. cit.*, pp. 26-27.

21. Garceau, O.: *Public Library in the Political Process*. New York, Columbia University Press, 1949, pp. 222-223.

22. U.S. Department of Health, Education, and Welfare: State Plans Under the Library Services Act, Supplement 2. *Bulletin*, 1960, No. 27, p. 97.

23. Garceau, *op. cit.*, p. 214.

24. U.S. Department of Health, Education, and Welfare, *op. cit.*, p. 22.

25. American Library Association. *Bulletin*, 54:709, Sept. 1960.

26. Link, H. C., and Hope, H. A.: *People and Books*. New York, Book Manufacturers' Institute, 1946, pp. 158-160.

27. Hauser, P. M., and Taitel, M.: Population Trends—Prologue to Library Development. *Library Trends*, 10:10-67, July 1961.

28. Fabricant, S.: Rising Trend of Government. *Occasional Paper 29*. New York, National Bureau of Economic Research, Inc., 1949, p. 19.

29. Council of State Governments. *Book of the States*. Chicago, [no pub.] 1960-61, Vol. 13, p. 161.

30. National Association of State Libraries, *op. cit.*, Appendix p. 6.

31. Mahar, Mary H.: *State Department of Education Responsibilities for School Libraries.* (U.S. Department of Health, Education, and Welfare, Misc. 35), Washington, D.C., U.S. Government Printing Office, 1960, p. 2.

32. *Ibid.*, p. 10.

33. *Responsibilities of State Departments of Education for School Library Services.* Washington, D.C., Council of Chief State School Officers, 1961, p. 16.

34. Joeckel, *Government of the American Public Library*, p. 50.

35. Eastlick, J. T.: *Sixties and After.* Special Report for Federal Relations Committee, Library Administration Division, American Library Association. Chicago, American Library Association, [1960], p. 4.

36. Ohio. State Library. *Library Laws of Ohio.* Columbus. F. J. Heer Printing Co., 1960, p. 86.

37. Ohio. State Library: *1960 Directory of Ohio Libraries.* Columbus, F. J. Heer Printing Co., 1960, p. 2.

38. Buffalo and Erie County Public Library. *First Annual Report of the Director, 1954.* [n.p., n.d.], p. 8.

39. Commissioner's Committee on Reference and Research Library Resources: *Cooperative Program for the Development of Reference and Research Library Resources in New York State.* Interim Report to James E. Allen, Commissioner of Education. (Mimeographed) November, 1960.

40. Ohio. State Library: *Annual Report, Part One, 1959.* Columbus, F. J. Heer Printing Co., 1960.

41. Missouri. State Library Commission: *Show-me Libraries,* 12:2, March 1961.

42. Joeckel, *Government of the American Public Library*, p. 53.

43. Schenk, Gretchen K.: Creating New Local Service in the United States. *Library Trends,* 4:399-411, April 1956.

44. Moloney, *op. cit.*, p. 4429.

45. Hamill, H. L.: Metropolitan Area and the Library. *Library Quarterly,* 31:13-24, January 1961.

46. Eastlick, *op. cit.*, pp. 10-11.

47. University Circle Foundation. *Directory of University Circle Libraries.* [Cleveland, 1961].

48. Eastlick, *op. cit.*, p. 10.

49. Bowman, J. R., ed.: *Proceedings of the Second Assembly of State Librarians . . . 1960.* Washington, D.C., Library of Congress, 1961, p. 52.

50. Eastlick, *op. cit.*, p. 5.

51. Leigh, R. D.: Functions of the State Library in Research, Field Studies, and Surveys. *A.L.A. Bulletin,* 53:25-30, Jan. 1959.

County and Regional Libraries

JOHN D. HENDERSON

GUIDELINES FOR COUNTY and regional library service in the future may, with some hazard, be projected from data at hand concerning population growth and its effect upon local governmental services.

The pattern of rural problems will undoubtedly persist and, as pointed out in the recent article by E. A. Wight,[1] current trends in library extension programs will continue to emphasize service to people living in areas where none had previously been available. However, in the future, county and regional libraries will find their greatest challenge in offering a service articulated to the needs of the new and growing population centers embracing multiple jurisdictions.

According to U.S. Bureau of the Census projections, by 1980 the total population of this country will be in excess of 245,000,000, an increase of more than 65,000,000, or nearly 40 per cent more than the present population of over 180,000,000.[2] This growth will fill in and urbanize many areas now served by county and regional libraries throughout the country, particularly in the Great Lakes region, the South, Southwest, and West.

By 1980, less than a third of the population will be rural,[3] and by the year 2000, urbanites will compose about 85 per cent of the national total.[4] This figure does not mean, however, that the rural challenge during the next twenty years will be any the less significant.

The types of library organization designed to serve the urban-rural population will be clarified by definition: according to the *A.L.A. Glossary of Library Terms*,[5] a county library is "A free public library maintained by county taxation for the use of the whole or a part of a county, established as an independent institution, or combined with a municipal or other library; or, a municipal or other library which provides library service to a county by contract." The regional li-

The author is Los Angeles County Librarian.

brary is defined as "A public library serving a group of communities, or several counties, and supported in whole or in part by public funds from the governmental units served. Sometimes known as District Library."

The *A.L.A. Glossary* goes on to define "extension library service" as "The supplying of books and other library assistance to individuals or organizations outside a library's regular service area" and "library extension" as "The promotion of libraries and library service, by state, local, or regional agencies."

Illustrating these definitions are several patterns of organization, *viz*: (a) as a department of county government serving the unincorporated area and those cities electing to receive and be taxed for the service; (b) as an extension of city service through a contract whereby the City Librarian becomes the County Librarian and establishes service outlets throughout the county and operates them from contract funds; (c) through a contract by which one county provides another with library service; (d) through a special district with elected trustees having power to levy the library tax and administer the service within the defined boundaries of the service area, e.g., Dayton and Montgomery County Public Library in Ohio; (e) by a federation of city and county library jurisdictions on a voluntary basis, such as the recently established Pioneer Library System in New York State; (f) by a county library contract with established city libraries for specific services or full operation of branches, as provided by the Wayne County Public Library, Michigan; (g) in conjunction with supplementary or direct service through state regional branches, as in New Hampshire, where the entire state becomes, in effect, a single library system; or in Tennessee, in which eleven affiliated regional library centers are administered under contract with the State Library.

Success in promoting library extension service and in establishing library systems reflects professional leadership, nationally and in a number of states. Where there are active professional associations working closely with their state agencies, long-range regional and state-wide programs have been and will continue to be developed. Much pioneer work has already been done in the establishing of county and regional libraries in such states as New York, Michigan, Wisconsin, Louisiana, California, and Washington.

With the concentration at headquarters of purchasing, processing, and administration, and a broad tax base, large-area service has been comparatively inexpensive and has set a pattern for similar operations in the future. Traditionally, county and regional libraries have been supported by a low tax rate spread over a large area for a service designed primarily to reach readers outside the cities having independent local libraries. Some cities contract for service, whereas others have joined the system, or, upon incorporation, have continued the county service because of the low tax rate. Equalization is a feature of large-unit service since the unincorporated area with its increasing industrial development, oil fields, and productive land and utilities provides a high assessed valuation which produces revenue that can be spent in the poorer parts of the library's service area, including the small cities.

The question of equalization becomes crucial as the areas served by county and regional libraries develop into metropolitan complexes. Within the areas served there will be poor and wealthy communities, and all should receive library service that meets professional standards. Equalization will have to be provided through state and federal aid in the interests of a high level area-wide service.

In farm areas and in rural communities, there are still twenty-five million people without public library facilities; more than 250 counties are without public libraries.[6] Through state demonstrations and guidance and with federal assistance through the Library Services Act, in these unserved or poorly served areas, the major emphasis will continue to be upon the establishing of new facilities on a county or regional basis.

Progress in the establishing of county and regional library systems serving populations of 50,000 or more is reported by the Office of Education as a gain of 27 in two years, from 147 systems in 1957 to 174 in 1959.[7]

In West Virginia, Mississippi, and Arkansas, where there have been losses in population, and in states showing less than a 10 per cent gain, such as North and South Dakota, Nebraska, Iowa, Oklahoma, Tennessee, Alabama, and Kentucky, county and regional libraries will follow established patterns in reaching readers outside the cities with independent local libraries. The future in these states will undoubtedly see new library jurisdictions and service consolidations, and present operations will be strengthened and expanded through the Library Services Act and state aid.

Fourteen states have experienced more than a 20 per cent increase in population since 1950: New Jersey, Maryland, Delaware, Connecticut, Florida, Louisiana, Ohio, Michigan, California, Texas, New Mexico, Arizona, Nevada, and Utah. Of these, only five have adopted state standards, although others are at present working on their adoption or are following A.L.A. standards.

With the adoption of state [8] and national standards, the first steps have been taken toward the establishment of an overall national plan of library service with some variation in patterns of development. The stages of development to be achieved in furthering public library service are the following: (1) the adoption of standards and goals; (2) the recognition of specific needs, identified through a process of assessment and inventory of current library resources and services as measured by the standards; and (3) the action program, based upon a detailed and specific plan. Under the Library Services Act originally passed in 1956, a number of working programs for rural service have been set up. The demonstration programs supported by federal and state "seed" money are described in some detail in *State Plans under the Library Services Act, Supplement 2,* previously referred to.

Illustrating the second developmental step are the three combined reports of the California Public Library Commission,[9] which includes recommendations for the establishing of library systems throughout the state, based upon minimum standards for determining state aid. Ralph Shaw's survey of existing library facilities in metropolitan Toronto,[10] set up as the basis for grants-in-aid for extended service and setting forth minimum standards, also illustrates step two. Another is the comprehensive Library Development Project of the Pacific Northwest,[11] a study of the library services and facilities of British Columbia, Idaho, Montana, Oregon, and Washington, sponsored by the Pacific Northwest Library Association and administered through the University of Washington. A current proposal is Michigan's "State-Wide Plan for Public Library Development."[12]

The action program, step three, based upon a specific and detailed plan, is well exemplified in the New York State Library regional service program, which in 1959 comprised 17 systems providing supplemental and contract service to all or parts of 19 counties, including the city of New York as one region. The success of this multisystem concept is attributed to the leadership of the trustees and librarians of the state in obtaining the adoption of the state-aid legislation.[13, 14]

Since Los Angeles County, California, has already felt the population impact that is predicted for existing and new metropolitan areas, the growth pattern of library service and the problems of jurisdictional relationships experienced there should indicate what lies ahead in other parts of the country. The core city, Los Angeles, is well served by its long-established public library system.

In the growing outer areas, the Los Angeles County Public Library has been in an interim position in providing service, and flexibility has been one of its features. Until a community became strong enough to incorporate and support its local services, it looked to the county to provide them. Many mature and wealthy cities such as Beverly Hills, Burbank, and San Marino were once served by the County Library. As these cities grew in wealth and population, they desired and were able to support an independent service. County library service was continued in other cities since the low county tax rate provided a facility that would have been more costly to the city as a locally-supported operation.

According to census projections, more than 170 million Americans will be living in metropolitan areas in 1980, and 58 per cent of these will live within suburban rings,[15] a pattern similar to the present Los Angeles County complex. To provide libraries for these multitudes of people will require vision and leadership of all librarians, and all will inevitably be concerned with large-area planning. The summary of state standards, their development and special features and application,[8] is of particular value at this point. H. L. Hamill,[16] also stresses the importance of long-range planning, as well as the breaking down of local barriers to metropolitan-centered service and awareness on the part of librarians of every opportunity to see that library service is included in studies of metropolitan problems.

The point was well made by Leigh when he said:

It is one of the assumptions of the [Public Library] Inquiry that in a large-scale modern democratic, industrial society there are advantages both in local initiative and participation and in larger units of administration; that neither should be neglected, but that governmental structure should be contrived to give the greatest possible scope to both principles.

✿   ✿   ✿

The movement for building larger public library systems by consolidation, federation, or voluntary association has centered attention largely on less populous areas. It is equally desirable as a direction for development, however, in metropolitan regions. As we have seen, public library systems which cover the whole of a metropolitan area exist almost nowhere in the United States. The organization of libraries under municipal corporations here, as in less populous areas, militates against complete coverage of the area, and voluntary cooperation to provide an integrated service for the whole metropolis has seldom been carried out. But a pooling of resources in large urban areas has as much promise of economy as in rural regions.[17]

Since the completion of Leigh's study in 1950, several events have contributed significantly to the progress of public library development. The passage of the Library Services Act in 1956 with its five-year extension in 1960 accentuates the role of state library agencies and challenges them to continue the leadership they have demonstrated in their pioneer work for rural service. The adoption of the revised public library standards [18] in 1956, a major advance, must be periodically reviewed to be responsive to newly emerging problems and conditions. Still another event is the Ford Foundation grant of $5 million, establishing the Council on Library Resources, Inc., for the purpose of investigating library problems. It is hoped that the Council will act favorably upon a proposal submitted to it for the study of the implications for public library service in the metropolitan complexes of the present and the future.[19]

Although something of a controversial excursion into public relations, the inauguration of National Library Week in 1958 has contributed to a broader community- and nation-wide understanding of public library service, which is essential to the support of an adequate program for the future.

Whether or not Sputnik I is to receive the credit, it is a fact that since its launching in October 1957 there has been an upsurge in library use, with "increased stress on formal and informal education, particularly in the fields of science, foreign languages, and mathematics." [6] There has also been drastic change in the ways in which the public uses the library. Modern readers, particularly students, are in a hurry; the majority come on specific missions and expect prompt and complete service.

The experience of Southern California as one of the newborn, mushrooming areas suffering from overgrowth and immaturity indicates the problems that will confront metropolitan complexes now in the embryonic stage. Not only is student use increasing dramatically in the libraries of the area, but there is also an almost spectacular gain in general adult and juvenile service. Los Angeles

County Public Library, with its two-million-plus service area population, is faced with unprecedented demands for technical books and high-level fiction and nonfiction, and there is a growing need in the branches for full-time reference librarians for telephone service alone. Furthermore, children are reading as never before and in many cases at levels far beyond their school age.

Reference is made to the American Library Association's publication on standards, in which libraries are urged to band together formally or informally in the systems which "reach out to a wider world, drawing on even greater and more specialized resources offered by state and federal agencies." [20]

Not only must libraries be provided for the great metropolitan areas, but the service must also be adapted to the new population. It is predicted that the number of students in school and college will double. Their assignments will place heavier demands upon the library resources available to them—public and school or college.[21]

The working population will increase, though not at the rate of the young people of school and college age. The older element of the population, 60 and above, will also increase. This growth will mean greater demands for service by the nonproductive segments of the population, with a heavy burden of support upon the middle group that must carry the tax load.

As pointed out in *State Plans under the Library Services Act, Supplement 2,* "If any differences ever existed between the needs and interests of urban and rural citizens, such differences are now insignificant because of such factors as mobility of population, modern transportation, and communication. The requirements of the rural resident are as advanced and diverse as those of the city dweller. He needs to have access to good, up-to-date library service to the same degree, and the same standards of service should apply to both urban and rural areas." [22]

County and regional libraries are structured to serve large and complex areas. In the future the urbanizing rural areas and the growing unincorporated communities and member cities will continue to look to the county or regional library for book service if plans anticipating this growth are developed. If our standards are to mean what they say, the service areas will expect not only films, records, serials, maps, documents, and other special reference materials, but also the additional resources of the ultramodern public library, including microfilm and microfilm aids, facsimile and photo copy, closed circuit television, and rapid teletype reference service—even access to an international reference network connecting major libraries throughout the world.

It is predicted that the pattern of metropolitan expansion will continue, taking in larger and larger areas. It is indicated that central cities will undergo both structural and jurisdictional changes and that the periphery cities will multiply; that the areas between cities will continue to fill in; that some areas will be annexed by the existing cities; and that other parts will remain unincorporated. However, it is not foreseen that there will be any significant increase in the number of metropolitan areas. Rather, on the East Coast and in the South and West, where the population concentrations are greatest, there will be a fusion or conglomeration of these areas, as in the case of Greater New York or Greater London. Interurbia[23] is the name applied to these newly identified phenomena. It has much meaning for market analysts, sociologists, political scientists, and librarians, especially those concerned with county and region-wide services.

Unplanned metropolitan areas, however, might easily Balkanize into a complex of independent jurisdictions with duplicate services varying in standard according to the wealth of each. The desire for home rule and strong local loyalties have prompted many new as well as older communities to withdraw from county service and establish their own; this vertical development of service by multiple jurisdictions unrelated to neighbor or area could very well become a disastrous trend.

According to the Committee for Economic Development,

These major shifts of people and industry have strained the social fabric and overloaded time-honored political institutions. Sixteen thousand local jurisdictions in fewer than 200 metropolitan areas have struggled hard to maintain a semblance of orderly growth and to supply the increasing demands for public service of their area residents. But the unit costs of these efforts have been high; a team of 20 mules is not as efficient as a single diesel engine. And although our local governments have kept things going in metropolitan areas they have failed in one crucial area of public responsibility: they cannot plan, budget and program ahead for the entire metropolitan region.[24]

Implied in any comprehensive plan for regional library service and the establishment of library systems is a new philosophy of local government. Political wisdom will be needed to develop a plan that will combine local autonomy and diversity with the features of region-wide coordination.[25] Furthermore, the development of the region must be the concern and responsibility of all jurisdictions within it, and an awareness of the total needs of the area should be reflected in the program. The features of the plan must closely establish the gain to all participating jurisdictions, and provision must be made for formulating policy and goals on a comprehensive regional basis.

It should be feasible to program such a service, inasmuch as it is possible to envision an ideal area-wide library system. Bookmobiles would serve the outlying communities, particularly schools and small crossroad centers, and it is to be seen that with greater concentrations of people, special branches for children could easily be established. In settled communities having comparatively large populations, local branch service should be provided, with buildings ranging from 4,000 to 10,000 square feet in size, and with book collections averaging between 15,000 and 30,000 volumes.

Supporting the community branches, a regional facility housing at least 100,000 volumes should be established, with a fully trained staff and broad resources available to all readers and serving as a backstop to the branches within the respective region. This centrally-located regional headquarters would therefore constitute a reservoir for the region or even a group of regions within the library system.

Uniformity in rules, policies, forms, and charging systems would be possible in the overall system, and there would be no standing need for nonresident service, nonresident fees, or reciprocal service. Fortified by a borrower's single-card method, patrons would have full access to the material wherever they might live or work or attend school, or at whatever library facility happened to be the most convenient point for taking out and returning library materials.

Overall administration, as well as all purchasing, book preparation, and the warehousing of secondary materials, should be performed at the central services headquarters. Book selection, cataloging, data processing, information retrieval, interlibrary loans, region-wide service programs, and the more difficult reference work would likewise be concentrated at this point. It should also feature a bibliographical center for the region, if not a cooperative, interlibrary reference service, such as the San Joaquin Valley Information Service in Fresno, California, or the Denver Tri-County Project. Special bibliographies and reading lists could be prepared here for distribution to the cities within the area, including material on local government for city and county officials, special material of interest to business and industry, and reading lists of general scope. A regional union catalog would also be feasible, such as the electronically produced book catalog maintained by the Los Angeles County Public Library continuously since 1952.[26] Such innovations and adaptations are reflected in the findings and papers of the Institute on Cooperative Planning for Public Libraries [27] sponsored in February by the School of Library Science of the University of Southern California.

It is realized that such a concept of cooperative library service is idealistic and remote from realization in the immediate future. The ease of transportation and communication and the burden of taxation will do much to create favorable public opinion supporting a broad-based library service with the features described here. The crux of the matter lies in assuring to the local jurisdictions the services, the economies, and the degree of local authority that will enlist their support in the broad plan of operation.

Community support will be basic and the advice of lay boards or councils should prove an invaluable administrative tool in the future programs. Since demands upon the administrator will be exacting and challenging, a strong body of counselors or advisors representing the communities served should participate in policy deliberations regarding the scope and level of the service. It is fundamental that the advisory groups understand objectives and program standards and the basic operations of library service.

Two possible lines of development are indicated in serving metropolitan areas: the core city library, in the one case, serving as a resource for the region far beyond the city limits, as contrasted with extended county or regional service as such. In this sense, the city is involved in extension service as defined in the *A.L.A. Glossary*. It is concerned about receiving support and equalization from the state to offset the expense to which it is put in serving nonresidents for reference or other services. In some cases, the city library is the agency through which the county and rural areas are served, as has already been pointed out.

In the federated library system in New York, the Pioneer Library System is centered in the Rochester Public Library and serves a large area. In this connection, it is of interest to note a statement by H. Hacker dealing with the system and with the importance of county government:

In our judgment, county government in New York State is the key to the future development of local government. The cities are integral parts of county government, for example, the City of Rochester is the county seat of Monroe County, and the people in Rochester pay general county taxes. We have few programs on a county level that exclude the city, either from financing them or from sharing the program benefits. There are many functions, formerly performed by the cities and the towns, that now are provided by the counties—welfare, health, water supply, planning, probation, libraries, etc. There has been resistance to these transfers of functions. The towns fear increased county taxes. At the same time, the city people are concerned that the quality of services might be sacrificed. But the trend toward transfer and consolidation is growing and very likely will not be stopped.[28]

It would seem that the definition of "municipal" must be expanded, since the metropolitan area will include a group of cities and possibly unincorporated interurban areas that will be urbanized insofar as the concentration of people is concerned. Whichever line of development is followed will depend upon several factors, including the leadership of the state agency and the local authorities in planning future service, as well as the strength of the core city library and its attitude toward a metropolitan area-wide library system.

It is a professional irony that as librarians advance in their work, their responsibilities fall into fields for which they have received progressively less and less training. Administrators of public library systems obviously draw on the fundamental disciplines of librarianship, but their energies and judgment are largely devoted to questions and issues far beyond the techniques and subject content of their library school training. Consideration should therefore be given to providing more adequate training for the responsibilities that go with the profession's higher positions.

In the future there will obviously be a greatly accelerated demand for library administrators. The broad field of library service should be attractive not only to the book-minded researcher and the librarian who wishes to work directly with readers, but also to the action-minded individual who appreciates book service and book knowledge and is called to responsibilities involving supervision and the directing of personnel, as well as planning, budgeting and programming, public relations, building layout and design, and the other responsibilities characterizing administration. Since library service on a large scale combines the characteristics of an educational institution with the qualities of a public service department, the administrator of the program must also combine leadership in the professional aspects of library service with the related facets of administration involved in operating a government department. It is these governmental elements in public library service that should be given greater emphasis in library schools.

The service areas of the county and regional libraries will include several jurisdictions, which will mean continuous communication and involvement in matters of policy clarification and development, all of which responsibilities, including budget, cost controls, and the service program, will call for qualities of leadership—even statesmanship. Unless we take steps to train our future librarians for this kind of administration, we shall find the work taken over by professional public administrators and business managers. The pattern is clear in the cases of hospital service, road departments, and the engineering divisions of government where professional managers supersede the professionals in top positions of authority and responsibility.

The library systems of the future will serve millions of people in the megalopolitan centers and hundreds of thousands in many others. There will, of course, remain the ever-present problem of the independent libraries within the metropolitan area. Whether or not cooperative arrangements can be established that will bring these libraries into the local system will depend in large measure upon the ability and training of our new library administrators.

The opportunities in extension service and in the field work connected with the planning and developing of metropolitan area systems will multiply as the new areas emerge. Librarians of the future who wish to train and qualify for field work as members of state agency staffs should receive special instruction. Also the activities of state agencies should be incorporated into the general education of all librarians. Techniques of counseling and advising librarians and local officials as well as community groups are matters of day-to-day work in extension service, in addition to the setting up of demonstrations for bookmobile service and other programs.

The work of the Library Services Branch of the U.S. Office of Education should be well presented to library school students, including the scope of the official reports, its counseling and coordinating functions, and the assembling of library statistics, with emphasis upon their interpretation and value to the library profession as a whole. The legislation behind library programs and the limitations of legislation, where there are such, also deserve the attention of students, in addition to the establishing of service yardsticks and the techniques of surveying and assessing library resources, services, and activities.

Library service is as unique governmentally as the public schools, and as an educational facility it merits special identification for its financing and administration. In metropolitan regions it should properly function on as broad a basis as water supply, air pollution control, public transportation, and other area-wide public utilities and facilities that overlap jurisdictional boundaries and call for coordinated master planning.

In brief, county and regional libraries are serving areas predicted to undergo astronomical increases in population, in which drastic governmental changes will take place. Based upon minimum professional standards, planning is called for on a large scale to provide acceptable service for the expanding metropolitan complexes and their satellite communities. The large-unit type of operation offers the best solution to the service problem, through federation, cooperation, contract, special library district, or some combination of these organizational patterns that will provide the broadest possible coverage for the county or region to be served. There are already many examples of such broad-based library systems, and state and federal aid offers the most effective means of equalizing support for their high-level service, provided over a large area with an uneven tax base.

Today's challenging library problems are accentuated by the staggering projections of the demographers; the patterns of area-wide development now emerging indicate the urgency of a full-scale planning and action program and the gigantic educational task that must be undertaken if we are to provide an adequate library service for 1980's expanded population.

References

1. Wight, E. A.: Trends in the Extension of Library Service. *Library Quarterly*, 31:60-70, Jan. 1961.

2. U.S. Bureau of the Census. *Current Population Reports*. Series P-25, No. 187, Table 1, Nov. 10, 1958.

3. Hauser, P. M.: *Population Perspectives*. New Brunswick, N.J., Rutgers University Press, 1960, pp. 96-98.

4. Pickard, J. P.: *Metropolitanization of the United States* (Research Monograph 2). Washington, D.C., Urban Land Institute, 1959, p. 8.

5. American Library Association. Editorial Committee: *A.L.A. Glossary of Library Terms, with a Selection of Terms in Related Fields.* Chicago, American Library Association, 1943.

6. U.S. Office of Education. Library Services Branch: *State Plans under the Library Services Act, Supplement 2* (Bulletin 1960, No. 27). Washington, D.C., U.S. Government Printing Office, 1960, p. 2.

7. U.S. Office of Education: *Statistics of County and Regional Library Systems Serving Populations of 50,000 or More: Fiscal Year 1959.* Rose Vainstein and Doris C. Holladay, comp., p. 10.

8. U.S. Office of Education. Library Services Branch: *State Standards for Public Libraries* (Bulletin 1960, No. 22). Rose Vainstein and Marian Magg, comp. Washington, D.C., U.S. Government Printing Office, 1960.

9. California. Public Library Commission: *Reports, Pursuant to 1957 Statutes of California, Chapter 2328.* Berkeley, University of California, California State Printing Office, 1959, Nos. 1-3.

10. Shaw, R. R.: *Libraries of Metropolitan Toronto; a Study of Library Service Prepared for the Library Trustees' Council of Toronto and District.* Toronto, Library Trustees Council, 1960.

11. Campbell, R., *et al.*: The Public Libraries of the Pacific Northwest. *In* Pacific Northwest Library Association *Library Development Project Reports.* Morton Kroll, ed. Seattle, University of Washington Press, 1960. Vol. 1.

12. Michigan. State Board for Libraries: *A State-Wide Plan for Public Library Service* (Proposed). Lansing, 1960.

13. New York. State Education Department. New York State Library. Library Extension Division: *Excerpts from New York State Education Law and the Regulations of the Commissioner of Education which Pertain to Public and Free Association Libraries, Library Systems, Trustees and Librarians.* Albany, The University of the State of New York, Sept., 1960.

14. New York. State Education Department. Commissioner of Education. Committee on Reference and Research Library Resources: *A Cooperative Program for the Development of Reference and Research Library Resources in New York State; an Interim Report,* Nov. 1960.

15. Hauser, *op. cit.,* p. 98.

16. Hamill, H. L.: The Metropolitan Area and the Library. *Library Quarterly,* 31:13-24, Jan. 1961.

17. Leigh, R. D.: *The Public Library in the United States.* New York, Columbia University Press, 1950, pp. 227, 229.

18. American Library Association. Co-ordinating Committee on Revision of Public Library Standards: *Public Library Service; a Guide to Evaluation, with Minimum Standards.* Chicago, American Library Association, 1956.

19. American Library Association. Committee on Metropolitan Area Library Service: *A Proposal for a Study of Library Service in Metropolitan Areas.* (Ditto) Aug. 12, 1960.

20. American Library Association. Co-ordinating Committee on Revision of Public Library Standards, *op. cit.,* p. 7.

21. Trump, J. L.: *Images of the Future; a New Approach to the Secondary School.* Commission on the Experimental Study of the Utilization of the Staff

in the Secondary School. National Association of Secondary-School Principals, 1959.

22. U.S. Office of Education. Library Services Branch: *State Plans under the Library Services Act, Supplement 2*, ref. 5, p. 1.

23. *Interurbia; the Changing Face of America.* Prepared by the J. Walter Thompson Company, Los Angeles, and the School of Architectural Design, Yale University. (Mimeographed) 1960.

24. Committee for Economic Development. Research and Policy Committee: *Guiding Metropolitan Growth; a Statement on National Policy.* New York, Committee for Economic Development, Aug. 1960, p. 5.

25. Feldman, M. B., and Jassy, E. L.: The Urban County: A Study of New Approaches to Local Government in Metropolitan Areas. *Harvard Law Review,* 73:582, Jan. 1960.

26. The Book Catalog of the Los Angeles County Public Library. *Library Resources and Technical Services,* 4:208-232, Summer 1960. (Articles by Catherine MacQuarrie, Beryl L. Martin, and Theodore Hewitson).

27. Cooperative Planning for Public Libraries. *News Notes of California Libraries,* 56: No. 2, Pt. 2, Spring 1961. (Articles by Katherine Laich, W. S. Geller, et al.)

28. Hacker, H. S., et al.: A Federated Library System in Action: The Pioneer Library System in New York State. (Multilithed) Sept. 1959, p. 1.

ADDITIONAL REFERENCES

California. Governor's Commission on Metropolitan Area Problems: *Metropolitan California; Papers Prepared for the Governor's Commission on Metropolitan Area Problems.* Ernest A. Engelbert, ed. Sacramento, California State Printing Office, 1961.

Daniel, H.: *Public Libraries for Everyone.* New York, Doubleday and Company, Inc., 1961.

Eastlick, J. T.: The Sixties and After. *ALA Bulletin,* 55:556-558, June 1961.

Garceau, O.: *The Public Library in the Political Process.* New York, Columbia University Press, 1949.

Goldstein, H., ed.: Current Trends in Bookmobiles. *Library Trends,* 9:287-384, Jan. 1961.

Hacker, H. S., et al.: New York State's Pioneer Library; a Federated Library System in Action. *Wilson Library Bulletin,* 34:345-350, 354-356, Jan. 1960.

Joeckel, C. B., ed.: *Library Extension: Problems and Solutions.* Chicago, University of Chicago Press, 1946.

Joeckel, C. B., ed.: *Reaching Readers: Techniques of Extending Library Services.* Berkeley, University of California Press, 1949.

Kee, S. Janice, ed.: State Aid to Public Libraries. *Library Trends,* 9:3-128, July 1960.

Metcalf, K. D.: *Cooperation among Maine Libraries; a Report Prepared for the Larger Libraries of Maine.* Cambridge, Mass., 1961.

Metropolitan Area Problems: News and Digest. A Publication of the Conference on Metropolitan Area Problems. New York, Institute of Public Administration, Jan. 1957, Vol. 1, No. 1.

Reed, T. H.: The Metropolitan Area: Its Implications for Librarianship. *In Library Trends: Papers Presented Before the Library Institute at the University of Chicago, August 3-15, 1936*. Louis K. Wilson, ed. Chicago, University of Chicago Press, 1937, pp. 45-62.

Schenk, Gretchen K. *County and Regional Library Development*. Chicago, American Library Association, 1954.

U.S. Office of Education. Library Services Branch: *State Plans under the Library Services Act* (Bulletin 1958, No. 10). Washington, D.C., U.S. Government Printing Office, 1958.

U.S. Office of Education. Public Services Branch: *State Plans under the Library Services Act, Supplement 1* (Bulletin 1959, No. 17). Washington, D.C., U.S. Government Printing Office, 1959.

Large Public Libraries

EMERSON GREENAWAY

JUSTICE LOUIS D. BRANDEIS once stated that there was a curse to bigness, and many a taxpayer and governmental official in observing today's phenomena of an expanding population will tend to agree. This great development of rapidly burgeoning and expanding metropolitan areas is bound to have both its problems and its benefits. The question is one of solving major problems in sufficient time to insure real benefits, for if the problems are not solved, at least in terms of library services, there will be a collapse of public library service as we have known it.

Rather we should think of the great future in the use of the book by the large reading public—student, businessman, worker, professional career person, general reader, and all the others who make use of their public library. But we shall have to do some careful thinking about the libraries of the future in terms of what kinds of libraries we shall have, who is to use them, what is to be the extent or limitations of the collections and services, how they are to be organized, how they are to be staffed, and of greatest importance, how they are to be financed. Four of the most difficult problems to be resolved are these: (1) resolving the dilemma of political boundaries which tend to make for small areas of service and which result from a local pride or provincialism; (2) organizing for area services; (3) staffing the libraries; and (4) determining an equitable financing of area library services.

Growth of urban areas has been significant: in 1790, five per cent of the country's people lived in 24 urban places; in 1960, 70 per cent lived in 6,041 urban places. This 70 per cent accounts for 125 million persons. As Hauser and Taitel have already indicated,[1] the population explosion in the metropolitan areas has been even more dramatic, and there are now, according to 1960 data, 211 Standard Metropolitan Statistical Areas which contain 112 million persons, or

Mr. Greenaway is Director of The Free Library of Philadelphia.

almost 63 per cent of the total population. By 1980 these areas will be even larger, and it is projected that there will be an increase of about 58 million persons in these areas. This figure would result in close to 70 per cent of the total population being so located. Therefore, if the metropolitan areas increase by 50 per cent in the next twenty years while the total increase for the country is but 37 per cent, we will have a serious, but interesting problem on our hands.

There have, of course, been significant changes in the last decade in cities of 100,000 or more people. In 1950 there were 107 such places; in 1960, 130. During this period, nevertheless, there was a loss in population in some of these cities, and four cities which qualified in 1950, did not do so in 1960. In fact, 42 other cities lost in popula-

TABLE I

Comparison of Statistics for Public Library Systems in Cities with Populations of 100,000 or More: Fiscal Years 1950 to 1959[1]

| Fiscal Year | Operating Expenditures (Excluding Capital Outlay) | | | Volumes | |
	Total[2]	Salaries (Including Building Staff)	Books and Periodicals	Number at End of Year	Number Circulated[3]
1	2	3	4	5	6
1950	$ 56,767,000	$40,498,000	$ 7,146,000	49,636,000	146,625,000
1951	61,890,000	43,454,000	7,188,000	51,169,000	144,685,000
1952	67,751,000	48,094,000	8,491,000	52,517,000	151,544,000
1953	74,384,000	52,513,000	9,273,000	53,841,000	153,541,000
1954	77,507,000	56,491,000	9,643,000	55,566,000	163,888,000
1955	82,134,000	60,083,000	10,427,000	56,916,000	171,449,000
1956	88,952,000	64,286,000	10,893,000	58,090,000	178,788,000
1957	94,829,000	69,159,000	11,611,000	59,690,000	186,395,000
1958	101,085,000	73,199,000	12,050,000	61,921,000	200,888,000
1959	106,959,000	77,090,000	13,268,000	63,819,000	208,869,000
	Per Cent of Change				
1950 to 1959	+88.42	+90.36	+85.67	+28.57	+42.45
1958 to 1959	+ 5.81	+ 5.32	+10.11	+ 3.07	+ 3.97

[1] Data for the Reference Department of the New York Public Library and for the Honolulu Public Library are excluded. Since figures are rounded, detail will not necessarily add to totals.

[2] Includes expenditures for other categories not shown separately.

[3] In addition, public libraries circulated films, sound recordings, and other audio-visual materials.

SOURCE: U. S. Department of Health, Education, and Welfare: *Statistics of Public Library Systems in Cities with Populations of 100,000 or More; Fiscal Year 1959.* October 1960, p. 9.

tion while 58 gained—and some of the latter had startling increases. Roughly, the older cities in the East and Middle West lost ground; the cities in the Southwest and West gained. However, it is significant that there was no population loss in the Standard Metropolitan Statistical Areas. In fact, they gained by 48 per cent, while the cities as a whole increased only 9 per cent.

In some of these cities the increase was great enough to pose serious problems to existing libraries. For example, consider the problem of Houston with an increase in population from 596,163 to 938,319 and with a library expenditure of 65¢ per capita, or that of Anaheim, California, which in ten years increased in population from 14,556 to 104,184. The problem is not one of annual operating monies and services but also one of funds for capital growth—and for all city departments. Such increases call for orderly planning, and many municipal services are going to be taken care of before libraries. Faced with such problems, each metropolitan area should do careful planning of total library service on an area basis.

The trend of the last decade, which is likely to continue, indicates a steady rise in expenditures for large public libraries.

As the Library Services Branch has indicated, "Of particular interest is the 28.57 per cent increase in book stock (column 5) since 1950 as contrasted with the 42.45 per cent increase in circulation. Although expenditures for books and periodicals have risen 10.11 per cent from 1958 to 1959 (column 4), the actual number of books available in the large public libraries has increased only 3.07 per cent (column 5) during this same period. This small increase in book stock may be attributed to the increasingly greater cost of books (particularly nonfiction and reference titles) and to the rapid wearing out of books caused by a high rate of turnover." [2]

An additional reason for the small increase in book stock could be the heavy weeding of books because of crowded conditions resulting from lack of adequate stack space.

It must be pointed out that in the decade from 1950 to 1960, the total book stock increased from 49,636,000 to 63,819,000, or 28.57 per cent, while population in these cities increased from 47,382,000 to 52,226,000, or 10.22 per cent. Thus the increase in book stock has kept ahead of the increase in population for the large cities when viewed as a whole. Although individual statistics for all cities are not available at this writing, it is perhaps fair to say that those cities with the most rapid increase in population are not keeping up the same rate of increase for their book collections. Many of these cities had insufficient monies to operate 1950 libraries with 1960 budgets! For example, Houston with a 1960 population of 938,319 is spending $61,700 a year for books, while Baltimore with a population of 939,024 spends $310,100. The cities experiencing a population explosion are going to need outside help to meet their problems of capital outlay for both books and buildings.

Along with adequate facilities and proper staffing, the amount and kind of book stock determine the kind of services to be given any community. It is well known today, and the problem is becoming more acute with the rapid growth and merging of metropolitan areas, that it is the large public library that is attracting people from without the city, but within the defined metropolitan area, to the use, either for reference or circulation purposes, of the great resources of the large city library. Its collections of reference books, periodicals and serials, microfilms and educational films, government documents, and extensive collections of nonfiction, act as a magnet for the student and serious adult who, living outside city limits, can find no other public place to satisfy his reference and serious book needs. There is no substitute for the large public library.

As already indicated, there are a number of factors which are having a great influence upon the large public library. In 1960 there are more large cities than ever before, the greatest increase occurring in the West and South (twenty-one) with seven in the North Central states and one in the Northeast. The latter had three cities drop under 100,000 population and the South one.

At the same time, there was a loss in population in all of the twelve largest cities except Los Angeles, and most of these are located in the older areas on the eastern seaboard. It must be remembered, however, that the Standard Metropolitan Statistical Area is still growing and that for the large city library the decline in population has not been accompanied by a decline in use. Rather the opposite has occurred.

In many cities, as a result of redevelopment and reclamation of older sections of a city and because of technological developments such as air conditioning, many cities are finding that the older citizens, having reared their families, are moving back into the city and enjoying comforts not obtainable before. They no longer face problems with transportation, keeping up of grounds, or trying to get maids to commute equally long distances; these and other reasons have induced many older persons to return to the city. And the elder citizen is finding a better city, physically, to return to, as can be witnessed in such places as New Haven and Philadelphia. Not only are more older people moving into the city, but there are also more older people to serve.

The stringent laws relating to the amount of education, the raising of educational standards, the desire and need of more people to go to college have definitely raised the level of education in this country. It is well known that the higher the level of education, the greater the use of the public library. But the greatest effect to date upon this type of library has been the intensive use of the public library by the student—both in the secondary and higher levels of education. This striking use of public libraries is due to a number of factors, for example: (a) insufficient book stock in school libraries; (b) in many instances the nonexistence of school libraries; (c) lack of sufficient books in the college and undergraduate libraries; (d) lack of study or seating space in educational institutions; (e) restricted hours of opening of school and academic libraries as compared with those of public libraries; (f) disinclination of students to return to the school library after classroom hours; (g) lack of sufficient professional staff in the formal educational institutions; (h) change in educational methods and requirements, placing greater emphasis upon nontext materials; and (i) lack of understanding as to the true role of libraries, school, college, and public, on the part of educators. Many of these factors can be improved or eliminated as problems by librarians themselves, who are now being forced to this realization. It will, however, take an equally serious effort on the part of those in the field of formal education at all levels to arrive at a solution to our many library problems and the challenge of giving the best service we can to our many and varied patrons.

In more instances than not, it is only the large city library that has the resources that the metropolitan resident, living outside city limits, must have access to in order to fulfill his needs. The question resolves itself into one of who is to organize, provide, and finance this service. People in a Standard Metropolitan Statistical Area live not only in the central city but also in the neighboring counties, adjoining states, and even, as in some areas such as El Paso and Detroit, in adjacent countries. It is a librarian's professional obligation to furnish as many people as possible with library resources, but it is also a librarian's responsibility to see that the cost of these services is met to a great measure by the governing unit in which the library user lives.

Almost as dramatic as the increased use of reference and informational services and the growth of the use of nonfiction collections, has been the sharp increase in the use of the telephone for reference and informational services, or to save a useless trip to the library if the specific book wanted is out of the library and being used by someone else. Because of the volume of telephone business, some libraries have established separate telephone reference service in order to avoid interference with the service to patrons already in the library. It is certain that telephone reference service is bound to increase.

Another significant and baffling problem facing the librarians of the largest city libraries is the nonuse of libraries by the largest per cent of the population. Registration figures for smaller cities and towns are always higher than for the largest cities. If metropolitan library service is developed extensively, it may be predicted that the outlying and neighborhood libraries will be used extensively for general reading and for quick information, but the large central library will be the active, heavily used unit for resources in depth, research, and housing the lesser-used materials. Both types are absolutely essential to good metropolitan service. Little in the way of effective studies has really been done concerning the potential use of libraries by nonusers, and more attention should be given to the problem.

Unfortunately, along with the population explosion has come a long period of inflation, and there seems to be no signs on the horizon of any leveling off of this inflationary spiral. Gone are the days of our thinking in terms of $1.00 per capita library support; gone are the days when library school graduates could be hired at $1,200 a year. Yes, we are handling more money each year, but are we really making the progress essential to good and adequate public library service? The answer can be a qualified yes, for while the population of the United States has increased in the last decade by 18.5 per cent, operating expenditures for large libraries have increased by 88.4 per cent, book stock by 28.6 per cent and home reading by 42.5 per cent. Part of this increase in expenditure for service and increased use has resulted from the organization and development of new library services and the strengthening of existing services, but a large per cent is the direct result of inflation.

Some of the largest library systems, e.g., Buffalo, St. Louis, Queens Borough, San Francisco, Los Angeles, Washington, D.C., and Philadelphia, have increased their budgets by more than 50 per cent in the last decade. This increase has offset any inroad in the budget as a result of inflation, but capital growth within these cities may have offset some of the gains from an increased budget, for part of the increase would have been used to operate new agencies or services.

One of the serious fiscal problems about financing library service on a metropolitan basis is the inequality between the libraries involved, not only in the collections and services given, but also in the financing of these services. Small town or county libraries, not having great stock or specialized reference and research collections, do not have the fiscal obligations to service or provide them. In the Philadelphia area, the average per capita expenditure in 1959 for public library service was Bucks County 31¢, Chester County 34¢, Delaware County 39¢, and Montgomery County 80¢. Even Philadelphia's expenditures of $1.71 were considerably below the average $2.26 expenditures for libraries serving over 100,000 population. Equalization will have to come in the nature of state aid. There is no doubt that a means must be found to provide increased financing of metropolitan libraries in order to bring substantial financial relief. We cannot be placed in a position of denying information and education to our people whether in this generation or the next.

For many years we have talked about larger units of service, and it is only now that we are being forced into a situation that something is actually being done about it in an extensive way. Increased thought and study are being given the problem, and an excellent roundup on the subject is to be found in Part 2 of *New Notes of California Libraries*, Spring 1961, titled "Cooperative Planning for Public Libraries."[3] Here is to be found the current status of bibliographical and reference services with some emphasis upon complete collections. It is strange that the development of large library systems has not had greater effect upon over-all planning for library service than it has. Undoubtedly, the cost factor has been the greatest restraint upon the development of metropolitan systems. The systems found between city and county such as the Public Library of Cincinnati and Hamilton County, the public libraries of Seattle and King County, Minneapolis and Hennepin County, Rochester and the Monroe-Livingston-Wayne Tri-County (Pioneer) System, Cleveland and Cuyahoga County, although not all have survived, have at least pointed the way toward larger units of service and a means for financing them. Indeed, twenty-six cities participate in a city-county library setup, examples being found mainly in the South and Middle West. But much more study is needed to determine the best method of servicing and financing.

At the moment, as indicated by Katherine Laich,[4] systems are developing along three levels: city, metropolitan or submetropolitan, and state. Eventually there will have to come under consideration the development of a fourth plan, i.e. national services. All the plans are to result from cooperative efforts and coordinated planning, and all the state and city plans are based upon three levels of service: local, regional, and central. The conception seems to be a sound one, with increasing emphasis being placed upon meaningful bibliographic, reference, and nonfiction collections being established at the regional level and with, of course, the central libraries having the extensive files and important titles needed on an area basis.

Although the various city plans are very similar in organization, the size of building and collection, the hours of opening, etc., vary considerably. Regional book collections vary from 37,000 in a Los Angeles city regional library to a proposed 200,000 in Philadelphia; from a building of 6,000 square feet in Los Angeles to 39,000 in Philadelphia. Obviously, planning is still in the experimental stage, and much thought should be given to the establishment of objectives, standards of service, collections, staffing, hours of opening, and square foot areas before a final evaluation can be made.

The development of the neighborhood branch as a general reading center has had interesting developments in recent months. The organization of Family Reading Centers in Brooklyn will be watched with great interest by the profession. It may well be, with the tremendous expansion of library services, that our smaller neighborhood libraries in the cities (and also in a state plan) will be staffed by nonlibrary school but college graduates, and clerical assistants. The regional center and central library positions, calling for a high degree of professional skill and knowledge, will be staffed by library school graduates. This kind of staffing will require the establishment, probably on a local basis, of a program for the training of readers' advisers and administrators of the neighborhood libraries. The neighborhood library staff would funnel to the regional library centers the patrons for reference, information, and the intensive use of nonfiction collections for subject use. The neighborhood libraries would then become centers for good, but general reading.

Such a plan poses a problem of reference service to children, and this is a factor to be reckoned with by both the school and the public librarian. But perhaps of greater importance is the need for a full study of the total needs of the community before any one type of library goes too far in a single direction. The formation of a metropolitan library council to plan, organize, and develop total library service may produce noteworthy results.

The development of levels of service in the large metropolitan cities has its counterpart in several of the metropolitan library plans. However, the development of these systems calls for cooperation and local financing. As in Toronto, the individual libraries are to maintain their own identity when different libraries are involved and may have but two levels of service (as in Los Angeles County) or may depend upon one central library (as is proposed in Toronto). Baltimore County is to rely upon Baltimore City's Enoch Pratt Free Library, through a state contract, for its specialized resources and materials. Eventual developments must include all three levels of service, with state fiscal support, to insure complete library service.

Possibly the most exciting state plan for public library service is the one now (1961) enacted into law in Pennsylvania. The system will include *local libraries*, regardless of size, within 15-20 minutes driving time of each resident, which, if they elect to join the plan, will receive twenty-five cents per capita for each resident in the local political unit. *District library centers*, located within an hour's driving time of each person in the district, will receive in addition to state subsidy as a local library, an extra twenty-five cents per capita for each person in the prescribed district but outside of the local taxing authority. Finally, *regional resource libraries* would be designated within a one day trip for those wishing to use these resources, except for some very specialized subject materials, which would be located in one of four of these libraries. These resource libraries will each receive $100,000 annually toward the building up of resources and services in this type of library. Of interest is that the Philadelphia regional libraries and the state district libraries will be of comparable size and with similar service goals. Thus, in the Philadelphia metropolitan area there can be close cooperation with the two kinds of libraries serving very similar functions. It is entirely possible that all states will not want a state program as extensive as that for Pennsylvania and that in certain regions of the United States a library plan based upon a multistate program will be a practical and economical approach to the problem.

An interesting proposal has been forwarded in New York for the development of reference and research resources in that state. Subsidized by state aid, this plan provides for the establishment of five regional reference and research libraries working closely together. It will be a part of the overall plan of library service for New York residents, thus supplementing the present plan of public library service.

Both the Pennsylvania and New York plans are to use existing libraries—Pennsylvania, public and college or university libraries; New York, college, university, and special libraries. There still remains the study of the interrelationship of the elementary school requirements and to a lesser degree the secondary school, with the services of the public library.

Plans are wonderful, but unless their financing can be adequately taken care of, they will not accomplish their purposes. Development of metropolitan and regional services will require the combined fiscal efforts of local, state, and federal government. C. B. Joeckel years ago recommended a division of fiscal support—local 60 per cent, state 25 per cent, and federal 15 per cent. This is a neat division and should be a good base from which to operate. It is interesting to note that Maryland has proposed legislation that would permit the state to supply about 30 per cent of the cost for local library service. There is good reason from the point of view of the metropolitan library for some such division. No one metropolitan city area is within one taxing unit; all include one or more counties in their area, and several include two or more states in the territory included. It will take federal leadership to bring those involved together, to gather the information and statistics required to assess the situation, and to aid in the development of necessary legislation. Until this time comes, the only alternatives are informal cooperation, which really means trying to accomplish a program with no funds, or development of contracts for library service with neighboring communities or on a state-wide basis as in Maryland. But the $64,523 which the Enoch Pratt Free Library receives by contract for supplying nonfiction to libraries in the state, while a good beginning, is not a significant sum with which to build up extensive collections and personnel for state-wide services.

An extensive public relations program must be developed to acquaint people with the problem of library service to the kind of population growth we are to experience in the years ahead. The growth of circulation and book stock has been steady in the last decade (see Table II), and there is no reason to believe that this growth will diminish.

TABLE II

*Growth of Circulation and Bookstock, Large and Medium
Sized Public Libraries, Actual 1950 through 1959 and
Projected 1960 through 1980*

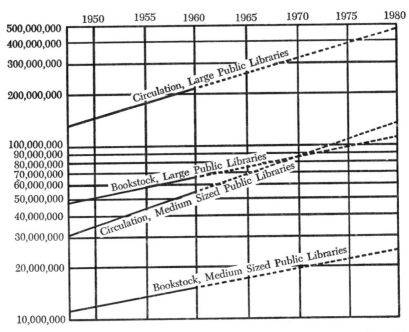

Source: Figures for 1950 through 1959 from data in U.S. Department of Health,
Education and Welfare reports, *Statistics of Public Library Systems in Cities
with Populations of 100,000 or More,* and *Statistics of Public Library Systems
in Cities with Populations of 50,000 to 99,000.*

The educational level of the population will continue to rise, con-
tributing to a progressive increase in the use of libraries. National
Library Week, which is likely to continue for the next few years, will
not only keep people informed about library needs, but will also present the profession with an excellent vehicle to make library needs
known to broad segments of the community. Librarians must also remember that library service is but one segment of local, state, and
federal government and that other divisions of governmental services
are also affected by the growth of metropolitan areas. Already some
states have begun to study the problem through legislative committees.
It behooves state library associations to be alert to such activities and

to request the inclusion of library problems in the legislative studies.

In conclusion, there is no question of the continued growth of the United States and of libraries of all kinds within the country. Barring war, this growth will continue on a steady and increasing basis. Librarians, by watching the population changes, can plan accordingly. Their problem is, at one and the same time, to secure personnel, facilities, and funds for a growing use by present population as well as for future needs.

At this writing each Standard Metropolitan Statistical Area might be urged to create a Metropolitan Area Library Council to study, recommend, and coordinate the area library needs. These metropolitan requirements and recommendations should be coordinated with state planning in all the states involved. Included in the constituency of such a council would be representatives of all library systems and individual agencies relating to libraries such as union library catalogs, etc., and individual libraries, both public and private. In addition there should be lay and governmental representatives to insure a full representation from all groups involved.

As librarians look to the future of public library service in metropolitan areas, the trend seems to be, and with justification, toward the development of three levels of library service providing for (1) local but limited resources and services; (2) regional district services with larger collections and varied, more intensive services; and finally (3) large collections, with emphasis upon reference books, serial publications, educational films, and intensive nonfiction collections with subject specialization to meet area needs. It is to be hoped that a means will be found to coordinate the services and resources of other libraries into a well integrated pattern that will answer the needs of the library public of tomorrow with service that will measure up to both their quantitative and qualitative needs.

References

1. Hauser, P. M., and Taitel, M.: Population Trends—Prologue to Library Development. *Library Trends*, 10:10-67, July 1961.

2. U.S. Department of Health, Education, and Welfare: *Statistics of Public Library Systems in Cities with Populations of 100,000 or More; Fiscal Year 1959.* October 1960, p. 3.

3. Cooperative Planning for Public Libraries. *News Notes of California Libraries*, Vol. 2, No. 2, Pt. 2, Spring 1961.

4. Laich, Katherine: Regional Reference Library Service. *In News Notes of California Libraries, op. cit.*, pp. 254+.

Small and Medium-Sized Public Libraries

RANSOM L. RICHARDSON

CURRENTLY THE HUMAN POPULATION of the world is increasing at about 45 million people a year. This figure becomes more meaningful when we reflect that a mere four years of such growth is all that is necessary to equal the population of the United States. Indeed someone with a fondness for mathematical computation has calculated that at the end of six hundred years there will be one person for every square meter of earth.

In the United States alone the next four years will see an increase of more than 11 million people or enough to match the 1960 population of Pennsylvania. In the next 20 years this country will add about 66 million people, or enough to equal all those now populating the four large states of New York, California, Pennsylvania, and Illinois, plus those in the whole East South Central Division, comprising the states of Kentucky, Tennessee, Alabama, and Mississippi.

For convenience, the medium-sized public library is defined here as one serving a city or place with a population of 35,000 to 100,000 and the small public library as one serving a village or place with a population of fewer than 35,000. A third group may occasionally be identified as very small, to indicate those public libraries serving populations of fewer than 5,000.

In 1960 there were approximately 8,190 public libraries in the United States. Latest available estimates supplied by the Library Services Branch, U.S. Office of Education, show that 4,657 of these served populations under 5,000, 2,625 served between 5,000 and 35,000 people, and 657 served populations between 35,000 and 100,000.

The Hauser-Taitel article appearing in the previous issue [1] discusses in detail the implications of the 1960 census, emphasizing those demographic aspects which have particular significance for the development of libraries. The Hauser-Taitel projections are based upon key

Mr. Richardson is Director of Libraries, Flint (Mich.) Public Library.

assumptions regarding fertility levels, death rates, immigration, and national catastrophe.

By and large, public libraries serving population groups under 35,000 have insufficient funds to provide recognized minimum standards of library service. Book collections are small, hours of service inadequate, and trained staff nonexistent or spread too thin to be truly effective. The most significant effect of population change upon these libraries during the next twenty years will be the one of growth. Many of them will become "medium-sized," and hence, with increased income along with other factors, a little better able to provide for library needs of the community.

The places and the libraries which will be most affected by the sheer impact of growth will of course be those which are now a part of the great urban fringes. If the current trend in suburbanization continues, as it is predicted, in two decades many of these small libraries will be serving population groups several times their present size. As these libraries slip over 35,000 into the next population class, those with commensurate incomes may well develop a depth and flexibility of service capable of responding to some of the more subtle demands of population change. The potential extent of this growth nation-wide may be roughly gauged by noting that from 1950 to 1960 the number of places in urban fringes with populations of 35,000 to 100,000 increased from 244 to 380. That this movement will continue at an accelerated pace is borne out by the predictions of population increase in and around urban areas.

Some of the smaller governmental units in urban areas, however, have already approached maximum growth within their boundaries and are so hemmed in by surrounding units that there is little or no opportunity to annex and expand. In the nonurban areas, many of the small places, especially those in the 5,000-or-less population group, will not gain a sufficient tax base under the predicted patterns of growth to permit their public libraries to achieve the minimums of service. Again, some measure of the growth of small places may be gained by noting that from 1950 to 1960 the number of places of fewer than 35,000 population increased from 18,264 to 19,279, while about 161 such places moved beyond the 35,000 mark. It is important to note that these figures refer to *places* and make no distinction between those with and those without public libraries.

Although the libraries in these small places may not have sufficient breadth and flexibility of service to respond to other kinds of population change within their boundaries, they will nonetheless feel the effect of such change. Change in age structure is a prime example. The population projection to 1980 shows for all age groups an increase of 37 per cent over 1960. Against this figure can be compared the increase of 48.9 per cent for the age group 65 years and over. Further, present trends indicate that members of this group tend to retire to suburban and rural nonfarm areas.[2] Since our senior citizens are reportedly devoting more of their leisure hours to a wide range of recreational, cultural, and educational activities, the implications to library service are clear. Where library service is comprehensive, suitable adaptations may be made to serve the special needs of the group; in smaller places, although some adaptation may be possible, it is likely that the more significant effect will be an exertion of pressure upon local authorities for an improvement in library service.

Even greater demands for public library service may be expected from the other end of the age structure. While the middle-age groups remain relatively stable until 1980, those under 30 years of age show sharp increases over the norm. Particularly significant projections are those for the age groups 14 to 17, 18 to 21, and 22 to 29, which show respective increases of 44.4, 73.0, and 83.8 per cent as compared with the norm of 37 per cent. When these projections are visualized in terms of school enrollment, it becomes clear that student demands upon the public library as a supplementary and, in some cases, as a primary resource will reach proportions unknown to present experience. To this should be added the greatly increased population of children below the age of 14, which will also require increased public library services and expenditures.

Changes in educational attainment for all persons in these two decades are predicted in terms of high school and college graduates. In 1960 51.5 million people over 18 years of age, or 44.7 per cent of the total, were high school graduates. The projection for 1980 shows 95.1 million, or 58.9 per cent, with high school diplomas, an increase of 14.2 per cent in twenty years. Although less rapid in growth, the number of college graduates shows a steady increase from 7.6 to 10.4 per cent of the population over 22 years of age during the same period. Even though a correlation between educational attainment and the use of public libraries would be too complex to express in a single quantitative ratio, it seems safe to assume that the upward trend in the educational level of the people will in general produce an increased demand for library service.

[134]

Small and Medium-Sized Libraries

During the decade 1950 to 1960 several changes occurred in the major occupation groups of employed persons which have significance to the use of libraries. Against an increase of 11.6 per cent shown for all employed persons 14 years old and over, there is an increase in professional and technical workers of 66.4 per cent or nearly 55 per cent over the norm.[3, 4] If the number of professional workers continues to increase at this rate or, indeed, if they simply hold to the norm for the next two decades, libraries may also expect from this source a considerable increase in the demand for service.

The combined effect of these projected changes in population upon the small library must inevitably be to emphasize further the inadequacy of its service or, to put it in another way, it will become increasingly clear that an acceptable level of modern library service can rarely be achieved by a taxing unit with fewer than 35,000 population.

The medium-sized public library will be exposed to much the same effects of population change. If it is assumed, however, that the medium-sized library more nearly meets minimum library standards for housing, organization, and service, it is obviously in a better position to tackle the problems of increased demand. While the small library will still be very much concerned with increasing, say, hours of service, the medium-sized library will be able to turn some of its attention to the more special needs of the senior citizen, the professional worker, and the student.

Many small and the medium-sized libraries will be affected by their proximity to urbanized areas. Any suburban library may expect demands upon its services according to the population characteristics of the central city and its pattern of library service. And those public libraries lying within fringe and potential fringe areas of the great urban developments must expect their communities to mushroom to near absolute capacity by 1980.

Hauser and Taitel indicate that growth patterns during the two decades will vary widely among the major geographical divisions of the country, from a low of 7.8 per cent increase for the East South Central Division to a high of 62.2 per cent for the Pacific Division. Here, of course, migration is the significant factor with climactic and economic advantages providing the major incentives.

Since projections for each geographic division show absolute increases in population, it follows that libraries generally will experience increasing demands for their services. Changes in age structure, school enrollment, educational attainment, and occupation must necessarily affect all libraries to some degree, and where these factors of normal growth are combined with a strong pattern of in-migration, the library may count on a dramatic increase in the demands that will be made upon it.

Library trustees and administrators must view these changes with considerable concern. Any assumption that present levels of service will do for tomorrow ignores the basic implications of the projected population changes. It is not simply a matter of more population but one of more population differently structured. A constant per capita income will not provide for an increasing per capita demand.

A more serious concern is manpower. Today we know from experience that funds to hire qualified personnel are useless if these people are unavailable. If the current trend toward personnel shortages continues, and the evidence is that it will, the problem of supplying increased demand for library service during the next two decades assumes gargantuan proportions.

Let us consider for a moment the small public library. Under the most benign circumstances, the small public library today is already losing ground in its efforts to provide minimum standard service to the community. Turn as it will, it cannot escape the fact that basic library service costs more than the small community can afford to pay. This is scarcely a new problem, but the trustees and administrators of small public libraries must expect it to be considerably aggravated during the next twenty years, and they must find solutions to cope with it effectively.

In the opinion of this author, the future of the small public library lies through affiliation with the expanding development of larger units of service. Granted that present library service patterns for the multijurisdictional areas produce some very real problems of their own, it is equally evident that they provide a greater number of people with more library service.

The authorities responsible for the small public library, therefore, will be wise to plan now for cooperative library services in whatever pattern is most feasible and appropriate to the communities and jurisdictions involved. (Particularly à propos is the Henderson article in this issue). They will do well to discover as quickly as possible that centralization of some services does not necessarily mean loss of ownership and autonomy and that it does mean a greatly improved library service for the community.

The medium-sized public library must be concerned equally with centralization of services and financial support if it hopes to cope successfully with increased demand. The medium-sized community that serves as the center of a large area may well consider itself the nucleus in the establishment of a larger unit of service and may hope to strengthen its own service thereby. Where several medium-sized communities exist in relative proximity, some form of library consolidation or federation may be indicated. Again, the medium-sized library serving a suburban community may find cooperative or contractual arrangements with the central city productive of improved service.

Any consideration of the projected growth and changes in population during the next twenty years yields the one general but inescapable conclusion that the per capita demand for library service must greatly exceed that of 1960. This demand will make it more necessary than ever before for the small public library to seek a means of increasing its service through some form of cooperation with other libraries—or face the fact that its resources will become ever less capable of meeting the needs of its community.

The medium-sized public library may be faced with the same problem—except for those whose communities will grow so rapidly that they move well into the class of the large public library. While the medium-sized public library might be able to make some adjustments in depth, it will not find it easy to cope with a sharp increase in per capita demand. The sheer quantity of service required may so burden the medium-sized public library that it, too, will have to look for assistance through large-scale cooperation or become less and less able to supply the community.

It seems evident that the small public library will virtually disappear as a self-contained unit. State laws and state and federal aid will so encourage the development of large units of service that the small library will not be able to justify an unaffiliated status.

In these large units, the small public library, serving as an outlet, will be almost wholly devoted to patron services. While it may retain local leadership, its administrative and technical services will be centralized. Comparatively speaking, it will be giving the best possible service for the dollar spent.

The medium-sized public library will also be a part of a large unit of service or a system of libraries. It may differ here from the small library only in the form of participation. Medium-sized libraries which are dominant in the unit of service will act as headquarters for administrative, technical, and related services. Particularly those in the metropolitan areas will be members of a system of libraries in which each will retain desirable minimums of local control.

In systems or larger units of service, much of the work of professional librarians will be to direct untrained or semitrained personnel in the improved performance of their activities. Personnel in the administrative, technical, and distributive services will be largely non-professional.

The large unit of service will engage in economic mass production of technical aids and tools. It will unite and make available the total library resources of the unit through the most economical and effective means of communication.

These directions toward total library service are actually current. It is idle to guess how many years must pass before they will be common throughout the land, but it seems certain that in the next twenty years the movement will have become necessary and massive.

References

1. Hauser, P. M., and Taitel, M.: Population Trends—Prologue to Library Development. *Library Trends*, 10:10-67, July 1961.

2. Bogue, D. J.: *The Population of the United States*. Glencoe, Ill., The Free Press, 1959, p. 100.

3. U.S. Bureau of the Census: *Statistical Abstract of the United States: 1960*. Washington, D.C., U.S. Government Printing Office, 1961, pp. 205-216.

4. U.S. Bureau of Labor Statistics: *Monthly Report on the Labor Force: December 1960*. Washington, D.C., U.S. Government Printing Office, 1961, Table 20.

◇◇◇

Rural and County School Libraries

MAE GRAHAM

Part I: Educational Trends in All School Libraries

MORE THAN A QUARTER of a century ago, speaking at an institute at the Graduate Library School at the University of Chicago, W. F. Ogburn reminded his listeners that "The library is a part of society as a whole and does not in any sense exist in a vacuum, nor does it pursue its own course isolated from the happenings around it." [1] This is peculiarly true of the school library. The school library has no existence—no reason for existence—except as it serves the school in which it is located. It has no board of trustees, no independent tax income. Its broad principles and policies are those of its school; its clientele is the faculty and student body; its professional staff is considered part of the instructional or administrative staff of the school; its budget comes from funds allocated to the school.

Since the society in which the school library exists can be defined so specifically, it would seem to be a simple matter to predict its role for the next twenty years. In 1936, when Ogburn made his statement, it would have been, but not so today. There is no segment of our total society which is now under such close scrutiny, which has so many critics, which is being studied any more carefully than elementary and secondary public education. The *Readers' Guide to Periodical Literature*,[2] March, 1955–February, 1956, lists 5 articles under the subject *Secondary Education* and 11 under *Aims*; the March, 1959–February, 1960, volume lists 18 articles on *Secondary Education* and 32 on *Aims and Objectives*. The widespread, vocal interest seems to have begun with the first Russian Sputnik in 1957, although undoubtedly it has a sounder basis in our very real concern for the explosion of knowledge and the increasing school population.

To try to anticipate school library needs for the year 1980 is to

Miss Graham is Supervisor of School Libraries, Maryland State Department of Education.

prophesy trends in education for these years, and a scanning of current literature concerning education makes these needs anybody's guess. The one point upon which all writers and speakers seem to agree is that, barring total destruction, we will have schools. J. B. Conant says, "I am convinced that American secondary education can be made satisfactory without any radical changes in the basic pattern." [3] J. L. Trump says, "Changes are especially urgent . . . The task calls for a realignment of educational priorities and a re-examination of school functions and needs." [4] While there is little agreement about the pattern of the school of the future, there is almost complete unanimity of opinion about three factors which will influence education.

First, there is the basic philosophy of a free society, concerned with the worth of the individual and his opportunity to develop his full potential: "The danger is that we may forget the individual behind a façade of huge and impersonal institutions. The risk is that we will glorify science and forget the scientists; magnify government and ignore the men and women who discharge its functions; pin our hopes on education, business or cultural institutions, and lose sight of the fact that these institutions are no more creative or purposeful than the individuals who endow them with creativity and purpose." [5] Even the severest critics of our public schools seem to have no quarrel with this premise though some of them accuse the schools of confusing equality with excellence and of sacrificing the latter for the former.

A related responsibility of public education which is seldom spelled out in detail, although it is basic to our concept of both individual freedom and of our democratic society, recently was stated clearly by Sterling McMurrin,[6] U.S. Commissioner of Education:

Traditionally, while we have recognized that the quality of our national life has depended on an intelligent and informed electorate, the aims and purposes of our educational program have been determined almost entirely by the interests of the individual as expressed in his vocational, cultural, or other purposes. It has been more or less assumed that the interests of our society taken as a total entity would take care of themselves. Indeed, it has not been common even to define what might be called the large educational needs of the Nation beyond the necessity of adequately satisfying the proper demands of the individual and local communities.

But now we are confronted by problems of a new order that place upon the educational establishment a social responsibility of new dimensions and greater proportions and that must claim from us a maximum of effort for their solution. Internally and in our relations with the world we are involved in increasing social complexities that pertain especially to vast industrial expansion, the new technologies, and increased intercommunication of all kinds, and it is becoming increasingly clear that we face the risks of serious shortages, misplacements, and imbalances in the education and training of our people that may affect the stability of our economy and the quality of our culture.

Second, the explosion of knowledge makes it not incredible that the man of 40 in the year 2000 may spend a weekend on the moon, that deserts will be fertile lands irrigated by sea water, and that the strides in parapsychology may revolutionize our concept of time. The schools are already faced with the task of helping students develop inquiring minds and habits of independent study and to realize that, unless learning is a continuous process, knowledge and understanding are quickly outmoded.

The third factor is the growth of the school population. In 1960, 42,627,000 pupils were enrolled in grades K-12 in the 50 states and the District of Columbia. Fifteen per cent, or 6,457,000 were enrolled in nonpublic schools, leaving 36,170,000 enrolled in public schools.[7] The most conservative estimate of the Bureau of the Census is that in 1980 the school enrollment, K-12 will reach 66,290,000.[8] If the percentage of private school pupils remains the same, this enrollment will be 9,943,500, and the public schools will have an enrollment of 57,346,500, an increase of 58.5 per cent.

While it is not within the scope of this paper to predict the pattern of the schools of the future, there are certain discernible trends which will have bearing if not direct influence upon the library in the school.

Television as a teaching tool is viewed with alarm by some and enthusiasm by others. Evanston Township High School with its closed circuit television for one school, Washington County, Maryland, with closed circuit television for one school system, the New York State Regents Educational Television Project over a commercial television station, and the still experimental Midwest program on Airborne Television Instruction are outstanding examples of extensive use of this medium. Washington County, Maryland, reports "a marked increase in the use of school libraries and cultural resources throughout the community"[9] as a result of television instruction.

Teaching machines apparently are frightening to more people than is television, but it is reasonable to conjecture that as they become less expensive, they will be used more extensively for teaching skills, for review, and for independent study. W. M. Alexander says,

We now find ourselves on the horns of a very real dilemma involving mechanization in the school. . . . Surely American citizens and taxpayers must recognize that automation can do more than replace teachers—it can release them from drudgery and make possible a concentration of fine teaching ability on pupils' learning needs. . . . With her time spent in teaching activities only and with adequate facilities for understanding each pupil well, the classroom teachers should be able to turn Johnny loose on materials which challenge him at any time. He should also be able to make full use of the wonderful storehouse of information available in the modern school library and in the surrounding community. Perhaps here the individual should find his greatest challenge in school in an age in which fact-finding becomes steadily more important than fact-memorizing.[10]

Broadened use of tapes, recordings, filmstrips, and slides will be brought about by an increase in independent study and will affect not only the school library collection but also its services and physical plan.

Numerous experiments in class size are being conducted. Large group instruction carries with it the implication of small group instruction as well as independent study. For a school of 1,200, Trump says,

Several different kinds of spaces will be used for independent study. The largest will be the library reading room, furnished with enough tables and chairs to seat 60 students. Adjacent to the library will be a listening room and also a viewing room, each to seat 40 persons, and 10 conference rooms each big enough for five persons. Also in or near the library will be five soundproof booths for study with electronic devices and a 1200 square foot room for automatic instruction devices (teaching machines). A total of 300 study cubicles, each with 24 square feet of space, will be constructed near the library.[11]

The content of the elementary school curriculum has expanded. It is encouraging to find this sentence in *Contemporary Issues in Elementary Education*: "The elementary school has a unique opportunity to influence the course of a child's further schooling and of his intellectual life in general. Here his knowledge and understanding of himself and his world, his habits in the use of his intellect, his skill in language and numbers, his ability to seek out further learning, and his sense of the aesthetic receive their first formal impetus." [12] One can only hope that this concept of elementary education will mark the end of all of the middle-class sibling teams in elementary readers with controlled vocabularies and without ideas. Whether it does or not, the concept has implications for the school library, because the same publication contains this paragraph: "An elementary school needs a library available to pupils individually, in groups, and in classes. It needs also a carefully chosen and catalogued supply of audio-visual and other instructional materials for classroom use. The library should be a place of discovery for the pupil where he learns to exercise his own judgment in the selection and use of a wide variety of reading materials, develops the habit of independent study, and broadens his own cultural horizons. It as an essential in a modern elementary school." [13]

It is not in the elementary school alone that curriculum content is expanding. High schools with multi-track curricula, honors courses, and new courses, particularly in the sciences and foreign languages, are adding breadth and depth to secondary education and place a responsibility upon school librarians to improve the quality and scope of the library's collection. Community colleges as a growing part of the public school educational program are creating the same demands for more highly-developed library services.

Experiments in the use of teacher aides and of team teaching have been successful in freeing teachers for full-time professional work. A study conducted by the librarians in the schools in Frederick County, Maryland, in 1959 showed that one-third of their time was spent on nonprofessional tasks. The use of library aides, properly guided and directed, would have the same advantage for the librarian as for the teacher. In team teaching the librarian has the same responsibility for supplying materials to the team as to the individual teacher and, in addition, in many instances the librarian himself should be an actual teaching member of the team.

Exploding population and knowledge and the already discernible educational trends will have a drastic and dramatic effect upon school administration. An article in *School Life*, January 1961, describes these changes in detail.[14] Selected from the article are nine changes in school administration which have direct implications for school library programs:

[143]

(1) Education will be extended both upward and downward. There will be more kindergartens. In 1955–56, 5 per cent of the total enrollment in public elementary schools was in the kindergarten, an increase of 1.8 per cent since 1944.[15] The number of publicly controlled junior colleges was approximately 200,000 in 1952 and 350,000 in 1959.[16]

(2) School days may lengthen to eight hours for intermediate and secondary grades and the school year to 200 days. Summer sessions will be extended and their programs expanded.

(3) The number of school districts will go below 20,000 (the estimated number is now 42,000).

(4) The organization structure of the intermediate unit will be altered to make it more effective.

(5) Many small high schools that unnecessarily operate as separate units will be consolidated.

(6) There will be more supervisory services, more efforts to improve instruction, more emphasis upon instructional materials.

(7) Advances in curriculum development and instructional materials and methods will necessitate the use of specialists and more flexible schedules from grade 1 through 12.

(8) Increased emphasis upon quality education and upon programs for identifying and developing talent will cause local schools to change expenditure patterns to meet new requirements.

(9) Federal support for public education will increase—both general support and support for special programs. If federal aid for schools becomes a reality, it is reasonable to think that it will have the same impact upon school libraries that a similar program has had upon guidance and counseling. In 1958, there were 69 professional staff persons employed at the state level in the guidance field; in 1960, there were 144. In the same period, 47 states indicated that counselors have been added to the staff of local schools; one state had an increase of 23 per cent in full-time guidance counselors and another 65 per cent.[17]

By 1980, the school library will have had a chance to prove itself. Informed and imaginative educators already are assigning to it an importance which it has never had before. The Council of Chief State School Officers in its recent policy statement on school library services has defined it as "an integrated materials instructional center, including books, periodicals, audio-visual equipment and materials" and an integral part of the instructional program.[18]

The American Library Association recognizes the school library as one of the basic requirements for quality education, where the many materials needed by teachers and students can be supplied efficiently and economically and whose program contributes to the overall education of youth and to the improvement of the instructional program of the school.[19]

If the school library profession is to fulfill these purposes, the individual school librarian must be enthusiastic, vigorous, flexible, intelligent, and imaginative. Leadership at national, state, and school system levels must be positive, dynamic, and informed. Positive action must be taken to provide the school librarian the education needed to assist him in meeting his dual responsibilities to the professions of teaching and librarianship.

Part II: Educational Trends in Rural and County School Libraries

Basically, rural schools differ from urban schools in two respects: size and location. The rural school is often small, or if it is not, it is a consolidated school which cannot be located near the homes of all pupils. The automobile, rural electrification, radio and television, and the extension of public library service to rural areas are factors which help to account for the lack of difference there is today between the rural child and his city cousin. Traditionally, the American people want equal educational opportunities for all children, rural or urban.

The problem of the rural school, therefore, is not the provision of a different kind of education for a different kind of child, but one of how to provide the same quality education for the same child when the difference is that the school itself is either small or relatively isolated.

There are two common patterns of public school organization that affect rural schools: the system-wide one and the small independent school district.

Any discussion of the needs of rural school libraries in 1980 must be based upon (1) a knowledge of what rural schools are today; (2) a prediction of what they will be in 1980; and (3) an understanding of how the school as it is presently constituted or will change, affects library needs.

Changes in patterns of organization will affect personnel needs for school libraries of the future rural school more drastically than will population changes. For these reasons this paper is divided into three parts: (A) Schools in Rural Areas; i.e., the rural school in the small administrative unit; (B) County-wide School Systems; i.e., the rural schools in one county under one board of education. There are many patterns of organization of the intermediate units, but the reason for their existence is always basically the same: to extend equal services to all schools, regardless of size. Because the principle is the same, only the county-wide unit is discussed in this paper. The third part, (C) Rural School Libraries, 1980, is a section which combines the predicted needs for both groups.

A. Schools in Rural Areas

As part of the *Biennial Survey of Education in the United States, 1954–56* the U.S. Office of Education made its first statistical survey of education in rural areas. There is no other one source with as detailed, well-documented, and pertinent information on the status of rural schools. The survey, therefore, is used here for definition of rural areas and description of the schools in those areas.

After an extensive study of available sociological facts bearing upon the environment of rural schools and a study of school accounting and reporting, "it was decided to base this first National survey of rural education upon county sources and draw upon state files and local district sources only where necessary." [20] Two criteria led to the choice of counties considered to be rural: (1) 60 per cent or more of the total number of inhabitants of each county had to live in rural communities (fewer than 2,500 in incorporated towns or unincorporated civil divisions and fewer than 50,000 in urban fringe areas); and (2) 50 per cent or more of this rural population had to live on farms if less than 85 per cent were reported as rural. [21]

All counties composed of a single county-wide school district were eliminated from the study, because a separate but coordinated survey of their schools was to be made and published as a separate report. [22] These are the counties included in the second part of this paper.

Table I shows the total number of counties in the Continental United States and by regions the number and percentage of counties defined as rural.

Table II is a summary of selected statistics in areas which directly affect school library service. Schools are small; expenditures for instruction (which include library materials) are lower than for the rest of the state; salaries for instructional personnel (which includes school librarians) average over $1000 per year less than for the non-

TABLE I

Total Number of Counties in the United States and Number
and Per Cent of This Total Selected for Rural County
Survey, by Region: 1955–56

	Total No. Counties in Region	Counties Selected as Rural— Number and Per Cent of Total	
		Number	Per Cent of Total
Continental U. S................	3070	1,199	39.1
Northeast......................	217	25	11.5
North Central.................	1055	609	57.7
South.........................	1387	419	30.2
West..........................	411	146	35.5

SOURCE: U. S. Office of Education: *Statistics of Local School Systems, 1955–56, Rural Counties.* Washington, D. C., U. S. Government Printing Office, 1959, pp. 10–11.

rural areas of the states. One significant fact not included in the Table is the number of "other instructional staff," which includes school librarians. To serve the more than 4 million pupils in 39,938 schools, there were only 1,955 persons employed as librarians, psychologists, guidance personnel, etc., and clerks for instruction.[23] While statistics are not available to show what percentage of this number is school librarians, it is a safe assumption that many—or even most—of these employees are not; even if all of them were, it would mean only one librarian to every 2,165 pupils, which is more than 1,000 more pupils per school librarian than the national average of one librarian to every 1,147 pupils,[24] in school districts with enrollments of 150 or more.

"There was a decrease of almost 17,000 in the number of independent school districts between 1952 and 1957. Most of the decrease may be attributed to the reorganization and consolidation of districts with an enrollment of fewer than 50 pupils." [25] Nevertheless, smallness remains an essential characteristic of the school in the rural areas. Table II again calls attention to this fact with the number of one room schools in operation in 1956.

Educators generally regard these small schools as unable to provide adequate educational opportunities. A survey made in Montana makes specific recommendations for larger school districts. Montana, which is included in the Office of Education's survey of rural schools, has 33.9 per cent of its schools classified as rural. In 1958, the Montana Taxation-Education Study Commission arranged for

TABLE II

Enrollment, Size of Schools, Expenditures Per Pupil for Instruction, Average Salaries, Number of One Room Schools in 38 Selected States and Their Rural Counties: 1955–56

	Total Enrollment [1] Public Day Schools		Average Enrollment [1] Per School		@ Pupil Expenditures [1] for Instruction		Salaries [1]		No. One-Teacher[2] Schools
	Entire State	Rural Counties	Entire State	Rural Counties	Entire State	Rural Counties	Entire State	Rural Counties	
38 States.........	26,527,250	4,233,143 15.9%	228.4	105.7	$199	$160	$4,155	$3,137	32,702
North East (6 States)......	5,346,017	100,821 1.9%	345.7	153	$235	$192	$4,719	$3,689	1,720
North Central (12 States)....	8,793,768	1,809,520 20.6%	164.7	71.6	$206	$185	$4,151	$3,193	23,099
South (10 States)....	7,750,040	2,025,262 26.1%	228.3	177.7	$142	$126	$3,316	$2,899	5,699
West (10 States)....	4,637,425	287,540 6.2%	348.0	109.9	$236	$224	$4,748	$3,863	2,184

SOURCES: [1] As for Table I, pp. 14, 38, 58, 52.
[2] U. S. Office of Education: *Statistics of State School Systems, 1955–56: Organization, Staff, Pupils, and Finances.* Washington, D. C., U. S. Government Printing Office, 1959, p. 86.

TABLE III

Selected Statistical Data of 743 County-Wide School Systems: 1955–56
Groups III–VI Considered Rural

	Group I Population 100,000 & Over	Group II Population 25,000–99,000	Group III Population 10,000–24,999	Group IV Population 5,000–9,999	Group V Population 2,500–4,999	Group VI Population Under 2,500
No. Counties (29 states)......	26	159	309	165	52	32
Per Cent Population Urban....	76.6	39.2	13.7	8.2	8.9	0.0
Per Cent Population Rural Farm	4.6	27.8	46.8	48.2	37.8	34.8
Total Enrollment............	1,136,961	1,657,963	1,280,392	320,534	48,569	11,065
Av. No. Schools Per County....	85.5	43.1	25.1	11.5	6.9	4.3
Av. Enrollment Per School.....	512	242	165	170	135	80
Av. Teacher Salary..........	$4,098	$3,417	$3,153	$3,092	$3,525	$3,608
Per-Pupil Expenditure— Instruction.............	$179	$145	$138	$143	$195	$254

Source: U. S. Office of Education: *Statistics of Local School Systems, 1955–56, County Units.* Washington, D. C., U. S. Government Printing Office, 1959, pp. 3–23 *passim.*

a comprehensive study of selected public school problems. Two recommendations call for larger units and have implications for school libraries: [26] (1) the state should require all school districts to operate schools from grades 1 through 12; (2) the state should revise upwards its definition of desirable minimum sizes for schools—(a) an elementary school of satisfactory *minimum* size should provide at least one teacher per grade (about seven teachers in a six grade school); (b) a high school of satisfactory *minimum* size should provide at least three sections of each grade taught . . . a total of ten academic teachers plus two vocational teachers for an enrollment of about 250-275.

With the trend toward consolidation of school districts or abolition of very small ones and of one room schools, it is certain that some such basic pattern will be the accepted one long before 1980.

B. County-Wide School Systems

"A county unit school system is one whose boundaries are coterminous or approximately coterminous with those of a civil county." [27] In 1956, there were 743 such units in 29 states, more than 89 per cent of all of them in the South. In 6 of these states 100 per cent of the counties are county-unit systems. In 1955-56, 14 per cent of the total public elementary and secondary day school enrollment in the United States was enrolled in these county-unit school systems. [28]

Table III shows these 743 school systems by population of counties and gives selected characteristics of the schools. A cursory examination reveals that the school systems are both urban and rural in character, and so are the individual schools. Since schools in county units are both urban and rural, their libraries are treated elsewhere in these papers. The purpose here is to try to show the advantage of the larger units of service.

The benefits of the county-wide system are administrative, instructional, and economic. Each unit has a single board of education to make policies and a single superintendent to carry them out. Policies apply equally to large or small, urban or rural schools. Supervision can be provided more easily and economically for all schools, even the small ones. The principal economic advantages are that there is a broader tax base on which to operate, and the purchasing of supplies and materials can be consolidated.

The school library program profits accordingly. Policies, standards, and practices for school library development for all of the schools in a system can be discussed with one superintendent and board of education staff. In this way, the state school library supervisor has direct communication with all the school libraries in the state. Overall plans for regional and state-wide in-service programs can be made with the same group. Most important of all, channels for communication are clear and simple, and thereby simplify interpretation and promote understanding.

Per-pupil allocations for materials are the same county-wide; there is a present trend, however, to establish minimum library collections in each school even when doing so calls for expenditures far in excess of the average per-pupil amount. Montgomery County, Maryland, for example, has recently taken a step in this direction, as well as in providing travelling elementary school librarians and clerical aides to work in small elementary schools. There is no difference between the salaries of rural and urban personnel in the same county; all librarians and teachers are paid on the same basis, depending upon education and experience.

County-wide materials centers and professional and curriculum libraries serve students, teachers, and schools according to the various needs. Supplementary materials are provided; little-used materials are housed in one center for the use of anyone who needs them. Any special service provided, such as supervision, is available at all schools.

A look at school library supervision at both the state and county level is interesting. Of the 38 states used in the Office of Education's survey of rural schools, 20 states, or 52 per cent, have state school library supervisors; of the 29 states used in the survey of county-wide systems, 20 of them, or 69 per cent, have state school supervisors; and of the 15 states with 10 or more county-wide systems 11 of them, or 73 per cent, have state supervision for school libraries.[29]

The American Association of School Librarians [30] lists 281 school library supervisors in cities, towns, and counties. Forty-six of these, or approximately 16 per cent are in the 743 county-wide school systems. The other 235 are in the other 40,720 school districts with enrollments of over 150. These figures mean that approximately 6 per cent of the county-wide systems have school library supervisors, while only 0.057 per cent of all the other districts have. It means that for the 36 million pupils enrolled in all the public schools in 1960, there was one supervisor for every 114 thousand pupils, and one for approximately each 26 thousand pupils in the rural county-wide systems.

In counties with local school library supervision, there are immediate advantages to the local school library: (1) The quality of materials is improved, not by imposed lists, but through the supervisor's organization of in-service education in the selection of materials to meet local needs. In addition, the supervisor provides opportunities to examine materials at convenient central locations. (2) Central purchasing of materials results in substantially increased discounts. (3) Central processing frees the local librarian to work more intensively with students and teachers. (4) Library quarters are more functional when there is a local supervisor to work with the county buildings' officer and the architects. (5) Morale of school librarians—an intangible quality to evaluate with precision, but nevertheless easy to recognize—is higher. The sense of a common purpose, the opportunities provided for working and learning together as well as for individual growth, and the guidance of qualified leadership account for this improvement in morale.

Table IV shows that the estimated enrollment in rural schools in 1980 will be 11 million. Either many more small schools, unable to provide adequate educational programs, will have to be built or some form of consolidation into large units will have to be effected. In 1956 there were 743 county-wide school systems in the United States compared with the 605 in 1942.[31] Educators predict this trend will continue and at a more rapid rate. Whether the pattern is the county-wide unit or some other form of a large intermediate unit, no single change in school administration could be more effective in the development of the school library program throughout the nation.

TABLE IV

Total Public School Enrollment in U.S. and in Rural Areas: 1956,
and Estimated Enrollments: 1980

Continental U. S., 1956 [1]........................	31,162,483
Rural Counties, 1956 [2].........................	4,233,143
County-wide Systems—rural, 1956 [3].............	1,660,560
Total—rural.................................	5,893,703
Per Cent rural..............................	18.9%
Estimated Total Enrollment, 1980 [4].............	57,000,000

SOURCES: [1] U. S. Office of Education, *Statistics of State School Systems, 1955-56: Organization, Staff, Pupils, and Finances,* p. 9.
[2] U. S. Office of Education, *Statistics of Local School Systems, 1955-56, Rural Counties,* p. 14.
[3] U. S. Office of Education, *Statistics on Local School Systems, 1955-56, County Units,* p. 23.
[4] U. S. Bureau of the Census: *Illustrative Projections to 1980 of School and College Enrollments in the United States.* Washington, D. C., The Bureau, 1961. (Current Population Reports, Series P-25, No. 232), p. 7.

C. Rural School Libraries—1980

Playing with figures is a dangerous but engaging pastime. Application of the current American Library Association's standards for school library service to the 1980 rural public school population of 11 million shows staggering needs. Even if the trend toward larger units of school organization continues with such rapidity that by 1980 no school would be smaller than 300, a minimum of 30,000 school librarians and 110 million books would be needed in the rural schools.[32] The proportion of one state school library supervisor for each of the 44 states with rural school population and one for each of the 1,942 counties calls for another 1,986 school library supervisors. Even this figure is not realistic in consideration of the development of adequate school library service. In 1961, seven of the states with rural population have more than one state school library supervisor; on the other hand, such large and populous states as Texas and California have only one each. Twenty-five hundred to 3000 school library supervisors will be needed by 1980 to develop the kind of library program envisioned by the 1960 Standards. In 1959 there were only 29,404 school librarians [33] in the United States, and in 1961 only 319 school library supervisors.[29, 30] The trend toward longer school days, extended school terms, and new services from the school library may make the present standards for personnel inadequate.

The increased variety and quantity of materials implied in discernible educational trends cannot be estimated statistically, though they probably mean that by 1980 the present ratio of $6 to $12 per pupil for books and audio-visual materials [32] will be insufficient. Even if the ratio stays the same, between 66 million and 132 million dollars would be needed for library materials if rural schools of 1980 were to meet 1960 standards.

The anticipated decrease in the number of school districts and in the number of small schools and the increase in the development of effective intermediate units are administrative changes which offer encouragement and possible solutions to the rural school library problems of 1980. Centralized purchasing and processing will be possible for large areas; instructional materials centers will supply seldom-used and supplementary materials to smaller schools; supervision which reaches all of the schools through larger administrative units will result in improved programs. In the Montana study, the following recommendation pertinent to school library development in this highly rural state is made:

As larger units of school organization are developed it should be possible—without too much increase in the amount of money now expended for library books—to develop within each county a fine central library which should be expanded into a central materials bureau. Delivery service for books should be provided to every school in the county at regular intervals. Certain isolated schools will need to be given larger collections at less frequent intervals, but circulation of books among several schools within the course of a year will mean many more available books for a school and much greater use of books already purchased. All elementary schools with twelve or more teachers should, as quickly as feasible, be provided with a central library . . . When financially feasible at least half-time librarian service should be provided for schools of this size . . . Units with eighteen or more teachers should have a full-time librarian–materials coordinator.[34]

Standards for School Library Programs [35] recommends a full-time librarian for schools with enrollments of 200, field librarians who spend part-time in smaller schools, maintenance of a centralized pool of printed and audio-visual materials, and central processing of materials. This service to the small schools could be provided through contractual arrangements between small school districts and legally established intermediate units, between small and large districts, or between small school districts and public, county, or regional library agencies.

The increased enrollment in the rural schools coupled with the need to meet even presently-accepted school library standards in professional personnel leads to the conclusion that educators, including those engaged in library education, must face facts realistically and with determination to take action in providing school librarians. Even the most obtuse optimist might doubt that by 1980 there will be 30,000 school librarians and 3,000 school library supervisors to serve about 19 per cent of the public school population. School librarians, therefore, seem to be faced with the dilemma of never having enough qualified personnel to meet existing needs or of taking a fresh look at the role of the school librarian.

An example of how redeployment of library personnel could benefit whole areas can be drawn from the ten most rural counties in Maryland, one of the states in which all schools are organized on the county unit basis, and one of the states included in the Office of Education's [36] study of county units. At present there are 24 high school librarians, one county school library supervisor, and no elementary school librarians in the ten counties. There are 22 elementary and high schools with an enrollment of 500 or more, only 2 of these with an enrollment of 1,000, a total of 179 schools, and 49,500 pupils. To meet present personnel standards, a minimum of 162 school librarians and 10 county school library supervisors would be needed. If, however, each county would decide to (1) employ a county school library supervisor for each 3,000 pupils or major fraction thereof; (2) place a full-time librarian in each school with an enrollment of 500 to 1,000 and 2 librarians in the schools with over 1,000; (3) place a half-time librarian in each school with an enrollment of 200-500 and use college graduates as assistants or aides in each of these schools; (4) place a librarian one day a week in each school smaller than 200; and (5) establish central processing of materials, school library service could be extended to all of the schools in each county by employing 86 school librarians and 17 school library supervisors.

In five of the counties there would be one supervisor, in three there would be two, and in two there would be three. There would be no advantage in such a drastically changed pattern unless there were equally drastic changes in the point of view of the school librarians. This change could be accomplished for the presently employed personnel through in-service education programs which might well be the responsibility of the State Department of Education. But the burden would fall upon the library schools, which would need to see future school librarians as administrators and materials experts whose chief responsibilities would lie in working with adult teachers in guiding and directing selection of materials, in providing in-service education for library aides and clerical assistants, and in organizing, administering, and using centralized services for ordering and processing materials. Teacher-education institutions would also need to take cognizance of the changed role of the school librarian; the teacher would have added responsibilities for the selection and use of materials with the individual pupil. In many cases, the librarian's only contact with the pupil would be through the teacher.

The example used here is not suggested as a pattern for school library organization. All of the facts, however, lead to the conclusion that unless dramatic changes are made in the role and education of the school librarian, many rural schools will have no school library service simply because there will be no personnel to provide it.

References

1. Weintraub, K. J.: Recent Social and Cultural Developments. *Library Quarterly*, 31:2, Jan. 1961.

2. *Readers' Guide to Periodical Literature.* New York, H. W. Wilson, 1956, 1960. Mar. 1955-Feb. 1956, pp. 5, 11; Mar. 1959-Feb. 1960, pp. 287, 292.

3. Conant, J. B.: *The American High School Today.* New York, McGraw-Hill, 1959, p. 96.

4. Trump, J. L., and Baynham, Dorsey: *Focus on Change. Guide to Better Schools.* Chicago, Rand McNally, 1961, pp. 4-5.

5. *The Pursuit of Excellence: Education and the Future of America.* New York, Doubleday, 1958, p. ix.

6. McMurrin, S. M.: *Education and the National Goals.* Address delivered at Annual Harvard School Conference on Educational Administration. Cambridge, Mass., July 20, 1961 (Mimeographed), pp. 2-3.

7. U.S. Office of Education. Educational Statistics Branch: *Projected Enrollments in full-time Public and Nonpublic Elementary and Secondary Day Schools* . . . Washington, D.C., 1960 (Mimeographed sheet).

8. U.S. Bureau of the Census: *Illustrative Projections to 1980 of School and College Enrollment in the United States.* Washington, D.C., Bureau of the Census, 1961, p. 7.

9. Morse, A. D.: *Schools of Tomorrow—Today.* New York, Doubleday, 1960, p. 86.

10. Alexander, W. M.: *New Challenges in the Elementary School Program.* Address delivered at the Conference on Elementary Education, Baltimore, Md., Nov. 12, 1959. Baltimore, Md., State Department of Education (Mimeographed), pp. 1, 3.

11. Trump, *op. cit.,* ref. 4, p. 39.

12. Educational Policies Commission: *Contemporary Issues in Elementary Education.* Washington, D.C., National Education Association, 1960, p. 4.

13. *Ibid.,* p. 20.

14. Educational Administration in the Decade Ahead. *School Life,* 43:5-10, Jan. 1961.

15. U.S. Office of Education: *Statistics of Public School Systems: 1955-56. Organization, Staff, Pupils, and Finance.* Washington, D.C., U.S. Government Printing Office, 1959 (Biennial Survey of Education in the U.S., 1954-56, Chapter 2), p. 58.

16. U.S. Office of Education: *Progress of Public Education in the United States of America.* Washington, D.C., U.S. Government Printing Office, 1960, p. 25.

17. *Ibid.,* pp. 7-9.

18. Council of Chief State School Officers: *Responsibilities of State Departments of Education for School Library Services.* Washington, D.C., The Council, 1961, p. 7.

19. American Library Association. American Association of School Librarians: *Standards for School Library Programs.* Chicago, The American Library Association, 1960, pp. 3-4.

20. U.S. Office of Education: *Statistics of Local School Systems, 1955-56,*

Rural Counties. Washington, D.C., U.S. Government Printing Office, 1959, p. 3.

21. Ibid., p. 5.

22. Ibid., p. 4.

23. Ibid., p. 71.

24. Mahar, Mary H., and Holladay, Doris C.: Public School Library Statistics, 1958-59. Washington, D.C., U.S. Office of Education, Library Services Branch, 1960, p. 13.

25. U.S. Office of Education: Progress in the United States of America, 1959-60. Washington, D.C., U.S. Government Printing Office, 1960, p. 15.

26. George Peabody College for Teachers. Division of Survey and Field Services: Public Schools of Montana: A Report to Montana Taxation-Education Commission. Nashville, The College, 1958, p. 13.

27. U.S. Office of Education: Statistics of Local School Systems, 1955-56, County Units. Washington, D.C., U.S. Government Printing Office, 1959, p. 1.

28. Ibid., pp. 2, 5, 8.

29. American Library Association: Membership Directory, 1960. Chicago, American Library Association, 1961, pp. 411-412.

30. American Library Association. American Association of School Librarians: School Library Supervisors: City, Town and Country. Chicago, American Library Association, March 1961 (Mimeographed).

31. U.S. Office of Education, Statistics of Local School Systems, 1955-56, County Units, p. 2.

32. American Library Association, Standards for School Library Programs, pp. 24-25.

33. Mahar and Holladay, op. cit., p. 12.

34. George Peabody College for Teachers, op. cit., p. 36.

35. American Library Association, Standards for School Library Programs, pp. 101-105.

36. U.S. Office of Education, Statistics of Local School Systems, 1955-56, County Units, p. 3.

School Libraries in City School Systems

ELIZABETH O. WILLIAMS

THE SCHOOL LIBRARY as an integral part of the modern school is such a well-accepted fact today that the beginnings of school library service in our country are looked back upon with a degree of awe that so much has been accomplished in such a brief span of time. Then as one reviews current surveys and statistical studies, he recognizes the limitations of this program and is somewhat overwhelmed at the tremendous needs still to be met if quality education is to be brought to all students. For "education in a democracy requires the resources and services of school libraries; the philosophy of democracy maintains the right of every boy and girl to have these resources and services." [1]

According to a statistical report of the United States Office of Education in 1953–54,[2] about 47 per cent of the schools in the United States received service from classroom collections only; about 37 per cent had centralized libraries; and 11 per cent of the schools in the United States received service designated as "any other type of library service." Five per cent of all schools reported no library service.

The greatest lag was at the elementary level. Seventy-five per cent of the elementary schools were without school libraries in 1953–54, although most city schools had some type of book service through classroom collections. However, these were not the equivalent of school libraries with a varied and adequate book collection and the educational services of a school librarian.

A recent statistical survey by the Library Services Branch of the Office of Education entitled *Public School Library Statistics, 1958–59*,[3] revealed that only about 50 per cent of the 82,222 schools studied had libraries. Of approximately 34 million public school pupils included in the survey, more than 10 million attended schools without libraries. Sixty-six per cent of the elementary schools, about 60,000

Miss Williams is Head Supervisor of School Libraries, Los Angeles City Schools.

schools, did not have libraries. Although only 3 per cent of the secondary schools were without libraries, many of the libraries were inadequate with regard to staff, quarters, collections of materials, and financial support.

Enrollment in kindergarten and elementary schools increased by 11 million during the 1950's. According to statistical studies of population growth,[4] the pressure in the grade schools will be much less during the sixties and seventies but it will not disappear. Between 1960 and 1980, enrollment may be increased by over 9 million or by 29 per cent over two decades by contrast with more than 50 per cent over one decade in the fifties. During the 50's, high school enrollment increased by about 54 per cent, roughly about the same rate as the rise in grade school enrollment. But while the pressure on grade schools will decline in the sixties, that on high schools will continue unabated. Between 1950–1979 the 14 to 17 year olds (potential high school students) will nearly double in number. By 1980 this group will amount to over 18 million. The explosion of population which has challenged educators in the past decade will bring increasing problems in the years to come. Building programs for new schools, including school libraries, personnel, and materials, will continue to be major issues.

In accordance with statistical studies and projections, over three-fourths of the increase in public school enrollment will be concentrated in fewer than 200 metropolitan areas.[5] The great increase in the size of metropolitan school systems will create problems of organization, facilities, finance, staff administration, and problems of adapting programs to meet new needs. "Metropolitan areas will be the new frontier in educational administration; decentralization of administration will become increasingly common in very large school systems."[5]

Transportation problems in congested city areas require that libraries and instructional materials be available within the school. Library services in schools will have to expand if we are to reach the goals in quality library service.

Our society has changed vastly in this century, in regard to both technological developments, and social and cultural organization. A new emphasis upon learning, a desire for knowledge, and the recognition of the utilitarian value of research are bringing an increased incentive in to the use of library resources. Our expanding, changing world has brought about new and significant educational trends, new methods, and new philosophies. Changes in concepts and purposes

have come about in the effort to pursue the knowledge and understanding necessary to living in today's world and in that of tomorrow.
Learning has become important; study and research are universal.
Knowledge must be current and worldwide. Even the moon, formerly
the special interest of astronomers and the poets, has taken on political significance. The children of today will be participants in the
space developments of the future.

The many changes in our 20th-century living and the rapid growth
of population have challenged educators to renewed efforts to explore
ways to make learning and instruction more effective. They have
turned to the new media of instruction. Motion pictures and closed
circuit television are meeting the needs for mass instruction by teacher
specialists. More recently, teaching machines and programs are being
developed which provide for individualized instruction at the student's own rate of speed and ability. Simple as well as complex subjects are being programmed by expert teachers with the claim for
an unusual degree of success on the part of the student. Language
laboratories are being widely established, bringing individualized programs of foreign language instruction and conversational drill direct
to the student through electronic devices. The audio-lingual method
claims to help students acquire a "near native" pronunciation of a
foreign language. These new devices together with filmstrips, slides,
tapes, recordings, and radio have added interest and given impetus to
learning as they supplement the traditional printed material in libraries.

These new teaching methods have implications for the school
library. Team teaching is being used as a device to direct student
learning through lecture, demonstration, and discussion by the best
qualified teachers. Other members of the team serve as teacher aides
or clerical assistants to relieve the teacher specialist of many routine
and clerical duties. Team teaching with variable scheduling and the
use of electronic devices releases teacher time for planning and study
in the library. The student, under the variable scheduling, is free
to explore on his own and will turn to the library and the librarian
for guidance and encouragement in his efforts at independent study
and research. Directions will be personally adjusted in accordance
with the ability and experience of the student.

Modern educational methods call for the use of many books, still
the most inexpensive and adaptable tools of learning. If the current
challenge of accelerated education is to be met, schools must provide

through libraries the variety of titles needed to encourage wide reading and research, to develop reflective thinking and independent judgment, and to deepen understandings. No longer can the school library be considered a luxury, for it has become an integral part of the educational program in the school. The librarian's responsibility is to expose young people to the best in literature during their school years, to assist them to capture the magic of the written word, to stimulate their imagination and natural curiosity, and to provide the materials and the skills for independent study and research.

For accomplishment of the goals now set for modern education, a full program of library services is essential in all schools, elementary and secondary, small and large, rural and urban, public and private. Separate classroom collections are neither economical nor adequate to meet the wide variety of reading levels and interests in each class; a library outside the school can provide services but not a program. For, to quote from *Standards for School Library Programs*,[6] "The true concept of a school library program means instruction, service and activity throughout the school." The library must contribute to the guidance program, to the program for exceptional children, to the advanced placement program; to a program that encompasses reading guidance for all levels of ability, instruction in the use of the library, reference, and research techniques; a program that touches all aspects of the curriculum, each classroom, every student and teacher; a program geared to the abilities, needs, and interests of all.

The quality of the library is one of the determining factors in the quality of any school. There must be an adequate and well-trained staff, functional physical quarters and equipment, a wide variety of printed and audio-visual materials, and the necessary financial resources. The active support of librarians, school administrators and teachers, boards of education, parents and other lay persons is needed to develop successful school library programs.

Although good teaching and learning programs require the resources and services of good school libraries, the inequality of services was revealed in a statistical study conducted by the Library Services Branch.[3] The evidence contained in this study showed the marked differences between actual conditions and the national standards published in 1960 by the American Library Association in *Standards for School Library Programs*.[6] The new standards state: "All schools having two hundred or more students need well-organized school libraries with functional programs of service directed by

[161]

qualified personnel." We have already noted the lack of libraries in 50 per cent of the schools studied.

In *Standards for School Library Programs,*[6] today's library is described as the instructional materials or learning resource center of the school, where audio-visual materials are also housed or made easily available. One reading room is not enough in large schools. In addition, the library area should include conference space, listening and viewing space, space for a teachers' professional library, space for the storage and production of materials, for library instruction, for individual study, for displays and exhibits. Fluid classroom collections must be provided.

How will the school plant of the future and more specifically the school library meet the challenges of the new instructional media, teaching methods, and ever-changing curriculum? Architects predict significant changes in school design. Our future schools must be planned with adequate space to serve almost overwhelming numbers of students and to function throughout the year and possibly 12 hours a day. Twice as many schools will be needed in the fast-mushrooming metropolitan areas, as space is diminishing with costs rising. Will we build skyscraper schools and underground classrooms, all a part of an apartment dwelling as one architect has suggested? Transportation problems would be simplified. Pupils would step out of their homes into elevators which would deliver them direct to their classrooms below.

Another architect describes the big-city school as the "Tower School of Tomorrow," an eleven story tower with a windowless lecture room, a smaller seminar room, and a number of compact individual cubicles, each enclosed on three sides, and equipped with the latest technological devices. He calls it a space saver and an economic necessity as land and building costs skyrocket in big cities. Other architects suggest a "school in the round" which requires less building material, less corridor space and more outside glass; or a windowless school with artificial lighting and mechanical ventilation, movable rooms made up of modular sections. Experiments are going forward with circular libraries as the hub of the school plant. Libraries with high windows above wall stacks are proving economical of space. Some architects recommend the cluster or satellite construction which breaks rooms into smaller units. Schools constructed today must have a "built in" flexibility for tomorrow: for example, each room easily darkened for visual aids, reversible chalk boards, an intercommunication system in each room, and portable walls to provide for smaller or larger groupings.

Whatever the outward physical plant, it is today generally recognized by educators and librarians that library plans must provide for individual study and the use of resources; they must be larger; conference rooms for group discussion and class instruction must adjoin the general reading room. There should be flexible partitions providing for many small groups or expanding for full classes, cubicles for individual study, listening posts for independent use of tapes and recordings, areas for viewers and teaching machines, new planning for the storage of microfilm and records, and work rooms for teachers.

The librarian will be a specialist with professional training in the organization and use of instructional materials of all kinds. He will work with teachers, administrators, and supervisors as a consultant in the evaluation, selection, and use of materials. He will provide leadership within the total instructional program and be a member of the administrative staff. He will instruct teachers as well as students in the resources of the library and prepare film strips and skill programs and tests for teaching machines. He will have technological knowledge and skill in the use of automation for ordering, cataloging, and distribution of materials.

Not only will the librarian be a member of the teaching team, he will also be a part of the library team, for more than one librarian will be necessary to carry on the myriad activities of a functioning modern library. As schools in cities reach an enrollment of several thousand, there will be a need for many librarians, as well as for clerical assistants, teacher aids, and technicians for supervising the machines housed in the library. The head librarian will coordinate the library program in the school, working directly with the administration, department heads, curriculum supervisors, and community agencies. Duties related to reference and bibliography, instruction of students and teachers, and reading guidance will be assigned to professional assistants.

When the school library of the future is open longer hours, possibly the year around, and as services are increased, more personnel will be required. With the expanding need for manpower in libraries must come an awareness of the need to recruit a steady flow of competent young people into the profession. The rewards of working in a field of service and personal growth should be suggested to promising student assistants, and the availability of scholarships should be called to their attention. Library education should provide courses for those specializing in school librarianship with more emphasis upon supervision and administration.

Much needs to be done in directing teachers in the knowledge and use of materials. A study of *The Secondary School Teacher and Library Services* made by the N.E.A. in 1958 [7] found that only 13.1 per cent of 1,448 teachers who participated in the survey had received instruction in the role and function of the school library as a definite part of their professional training. Principals and teachers have personally expressed their interest and have recognized the need for improved methods and training in the use of library resources. Every librarian should be dedicated to the task of improving instruction in his school. Courses must be established in teacher training institutions and librarians must hold city-wide workshops on library resources and their use.

This kind of training is basic to solving some of the important problems in student use of the public library. Pressures on both school and public libraries continue to mount. These will not diminish, but as teachers are directed into the more efficient use of library resources and in turn direct their students, the work load will be lightened. In addition to pre-service training courses, each librarian must assume a responsibility for establishing better communication between schools and public libraries. Through planned conferences, workshops and institutes, teachers can be made aware of good library techniques and available materials, and in turn public librarians can be informed about the curriculum in the schools. This use of libraries which has been given emphasis under the pursuit of excellence in education should not be discouraged, but this interest and enthusiasm should be directed for the greatest good of all.

In 1960 the publication of *Standards for School Library Programs* [6] was a distinguished service to school librarians and administrators and a timely aid to the accelerated educational program. With the publication of this document has come a new challenge and a renewed interest in providing better education through strengthening the library services of the school. It sets forth a long term plan for school libraries and establishes qualitative and quantitative criteria. A basic tenet of the philosophy of the standards is that the most important part of the library program is the work with students and teachers, those activities and services that make the library an educational force in the school: "The objectives of very good schools require that the library program be in full operation, which can be done only when the school meets standards for the personnel, materials, funds, and quarters of the school library." [6] School librarians are indeed fortunate to have this guide to future implementation of good school library programs. The support of boards of education and administrators in financing such programs is essential to their continued success.

Education has a tremendous task today to train youth to assume their responsibilities in an ever-changing world. School librarians have a share in this endeavor. With the guiding principles set forth in the A.A.S.L. publication, *Standards for School Library Programs*,[6] and with an aggressive plan for their implementation, librarians may hope to contribute to the success of this educational challenge and carry out the ideal expressed at the White House Conference: "America's determination to help children and youth realize their full potential for a creative life in freedom and dignity."

In a democracy, the development of the individual to his full potential is the right of each person. As stated in The Report of the President's Commission on National Goals, November 1960, "The paramount goal of the United States was set long ago. It is to guard the rights of the individual, to ensure his development, and to enlarge his opportunity. It is set forth in the Declaration of Independence." [8]

One of the most challenging tasks in education today is that of the school librarian whose responsibility it is to provide the materials of learning and a program of service which will fully develop the potential talents of each and every student and provide the materials of instruction required in the modern educational program.

References

1. Henne, Frances: School Libraries and the Social Order. *Library Trends*, 1:263, Jan. 1953.

2. U.S. Office of Education: Statistics of Public School Libraries, 1953-54. *Biennial Survey of Education in the United States, 1952-54.* Washington, D.C., U. S. Government Printing Office, 1957.

3. Mahar, Mary H., and Holladay, Doris C.: *Public School Library Statistics, 1958-59.* Washington, D.C., U.S. Department of Health, Education, and Welfare, 1960.

4. Hauser, P. M., and Taitel, M.: Population Trends—Prologue to Library Development. *Library Trends*, 10:10-67, July 1961.

5. U.S. Office of Education. School Administration Branch: Educational Administration in the Decade Ahead. *School Life*, 43:5-10, Jan. 1961.

6. American Association of School Librarians: *Standards for School Library Programs*. Chicago, American Library Association, 1960.

7. National Education Association. Research Division: *The Secondary School Teacher and Library Services*. Washington, D.C., National Education Association, 1958.

8. *Report of the President's Commission on National Goals*. New York, American Assembly, Columbia University, 1960.

Suburban School Libraries

SARA I. FENWICK

SCHOOL LIBRARIES OF ALL TYPES, and in all
settings, have been suffering from the growing pains of rapid school
enrollment increases, but the library in the suburban school finds its
problems brought into sharp focus when the implications of demographic changes are charted for future planning. The migration to
the suburbs that has taken place in the past twenty years has placed
unusual stresses upon the suburban school system and has posed problems unique among school libraries.

It is not the uniqueness of the suburban school library facilities
or program that sets it apart but, rather, the character of the school,
which is determined by the suburban community; and the character
of the community determines the goals of the school program, the
backgrounds that students bring to their formal schooling, and the
quantity and quality of materials and services needed. The pattern
of living in the community determines the curriculum, the organization of the school day and year, even the routines of library management. Therefore, to discuss the suburban school library one must
discuss the suburban school, since the library is an integral part of
the school system.

Suburban is used to describe a district, especially a residential district on the outskirts of a city, usually incorporated as a separate
village, city, or town; in this paper it refers to those communities
that are part of a Standard Metropolitan Statistical Area but not the
central cities of such an area.

Twenty years ago *suburban living* was a term connoting comfortable homes on wide streets, spacious lawns, upper level incomes that
provided superior schools with well-equipped gymnasiums, auditor-
iums, libraries, and laboratories; schools that attracted competent
faculties and provided many educational models for the entire

Miss Fenwick is Assistant Professor, Graduate Library School, University of
Chicago.

country. Such suburbs have developed in an outer ring around the large metropolitan centers and have served as bedroom communities for executives and professional men in upper income brackets. The communities are of particular importance to the development of schools because they have been the scene for some of the outstanding school programs, notably the North Shore communities of the Chicago area and the Westchester and Long Island towns.

The image of the privileged life of the suburb has not been erased by changes of the past decade, but new aspects of the picture have become apparent. The percentage of the population of a metropolitan area living in the suburbs has greatly increased. During the first two decades of this century approximately one-third of the people living in a metropolitan area lived outside of the central city in a suburb, but by 1960 this percentage had increased to just under one-half, as an accelerated migration from the city cores continued. A population of 58 million has been projected as the increase in population of the Standard Metropolitan Statistical Areas, of which 45 million will be in the suburbs.

Within the Chicago Metropolitan Statistical Area there have developed suburbs that represent the full range of historical, economic, cultural, and social patterns. The suburban areas in this Metropolitan Area increased from 2,500 in 1920 to 20,000 in 1960, with a density today that ranges from 200 to 20,000 persons per square mile. Some of the unincorporated interstices, or fringe areas, are almost as densely settled as the towns, and these are rapidly becoming fully occupied. Selecting representative samples of different types of communities, one finds:

(1) the long-established, stable and relatively homogeneous suburbs that are largely high-income communities, e.g., Oak Park and Evanston;

(2) the communities of comparative size, also long-established and homogeneous, but less stable because the average income level is lower and the dominant function is industrial rather than dormitory, e.g., Cicero.

Until 1940 these two types of communities included the majority of suburbs. It was in the following decades that the next types emerged:

(3) the newly-developed suburbs—scenes of the tremendous building boom of the past decade—most of them with modest homes owned

by residents with only moderate-to-low incomes; communities too new to have much identity and whose economic function is mixed dormitory and industrial, e.g., Oak Lawn.

(4) one community that is unique in the Chicago area and fairly unusual in the country as a whole—Park Forest. This is a planned community that was founded in 1949 and has grown in eleven years to 30,000, with a strong community identity, moderate income level, with a majority of wage-earners being professional, executive, and business men, commuting into the Chicago Loop. All of the families living here have high aspirations in education for their children and the problems and achievements of Park Forest in realizing their goals provide an interesting pattern for understanding suburban development.

What has happened in the Chicago Metropolitan Area has been repeated to a greater or lesser degree in every such area in the country. The face of suburban living has come to have many aspects with the rapid exit from crowded cities to suburbs.

What has happened to change the aspects of life of the suburbs is apparent from a comparison of public school populations and level of support of the educational programs.

A comparison of gain in enrollments in representative high school districts of the four types of suburban communities in the five years between 1954 and 1959 reveals the pattern of growth. Evanston Township High School—the high school district in the first type of long-established, high economic level suburb—had a gain of 38 per cent enrollment; J. Sterling Morton High School (Cicero)—school district serving an industrial suburb of the second type—also had an enrollment gain of 38 per cent; Bremen Community High School—in an area of recently accelerated growth—had a gain of 93 per cent; and Rich Township High School (Park Forest) gained 146 per cent.

Projections for growth in the next six years, 1959–65, are 13 per cent for Evanston Township High School (Type 1), 16 per cent for J. Sterling Morton High School in Cicero (Type 2), 56 per cent for Bremen Community High School (Type 3), and 100 per cent for Rich Township in Park Forest (Type 4). Looking at this small, representative sample of pupil populations and degree of change against the per-pupil assessed valuation of each high school district provides an estimate of the magnitude of the financial problems involved in the school of the suburbs.

Per-Pupil Assessed Valuation

(June 1959)	All Funds Tax Rate (Combined)
Evanston Township $95,360	$ .98
J. Sterling Morton (Cicero) $93,177	.93
Bremen $37,643	1.80
Rich $57,712	1.52

The wide range of per-pupil expenditures for schools in suburban communities is the result of a built-in inequality that is due to the nature of development of such communities. Sociologists are concerned with the stratification that results in communities homogeneous to the extent of representing one age group, one economic level, one cultural level. Lack of area planning finds a school district of small homes in a crowded residential area, with only a little more than $8,000 per child in property against which to levy a tax, while in the same county is an industrial district with almost a quarter of a million dollars behind each elementary child. These inequalities are increased as towns in fortunate location with respect to dormitory transportation and geographical attractiveness develop high-priced homes able to support the best schools, and the schools, in turn, enhance the property values and help to characterize the community as a deluxe suburb.

The out-city migration to the suburbs has been facilitated by higher average income levels, by shorter working hours, increased transportation (not by rail but by highway), broader credit financing of new homes, and decay of the central cores of cities. The recent migration has brought more young families and more families of medium and lower incomes to build and buy homes in the new suburbs. The aspirations motivating migration have been the same as those that brought families out of the growing central cities thirty and forty years ago—desire for open space, stable homogeneous neighborhoods, safe play areas, and good schools.

The importance of the aspiration for quality school experience for children has been dramatically illustrated by the resistance of the parents living in the newly-developed section of a wealthy Chicago suburb. There has been one high school in this suburb, and it has had one of the outstanding programs in the country, superior facilities, an excellent faculty, and an outstanding library. A proposal to build a new high school in the township to accommodate the increased

[170]

enrollment has been turned down by the voters. Residents in the area that would be included in the new school's territory were unwilling to accept the location of their children in any other than the nationally-famous New Trier High School. Many of them pointed out that this was the prime reason for their move into this particular suburb.

During the past decade the growth in the school population has been at its peak in the years covered by the elementary school that has just passed along the largest swell of the wartime and postwar "baby boom." This increase in elementary school pupils was a gain of 50 per cent in the 1950's and is expected to level off to approximately 29 per cent in the next 20 years. The early part of the next decade, however, will see an enrollment bulge at the high school level, and within 4-5 years at the colleges. The increase at the high school level may be less dramatic than at the elementary because there has already been a marked rise in the percentage of students who finish high school. This number will continue to rise to a predicted 60 per cent of the population who will be high school graduates in 1980, while the college graduates are projected to reach 10 per cent of the population in the same span of years.

The general effect of this rapid expansion of population in suburban communities has meant great pressures upon the existing school facilities, and the immediate need for many more schools, most of which were outgrown before they were completed. The immediate need in most communities has been for elementary schools, since the past ten years found the wartime and postwar babies at this level. If the prediction is correct that the rise in elementary population will be at a decreased rate for the next two decades, there are communities that have built enough classrooms for their elementary school enrollment and who may look for temporary respite from the overwhelming pressure to provide more elementary classrooms. It is conceivable that some classroom space may be available to provide elementary libraries, but the growing trend toward the education of four-year-olds will add to the elementary school load and absorb any available space.

The pressure will continue to be heavy upon the secondary school, however. Not only is an increase of 45 per cent projected for the 14 to 17 year old group, but the percentage of young people finishing high school is likely to continue to increase with the decline in unskilled labor force needed and the growing needs of industry and

[171]

business for skilled workers who can be trained to high degrees of competence on jobs requiring a minimum of twelve years schooling. The accelerated pace at which schools have been built in the past decade has all too often meant that, in the case of elementary schools, no library was provided, or, in the case of high schools, that the libraries provided minimum facilities in space, materials, and staff. Again at the range of suburbs in Cook County (Illinois), the Evanston Township High School on the north shore of Chicago is reaching for the 10 books per child figure recommended by the Standards for School Library Programs, with good elementary libraries in the area, but in the high schools in the newly-developed suburbs south of the city of Chicago, there is no high school that meets the national standard for printed materials, and there are no elementary school libraries, with the exception of the Park Forest district, where an elementary supervisor has been appointed to develop and to coordinate a library program in the schools of the village.

A community-wide scrutiny of the accessibility of materials for study and research by elementary and secondary school students underscores the serious shortcomings of resources for education in new suburban areas. In these communities public library facilities are likely to be far less adequate than those of school libraries. Wherever there have been developed systems of libraries, or cooperative arrangements of libraries, in these areas the materials and services are planned and organized on a sound tax basis able to provide for the needs of the citizens, young and old. But in the majority of our large metropolitan areas, such cooperative planning is only beginning. By far the most common pattern is for each village to organize a public library with book donations, to arrange for a minimum of service with volunteer help, and as soon as possible to seek a bond issue for a building. Only after this is achieved is a serious look given to the resources and the provision of a professionally trained librarian. Requests for state library books are usually the first answer to the empty shelves; the lack of a librarian is much more difficult to overcome.

In a suburban area of approximately 475 square miles, south of Chicago, there are 34 communities, of which 12 have libraries with some level of tax support. In addition there are 9 libraries operated on a voluntary basis, with no public money taxed or appropriated. Of the tax-supported libraries, only 4 are open as many as 50 hours a week. They report book budgets for 1959-1960 that range from $550 to $17,870, with a median of only $2,903. Obviously such public libraries are too weak to supplement the school libraries in meeting the many needs of young people and children, and yet the majority of them are called upon to supply classroom libraries for the elementary schools.

The solution for many residents of the suburbs where there is inadequate provision of materials for personal interests and curriculum-centered research is to travel to the public libraries in the metropolitan area where materials can be found. Most of the large central-city libraries, as well as the well-established libraries in other communities of metropolitan areas, report a heavy increase in nonresident cards. Many libraries, as a result, have been forced to raise the fee asked for such nonresident service. College, university, and special libraries are concerned about the amount of service which they are asked to give to high school students.

This, then is the problem of the suburban school library at this time: a community-wide lack of adequate facilities, materials, and staff, both professional and clerical.

Factors to be discerned that will shape the suburban school library of the future must be gathered from several sources. They are to be found in the projected development of the populations of metropolitan areas, the emerging goals of the school, the new dimensions being evolved for school library programs, and the new solutions forecast for metropolitan community problems.

These implications will need to be studied in a continuing examination of the effectiveness of the library in every school setting. The need for a much broader collection of materials is obvious. Equally imperative is the planning to accommodate flexible scheduling and grouping of students, decentralization of some materials while maintaining strong advantages of a centralization of materials, making accessible to teachers and students all kinds of learning materials and the equipment to use them, and planning for participation in team teaching in whatever way is most appropriate and meaningful.

Several new secondary schools have received nationwide publicity because they have been designed by close collaboration of architects and educators and to a greater or lesser degree provide for the kinds of staff and facilities utilization envisioned in "Images of the Future." [1] Most of these schools are located in a suburb of a large metropolitan area: Wayland, Massachusetts; San Bruno, California; Norridge, Illinois; Metaire Park, Louisiana. Such imaginative planning to accommodate new approaches to education will continue to multiply; they will be expensive, but they will put the suburban school in the forefront of experimental education.

There is evidence of a strong trend to plan new schools with consideration for their relationship to the entire community. This is being done from both points of view: the needs of the community at large that can be served by the school facilities, and the need of the school population—pupils and teachers—to experience more fully the activities of community life.

As an aspect of the planning for better utilization of school facilities, the opening of school libraries in suburban schools, for evening hours, Saturday hours, and during vacation periods, is being tried in some communities. Such extended hours would provide the opportunities for use of school library resources for school-related assignments and relieve some of the pressure on public library reference collections. It has been evident in studies of accessibility of materials within schools that one of the major deterrents to the use of the school library by students is the lack of time in the school schedule for needed library research and study. The extension of opening hours would seem to be one of the first means of providing for the study needs of students. Not all schools that have reported experiments with increased hours of service have found this solution to be successful, but in many cases the experiment has probably been of too short duration.

Newly-identified school and community needs for extended service will help to characterize future suburban school library service. Summer school programs of enriched educational experience are being planned in most metropolitan areas today, and these depend heavily upon full library service in the school. The trend toward increased use of school facilities for adult education and community projects will create needs for extended hours of service. Because public library service is not available or adequate in so many of the new communities, school libraries are recognizing their responsibility to provide library service in vacation periods and during the summer. Essential to the instituting of extended hours is the provision of adequate personnel. Location of the library within the school is another important factor and should be a consideration in designing new buildings. If the library is on an upper floor, or at some distance from the main entrance to the building, keeping the library open in hours that are outside of the regular schedule of the school may present very difficult problems of access and maintenance.

The needs of the total community are increasing in focus as more frequent proposals appear urging that consideration be given to providing library service to the whole community through the school library. In a school district located in the outer ring of the Detroit metropolitan area a plan was formulated to open the central library of the school to all the residents of the township. Financial arrangements would include a payment of $10,000 by the township for the first year's operation. In a newly-developed Chicago suburb the original bond issue for the construction of a secondary school was promoted with the promise that the school library in the new building would be a public library facility to serve the entire community.

Over the past twenty-five years, the profession has become well aware that the best school library program does not result from administration as a part of a public library organization. The location of public library branches in schools has provided neither the type of integrated school library program that modern instructional patterns demand, nor the dynamic service to the adults and pre-school population that a community hopes for.

In spite of the accumulated evidence that there are sound reasons for maintaining the two separate library services, it is impotrant that careful study be given to the acute needs of the new suburbs. It may be that some form of service can be provided by the school library to the community as a whole, as an intermediate step, but it behooves librarians to assess their objectives and to inform school boards and village trustees of long-range goals for adequate community library service. Such arrangements could be fruitful only where there is a strong community identity and mobilized public effort to provide the best possible environment for its residents, and where the school administration and faculty are committed to a role of leadership in the development of the community. It would be a stopgap arrangement that would become permanent in those areas that are not participating in long-range planning, or where the school maintains a position of isolation from the community.

The possibility of re-examining patterns of service to children has been recommended in two recent survey reports. In the study of public and school libraries in Hawaii by R. D. Leigh, there is this recommendation:

It might be worthwhile, however, if physical conditions make it possible, to initiate two experiments in the combination of a public library branch and school library, one in urban or suburban Oahu in a district where a new high school and a new public library branch are being planned; the other in a rural, sparsely populated area on one of the other island counties. For the urban experimental installation it would be necessary to have the accidentally favorable situation of a location making possible a separate library annex directly accessible to a shopping center and the library's school library section directly accessible to the high school's classrooms as well as to children and young people coming from other schools.[2]

In the study of the libraries of metropolitan Toronto, R. Shaw examines the inadequacies of both public and school library service to children and points out that "in Metro [Metropolitan Toronto] structure we have a mechanism for long range planning and development of equal educational and cultural opportunities for all children and adults in Metro, which makes possible more positive approaches than have been made in other places in the past."[3]

An aspect of planning for future service that seems to hold great promise for the improvement of suburban libraries is the development of district and regional materials centers that will serve as aids in the examination and selection of materials, that may perform the functions of a centralized acquisitions service, that will have resources for bibliographic control and services available to a wide area through the development of technological facilities. Such facilities should provide additional dimensions for all types of libraries in an area. A materials center could be a level of most fruitful cooperation between school, public, and special libraries. Reference libraries that serve as district or regional resource centers might help solve this problem of providing materials and guidance for the high school students.

The need for more finances for all levels of public schools in the next 20 years is likely to increase. The educational program itself will cost more. Enrollments will be increasing, and most rapidly at the secondary and junior college levels, where costs are greater than at the elementary level. More research is being sought in every area of education, and this will be an addition to the overall budget. Salaries are still far from the averages proposed recently by the Department of Health, Education, and Welfare and the Office of Education —$7,439 a year for instructional staff as a whole by 1961–62, and $7,216 for classroom teachers.

The financing of school facilities is a particularly difficult problem at this time. In 1959–60 the total national expenditures for schools increased 6-7 per cent, twice the size of the increase in the national income. This year has seen another increase in enrollment, and a rise in salaries will mean a similar increase. One of the particular problems of the suburban school district is the time lag of two or more years between the time at which pupils in newly-developed areas enter school and the tax money from their property is received.

A disquieting resistance of voters to school financing has been evident in the past two years. The office of the Cook County (Illinois) Assistant Superintendent of Schools in charge of research reported that of 24 bond issues put before voters between October, 1960, and May, 1961, seven failed. This failure represented a loss record of 29 per cent, whereas loss records of the previous three years were 15 per cent, 6 per cent, and 2 per cent. There have been a number of instances of new schools constructed without adequate planning for furnishings and operation, and which, as a result, have stood idle one or more years. Libraries in suburban schools have opened without a book on the shelves, or with the only books being those provided by State Extension services.

A super-school district for suburban areas has been discussed in one state, one that would have power to levy nonproperty taxes for schools. Similarly, a metropolitan area taxing unit of three, or even six, counties to supply school funds has been recommended in another. If there is a combination of enforceable standards for schools and the provision of equalization funds, state funds can often be used to bolster school libraries. "Twenty-one states provide some form of direct state aid to school librarians and/or libraries." [4]

In the area of scientific inquiry lies hope for future improvements in the suburban school and the school library. This area is particularly ready for some careful evaluation and experimentation. Many of the innovative practices hold promise for the suburban school, especially the fuller utilization of facilities and the new organization of classes and schedules. Librarians should take the leadership in preparing a comprehensive plan for the future. They should, in every case, make themselves thoroughly familiar with the factors of change in their community and the projections for future growth and change. With blueprints of the future in hand, librarians should be able to develop recommendations for the kind of library program that would best implement the goals of the school and community. Dimensions of such long-range plans would include the quantity and variety of materials needed to support the instructional program, recommendations for adequate physical facilities, provisions for students to engage in independent study, appropriate provisions for newer media, and provision for accessibility of materials throughout all areas of the school.

The increasing interdependence of all parts of the metropolitan area is underscoring the need for coordinated planning at the local, regional, and state levels. It is imperative that there be communication between the school and public library in the essential task of providing youth with the materials of learning. A status survey of the accessibility of materials for children and youth is an important first step in any planning for future development of library services. New blueprints for financing are imperative, but even before these can be drawn up, there must be an assessment of the resources and needs of the suburban schools in a metropolitan area, or part of that area, along with an identification of those processes and activities that could be centralized or performed cooperatively and those program aspects that must be strengthened in each school. Only thus can we begin to overcome the growing imbalance of the suburban schools and raise the level of all library service. Unquestionably, the new frontiers of school library service for the next two decades lie in the suburbs.

References

1. National Association of Secondary School Principals: *Images of the Future.* J. L. Trump, ed. Washington, D.C., National Education Association, 1959.

2. Leigh, R. D.: *Governor's Study of Public and School Libraries in the State of Hawaii.* Honolulu, Department of Public Instruction, 1960, p. 45.

3. Shaw, R.: *Libraries of Metropolitan Toronto.* A study of library service prepared by the Library Trustees' Council of Toronto and District, 1960.

4. Mahar, Mary H.: *State Department of Education Responsibilities for School Libraries.* Washington, D.C., U.S. Department of Health, Education, and Welfare, 1960.

Libraries in Larger Institutions of Higher Education

LEWIS C. BRANSCOMB

THIS PAPER DEALS WITH LIBRARY SERVICES to
the year 1980 in 163 four-year colleges and universities with enrollments of 5,000 or more students.[1] Catholic University of America,
Princeton, and Brown universities are included, though their enrollments are below 5,000, because the nature and extent of their
programs of graduate education and research strongly ally them with
this group.

As the outset let us view briefly a few of the more important national developments from the end of World War II to 1960. The space
age, so dramatically ushered in by Russia's launching of the first
successful man-made satellite in October of 1957, has had tremendous impact upon American higher education, as well as upon
other aspects of American society. Although a review of U.S. educational programs in the sciences and technology has received greatest
emphasis, all disciplines have come under close scrutiny, and the
nature of the findings has stimulated the greatest pursuit of excellence
which this nation has ever had. Comparison with the numbers of
engineers and scientists trained in the two countries has generally
favored the U.S.S.R. American educators, earlier lulled into dangerous complacency respecting educational programs, have been shocked
into a general awareness of the inadequacies of education from kindergarten through the doctorate, although general public recognition
still lags behind. As a result of J. B. Conant's contribution to the
intellectual reawakening by his high school study, most of the states
have upgraded the requirements for prospective teachers.[2] There is a
growing feeling that competition with Russia involves not only the
production of arms, but what is even more important in the long run,
education, economic productivity, a basic way of life, and perhaps

Mr. Branscomb is Director of Libraries at the Ohio State University.

survival itself. Although the cold war varies in degree from time to time, signs point toward an indefinite continuation of the struggle with the Soviet Union.

Concomitant with the end of World War II and the emergence of the United States as the leader of the free world, higher education began to assume far greater responsibility for teaching and research in far flung parts of the world. Area studies began to develop at individual universities, involving the Middle and Far East, Latin America, the Slavic countries, and more recently Africa. Northwestern University developed a strong African program, Florida concentrated upon the Caribbean, Texas on Mexico and parts of South America, California at Berkeley on the Far East. Columbia, through its Russian Institute, has a Slavic collection of well over 100,000 volumes, while seven or eight other institutions have similar or related programs built around substantial holdings.

With the growing concept of a shrinking world which can now be completely spanned in eighty-nine minutes, the development of area studies around the globe will expand to meet the demands of teaching and research. University libraries for the most part have somewhat belatedly acquired research materials upon which such studies are based after their institutions have made the decision to establish a particular program.

The late 1940's and the 1950's saw the rise of a number of significant cooperative ventures such as the Farmington Plan in 1948, designed to bring at least one copy of every book of research value published abroad into a known location in this country, the Midwest Inter-Library Center in 1949, the Hampshire Inter-Library Center in 1951, and the Southeastern Inter-Library Research Facility in 1955. The New England Deposit Library, begun much earlier, may be said to be the prototype of this kind of cooperation. More than sixty research libraries, dispersed through every region and most of them attached to universities, participate in the Farmington Plan. M.I.L.C. now has twenty member libraries, with prospects of broader support, and is beginning to exert an influence upon scholarship in the middle west and indeed nationally. The success of the Hampshire Inter-Library Center with its four members points the way toward further cooperation in the East. In 1956 the Association of Research Libraries began a cooperative program of foreign newspapers on microfilm pooled at M.I.L.C. for the use of some sixty widely scattered libraries throughout the nation. More than one hundred universities with graduate programs cooperate with University Microfilms in its program of centralizing film copies of doctoral dissertations at Ann Arbor from which copies can be purchased cheaply and promptly in lieu of inter-library loan. Many more examples might be cited, but this list is sufficient for illustrative purposes. The underlying intent in these and other cooperative ventures has been the extension of library services and resources within the framework of the limited funds available.

Another relatively recent major development in the large universities has been the rapidly expanding program of industrial- and particularly government-sponsored research. Approximately one billion dollars were spent on organized research in American universities in 1960—an increase of 126 per cent from 1954 to 1960, and well over half this sum came from the federal government in the form of contract research.[3] Graduate education and faculty research are feeling the impact of this new demand and new source of funds. One may well question whether this applied research, as it is in large part, as compared with basic or fundamental research, is producing an imbalance detrimental to the quality of graduate education and faculty research. The growing dependence upon this source of support of research will make it exceedingly difficult for most large research institutions to curtail the number of contracts it will accept.

Perhaps the most obvious postwar development, and one destined to affect substantially both higher education and the nation, is the steadily increasing student enrollment in the colleges and universities. Among the 18 to 24 year olds in the nation 72 out of 1,000 were enrolled in 1930, 91 in 1940, 168 in 1950, and approximately 250 in 1960, or an increase of approximately 247 per cent in thirty years.[4] The increases are the result both of population growth and the rising percentage of high school graduates who elect to go to college. The percentage of young people 18 to 24 years of age who were enrolled in college in 1960 is roughly the same, 25 per cent, as that of high school enrollment in 1917—a truly remarkable achievement in such a relatively short period.[5]

This short summary of some of the national developments and continuing trends since 1945 is suggestive of future patterns in large college and university libraries. A rededication to the pursuit of excellence, language and area studies, cooperative ventures among libraries, the great expansion of government-sponsored research, and the exploding college enrollment—all affect the library, most of them by demanding greater resources and services. But what are some of these future patterns?

One of the most difficult problems facing higher education is that of adequate financial support. There are other problems, of course, and money alone does not produce a quality program, but it is one of the essential ingredients. Costs of running colleges and universities are mounting, and the portents are that they will continue to increase in the foreseeable future. One may recall the storekeeper who said that he lost money on every sale, but that he was able to stay in business only because he made so many sales. Unfortunately, colleges do not have this golden touch. Since students at most institutions pay no more than half, or even less, of the cost of their education, steadily increasing enrollment requires continuously more funds from one source or another.

To make matters worse, the status of the college and the college professor in the United States is low. Both the salaries and the prestige of college and university professors in European institutions, considering the economics of their countries, are much higher than in the United States, although it is some comfort to note that the Russian sputnik has focused attention upon the importance of education and research with the result that "egghead" is no longer a popular term of derision.

Libraries, of course, share the general financial problems of their parent institution, but their plight is even greater. R. B. Downs has pointed out that in 1945–46, thirty university libraries were spending a median of 4.86 per cent of their institution's total education expenses for library services, but by 1958–59—fifteen years later—the figure for the same group had dropped to 3.7 per cent.[3] Efforts on the part of college librarians to secure a share of the overhead allowances from government contract research, despite a few bright exceptions, have been singularly unsuccessful.

It seems likely that the situation will get much worse during the 1960's before very much is done about it. A broad educational program designed to acquaint the public with the financial problem of higher education is badly needed. Only a beginning has been made in this effort. The American public may have to face the grim fact of failing to get Junior into a good college or even failing to get him into any college at all before the problem can be brought home. To finance higher education during the next two decades, not only must the student pay higher college fees, but substantial assistance must also come from the individual states, the federal government, foundations, alumni, friends, business, and industry. Although libraries receive some funds from a variety of sources, most of them will continue to face the difficult job of trying to secure adequate support from the parent institution as the major source of funds.

But the picture is not all dark. Efforts are currently in progress to persuade the National Science Foundation, an agency of the federal government, to assist college libraries to provide better and more extensive services to scientists and social scientists. The Association of College and Research Libraries has embarked upon a program to secure federal legislation to help college libraries, similar to the assistance so effectively given to rural public libraries through the Library Services Act. The President's Commission on National Goals calls for improvement in teachers' salaries, increased scholarship and loan funds, and a doubling of the annual public and private expenditure for education between 1960 and 1970, for a total which would then approximate five per cent of the gross national product.[6] The current proposals for federal aid to education are indicative of the growing concern among the people about the problem, and whether or not the bill passes at this session of Congress, the climate of opinion is improving. The United States can afford to provide a superior program for educating its youth to realize their full potential, but it cannot afford not to provide it. It is possible that during the next two decades this goal will largely have been reached.

One of the most baffling problems now facing librarians and documentalists alike is that of control over the tremendous flood of publications now issuing from the world's presses. Even the largest libraries long ago conceded defeat in the attempt to struggle alone against this tide of print and have cooperated with other libraries coping with the same problems. Research is proceeding at an explosive rate, the findings of which in turn result in the publication of books, articles, pamphlets, leaflets, and technical reports by the scores of thousands. Because of inadequate indexing, abstracting, acquisition, processing, and servicing, scientists are becoming increasingly frustrated in their efforts to keep up with progress in their own specialities, much less in their general area. Automation comes slowly to libraries, but the librarian of the large research institution now admits that his outdated manual procedures are no longer appropriate to the tasks at hand.

At least a partial solution surely lies in the development and use

[183]

of machines to do many of the physical and manual jobs involved in libraries, and all academic librarians are aware of the research in automation now being carried on by documentalists, librarians, physicists, mathematicians, engineers, and other specialists. The Western Reserve University Documentation and Communication Research Center is, among other projects, currently engaged in pioneering research and development of techniques and machines for storage and retrieval of educational research information. The Library of Congress is conducting a survey of possibilities for automating the organization, storage, and retrieval of information in a large research library financed by the Council on Library Resources. There is evidence to indicate that, while the complex of problems has not by any means been solved, some of the adaptations which are now capable of operation are not being utilized because they are not economically feasible, as, for example, the Michigan study on "telereference"—a system of consulting card catalogs by television. A high degree of automation for every academic library may never be financially justified, but state or regional centers will be established to serve as nerve centers from which information will be transmitted electronically to institutions within a particular area. On a given campus of a large university the library headquarters will be in communication with its branches by television, telefacsimile, and/or similar electronic devices.

It is not predicted here that the book as such will disappear by 1980. In many situations of the individual reader, it will remain highly useful and efficient. But certain categories of information, particularly in the physical and engineering sciences, must somehow come under machine manipulation if research is not to become submerged in its own unorganized literature.

Another problem faced by academic libraries is the very uneven or maldistribution of American library resources. The heaviest concentration lies along the eastern seaboard and in California on the west coast, with decreasing holdings in the Middle West, Texas, and Washington, and with the southwest, southeast, plain and mountain states bringing up the rear. R. B. Downs [7] has brought Wilson's [8] interesting study of 1935 up to 1955. The later study reveals that in general those that had the largest resources in the earlier period were also at the top in 1955, but that their lead over the rest of the country was not quite so great. The southeast grew most quickly with a percentage increase of 399, and the southwest most slowly with 86 per cent. However, among the seventy-six library centers listed, Dallas ranked second in the rate of increase, jumping from 70th to 37th position, a volumes increase from approximately 571,000 to 1,963,000, or 244 per cent during the two decades. The population of the entire United States increased by 18.5 per cent for the decade ending in 1960. If there is a positive correlation between population growth and college enrollment, it would seem desirable for library resources to increase along the same lines. Though not one of the worst problems facing libraries, this dilemma can be partially resolved by greater efforts on the part of those in less heavily concentrated areas to strengthen rapidly their library holdings, by imaginative cooperation among libraries, and by the establishment of state or regional centers as indicated above.

As we turn to education for librarianship and the shortage of trained personnel, we see it predicted that the largest increase in per cent of change in employment of various occupation groups from 1960 to 1970 will occur in the professional and technical group—40 per cent.[9] This group, including librarians, also requires the highest educational level of any group.

Librarianship shares with other professions a critical shortage of trained personnel. Already acute, this problem is going to become more serious in the 1960's because of exploding college enrollments and a much greater emphasis upon high scholastic standards. It has been estimated that while there were 10,000 professional positions unfilled by professional librarians in 1959, library schools are graduating fewer than 2,000 annually.[10] There are doubtless many factors responsible for this situation, but among the most important are inadequate salaries, lack of status within and outside the institution, a generally poor recruiting effort on a national basis, and a continuing failure to distinguish clearly between professional and clerical library duties (by contrast with the tightly-drawn distinction between the duties of physicians and nurses, for instance).

The salaries and status of academic librarians are inseparably linked with those of their teaching colleagues, and the solutions when found will apply largely to both groups. Librarians can, however, do more about recruiting personnel and sharpening the lines between professional and clerical duties. The latter involves in part shifting to high level clerks some tasks now performed by librarians, particularly in several aspects of acquisition, cataloging, and circulation work. Adoption of such plans as the cooperative "cataloging in source" would help substantially to make better use of the inadequate numbers of graduates of the library schools, as will the use of automation to perform routine chores.

The demand for specialization in the professions, including librarianship, is increasing. A high percentage of librarians have training in the humanities and to a lesser extent in the social studies, with relatively few having a substantial background in the physical and biological sciences or in technology. There is a paucity of linguistic skills especially in the Slavic and east European languages, Chinese and Japanese, and other less well-known languages. As institutions establish area programs and institutes on Russia, Africa, the Middle and Far East, not only will there be special language needs, but some knowledge of the country is also highly desirable. Of course some of this background will not be provided in the library school, but will be ancillary to it. Where it is not feasible for the university library to secure staff with such special knowledge, it may be possible for the institution to subsidize the general librarian while he is studying in the specialized area, particularly when this arrangement can be made on the campus where the librarian holds appointment. It is encouraging to note that the Library Services Branch of the U.S. Office of Education and the School of Library Science of Western Reserve University are sponsoring an institute on the future of library education to be held in Cleveland in 1962.

It has been suggested that while special librarians will still be serving in departmental libraries of large universities in 1980, the most highly-skilled special librarians will be in university-sponsored research institute libraries serving research foundations and industries adjacent to the campus.[11] This work will be on a fee basis, involving the total marshaling of university information, not merely the literature resources.

There are now more than thirty accredited library schools in the nation offering master's degrees, and about one-fourth of them offer doctorates. In these schools the talent is available in the form of students and faculty to carry on research in librarianship which could be of great value to the profession. To be sure, such research has been going on for some years, but during the next twenty years as the number of library school students grows, especially on the doctoral level, it should be sharpened to meet the demands of a practical, not a theoretical, discipline.

A minor problem faced by larger university libraries, especially those located in metropolitan areas with high industrialization, is

[186]

the growing demand for library service by industry and business. Even though there are many industrial libraries, these are not always adequate to the research or other needs of the companies which maintain them. The large university library, always hard put to provide optimum service to its own community, is asked with increasing frequency to assume this additional burden. Other categories of patrons requesting library privileges not traditionally associated with the college and university library are local secondary school students and townspeople. With the recent raising of school standards, the high school library in many instances is inadequately stocked for the demands made upon it, and when it closes at four or five o'clock, high school students besiege the university library on evenings and weekends.

Some private university libraries are charging fees to industry and townspeople for services rendered, although this partial solution is not as appropriate for the state-assisted as for the private institutions. While it is a problem for the university library to serve patrons other than its own, the reverse is also true. The public library in some areas serves large numbers of college and secondary school students. Studies are now being made of this problem of overlapping clienteles.

As already indicated, the exploding college enrollment problem is already here, but it will become even more acute in the future, especially in the decade 1960–1970, as indicated by the following data:

Estimates and Projections of Fall Enrollment in Colleges and Professional Schools [12]

1950	2,214,000	1965	5,720,000
1955	2,379,000	1970	7,805,000
1960	3,570,000	1975	10,092,000
	1980	11,948,000	

These data reveal a recorded increase of 61 per cent from 1950 to 1960 and projected increases of 119 per cent from 1960 to 1970, 53 per cent from 1970 to 1980, and an overall increase of 235 per cent for the period 1960 to 1980. The children are already born who will be of college age up until the year 1978, and only a major catastrophe or a radical and totally unexpected reversal of the increasing percentage of high school graduates electing to go to college can change this general picture. It is estimated that about 75 per cent of the increase is due to a larger percentage of high school graduates going to college and that about 25 per cent is due to increasing birth rate. Educators, state legislators, boards of trustees, and others are now studying the problem and are considering the establishment of new or additional junior and community colleges, trade schools, and technical schools along with the expansion of existing state-assisted and private colleges. Furthermore, academic institutions will be forced to make more efficient use of their facilities by scheduling classes from 8 a.m. to 10 p.m., six days per week and eleven months of the year. Some institutions are already well along in efforts to make summer sessions more nearly comparable to the quarters or semesters of the so called "academic year."

Libraries will feel the full impact of this tremendous enrollment growth and must provide for it in a variety of ways. The larger universities will continue the trend of establishing substantial and separate undergraduate libraries such as those at Harvard, Michigan, Texas, and South Carolina. They will also further disperse their main collections either in the form of departmental, school, and college libraries or in strong area libraries for the biological sciences, engineering sciences, and other areas as proposed at Ohio State.

A relatively sophisticated and well developed country like the United States demands more and more services of a professional nature. To meet this demand the enrollment in graduate and professional schools will continue to increase, and it is this growth which will put the heaviest strain upon the library for resources to support graduate and professional programs. In order to meet the great demand for college teachers, engineers, doctors, lawyers, and other professional people, some colleges will develop into universities, a process which already has been under way for some years, particularly among the state institutions. The libraries of these new universities will follow to some extent the library pattern of their predecessors, but they will be wise to experiment boldly in new techniques before they become so large that change is difficult and expensive.

Changing patterns of instruction, such as tutorial plans, expanded honors work, and similar programs, may well change markedly the student-teacher-library relationship. The relatively recent introduction of the teaching machine and programmed learning opens the door to exciting new techniques and methods of teaching. Should these devices enable students to proceed at their own pace, it seems likely that the more talented and more strongly motivated students will have time for enrichment of their courses by additional reading in the library. The use of television involving large numbers of students and outstanding teachers will also undoubtedly affect the relations among students, professors, and libraries. One currently popular device for accommodating a greater number of students with college level work is the plan of instructing some of the students at home by television. This program is already being carried out on a small scale, and it may well become one of the answers to student congestion on the campus. Such a plan relieves the classroom and teacher pressure, but does nothing to solve the library problem of servicing thousands of additional students.

With improvement in teaching and learning methods, heavier use of the university's libraries is inevitable. The very act of providing enough qualified teachers for the students flooding the campus in the next two decades will exert pressure to shift the emphasis from frequent lectures and use of a single textbook to self-instruction in the library among many books. A more radical departure is the continental method of lectures without class assignments, examinations at the end of the course, with emphasis upon direction of the subject matter rather than on the day-to-day instruction of students.[18] Such changes would call for far greater library resources than are now available in terms of physical facilities, books, and librarians with the ability to guide the student in his reading program.

Enrollment appears likely to grow more rapidly in public than in private universities because of two factors: private institutions will find it more difficult to finance increasing enrollments, and they are not obliged to take all or most of the high school graduates who apply. Slightly more than half of the total college enrollment is in public schools—probably a satisfactory situation on balance. But deleterious effects may accompany a ratio of, say, 65 per cent public and 35 per cent private. Private schools will undoubtedly make every effort to maintain quality programs and will become even more selective in admission requirements than at present, leaving the public schools with a higher percentage of relatively poorly prepared students. The great advantage of experimentation in educational techniques which the private school enjoys to a greater extent than its public counterpart—and which eventually enriches all higher education—will be dissipated in part because fewer students will be involved.

These are some of the problems—and some suggested solutions—which we will face in the larger universities and their libraries during the next two decades. But it is to be hoped that these thorny problems are also challenges which we will meet in such a way as to make this score of years the finest and most fruitful in the history of American academic librarianship.

References

1. U.S. Department of Health, Education, and Welfare: *Opening (Fall) Enrollment in Higher Education, 1960: Institutional Data.* Washington, D.C., U.S. Government Printing Office, 1960.

2. Hechinger, F. M.: *The New York Times,* Feb. 26, 1961, pp. 1+.

3. Downs, R. B.: Crisis in Our University Libraries. *College and Research Libraries,* 22:7-10, Jan. 1961.

4. Schick, F. L.: Facts about the Future. *Wilson Library Bulletin,* 35:219-221, Nov. 1960.

5. U.S. Department of Health, Education, and Welfare: *Progress of Public Education in the United States of America, 1959-60.* Washington, D.C., U.S. Government Printing Office, 1960, p. 11.

6. *The Report of the President's Commission on National Goals.* New York, The American Assembly, Columbia University, Nov. 1960, p. 7.

7. Downs, R. B.: Distribution of American Library Resources. *College and Research Libraries,* 18:183-189, May 1957.

8. Wilson, L. R.: *Geography of Reading.* Chicago, University of Chicago Press, 1938, pp. 118-123.

9. U.S. Department of Labor: *Manpower Challenge of the 1960's.* Washington, D.C., U.S. Government Printing Office, 1960, p. 11.

10. Eastlick, J. T.: *The Sixties and After.* Chicago, American Library Association, 1961, p. 5.

11. Jackson, E. B.: Teletype message dated Jan. 9, 1961.

12. Hauser, P. M., and Taitel, M.: Population Trends—Prologue to Library Development. *Library Trends,* 10:58, Table XVII, July 1961.

13. Branscomb, H.: Letter dated March 6, 1961.

Libraries in Smaller Institutions of Higher Education

EILEEN THORNTON

LIKE THE TAIL OF A COMET, panic about United States higher education soared with the first Soviet Sputnik, four years ago. As the air cleared, the tumult over the specific areas of science and technology gave place to a broader and perhaps more reasoned concern over the whole body of American higher education.

Many higher institutions found that traditional content and methods must be re-examined in the light of the need for quality of education, quite apart from the quantitative needs. Fear of throwing the baby out with the bath, plus the built-in inertia of large and complex social institutions (and even a small college is surprisingly large and complex) has made evolution rather than revolution the way of change for long-established colleges. There are, of course, notable exceptions, such as Dartmouth's shift from a two-semester multiple-course program to a three-term, three-course program and the attendant reconstruction of its whole curriculum. There are many educators who believe that though fundamental reforms are necessary, they will be achieved only piecemeal, too little and too late, unless new and distinctly experimental institutions are established. And new institutions are being established, experimental and traditional, and largely public.

It has become increasingly evident that in many subject fields students can learn at least as well as they now do with far fewer class hours than are commonly used. So far, because of the initial planning involved, the experimentation in this area shows little saving of faculty time, but once new patterns are set and in cycle, faculty time should be saved. There is broad interest in the best use of student time, too. In the smaller academic institutions, from one-fourth to one-half of the graduates may go on to graduate study; this constant extension of the

Miss Thornton is Librarian, Oberlin College Library.

years spent in preparation is exerting pressure to squeeze wasted time out of secondary education via advanced admission to college, and out of college years by means of proficiency and comprehensive examinations, round-the-year schedules, and other means of acceleration. Teaching machines, television, and other devices will be used increasingly. While the most traditionalist element in the faculty will continue to decry them, some educators will see over the top of the device-mountain to a land where such aids serve a middle purpose and can be turned to educational profit in skillful hands. All such explorations, while still unorganized and unsystematic, point to one conclusion: the next twenty years will see more students taught by relatively fewer and fewer teachers. The burden has to go somewhere; students and librarians are the obvious legatees.

Within twenty years we must know objectively what is and what is not effective teaching. In that time span, some of the present dissatisfaction with the nature of the preparation of college teachers will have been dissipated through research and experiment. For example, the Mathematical Association of America and the American Mathematical Society are already backing a program leading to the Doctor of Arts in Mathematics. This program differs from the traditional Ph.D. program with its emphasis upon a research project in that the candidate will seek instead a maximum of breadth in the field, with the intention of teaching it.

There is grave concern that our most promising young people be able to go to college and be financially able to stay in college, and that each get to the college that is right for him. There is concern that the less able student shall not be crowded out. Already students and their parents are discovering that college attendance for pure status reasons, or even for that extra $100,000 in life earnings which almost any college diploma is said to assure, has no blank allotted to it on application forms.

Colleges of known excellence will always have an obligation to attract superior students and to lead the way in demonstrating what can be done with first-rate faculties, superior libraries, and other outstanding facilities. But even the Sunday supplements of metropolitan dailies now call attention to the existence of dozens of undergraduate institutions where excellent education is available. These smaller institutions have a precarious future. Many feel that they will succumb, especially those under private aegis, because of the burden of costs and the terrible competition for personnel, but others believe that they can survive and gain strength if they achieve a better economic unit upon which to operate.

Studies on changes in attitudes and values between freshman and senior years indicate that the student culture in the college is the prime educational force at work.[1] Those who know smaller institutions know that they do tend to have an ethos, and that it is a truism that students are educated by each other as much as by the faculty. The interaction of all elements in college life, with special concern for educational implications, is bound to receive more study in the coming years.

There is confusion about the institutions needed. On the one hand, we find a passion to establish a community college at every crossroad, no matter what the prospects of quality and persistence of that institution may be. On the other hand, we see the perilous life and times of already established small institutions. Geographical handiness cannot explain away this seeming paradox. Study of the need for institutions of various kinds in various places is urgent and inevitable, and it is hoped that such study comes before old institutions are allowed to die or before too many new institutions are jerrybuilt on sand. This situation may call for the revamping of old institutions to meet new needs.

There are rumors of coercion. State agencies might control faculty licensing, curricula and specializations, admissions, and other central issues. There are statements like Beardsley Ruml's [2] that chill some faculties because administrators and trustees might wish to jump abruptly in the direction of Ruml advocates. There are voices decrying the traditional *laissez-faire* policies which permit the student to be largely the sole judge of the career he wishes to prepare for and stay with; these voices say that perhaps it is time to abandon this policy and direct the student forcibly into those vocations and professions where trained personnel are needed. Against such trends there are voices which urge voluntary cooperation, far more thoroughgoing than is common today, among institutions; the development of better guidance of potential college and graduate students; greater attention to the students not at the very top of measured promise; and thoughtful rather than sentimental preservation of the best aspects of institutional individuality.

A few years ago a grade school diploma was the union-card into adult employment. Shortly thereafter the high school diploma became the standard. Today college graduation—any college will do—has become the necessary mark. The next twenty years must recognize and dignify all types of higher education, or we shall have turned the process into a stamping machine. While we would welcome a certain standard of common excellence as the result of secondary education, advanced education should, in the eyes of many, provide a wide spread of kinds of excellence. And after sixteen years or more in the educational process, our young adults should emerge with an education suited to society's needs and to their own best talents.

If demographic and economic needs actually do prove the desirability of proliferating the two- and three-year institutions, the drain-off to such institutions will radically affect degree-granting institutions of all sorts. If some of these institutions are terminal/vocational and if they can achieve an attractive status, they will not only provide a body of trained personnel likely to be needed for many years to come, but they will also free the degree-granting colleges and universities of the heartbreaking problems of massive drop-outs. If some of these two- and three-year institutions are truly comparable to the lower levels of liberal arts undergraduate colleges, the influx of transfer students in their third and fourth collegiate years could profoundly affect colleges and universities. Whether the numbers of transfers would be large enough to alleviate one of the greatest problems current in higher education is difficult to predict: that problem is the very high cost of tiny enrollments in advanced course work. If a typical four-year college were to have more well-prepared juniors and seniors than it had freshmen and sophomores, the change in teaching assignments alone could make vast changes in financing, curricula, and library need. In fact, such change might create the lifeline many small but good older colleges may have to find if they are to stay afloat.

Some of these big questions facing all of higher education will have to be answered on a wider front than in the past. Education at any level is a national need. National research and national findings will give us a greater variety of educational choice rather than a narrower field, if the coming twenty years build on the scattered experimentation of the past and invest enough in real research in the future:

It is anomalous that through research and the training of research workers, higher education has made discoveries, developed techniques, and built devices which have literally made over most of

[194]

man's workaday world, but has not applied this same brilliance, imagination, and ingenuity to fundamental research on the educational process and to the development of ways in which schools and colleges may increase their own productivity. . . . It is unthinkable that the application of sustained, dedicated intelligence to the improvement of educational processes and procedures will not produce similar discoveries and changes. The investment in research on the country's problems of agriculture, business, labor, and health has yielded tremendous dividends. Basic research on crucial problems in education will be equally rewarding.[3]

Federal money, evidence of belated federal concern, is finally being invested in projects which aim to study American education—its content, its personnel, its methodology, its successes and failures—on a broad and serious scale. It is high time. As L. G. Derthick said in testimony before a congressional committee: "I pause, Mr. Chairman, to ask how much longer are we going to be satisfied with less information about our children than we have about our hogs." [4]

What happens to academic libraries in the next twenty years depends upon what happens in higher education, in librarianship, and in communications. And what happens in those areas depends upon what happens in population growth and dispersal, in the economic situation, in manpower needs, and in international relations. Librarians in smaller universities and colleges may well wonder what the future holds for the libraries and the clientele they serve.

We all know that the population tide is rising like the waters in the *Sorcerer's Apprentice.* We all know that now a larger part of the college-age population wants to go to college than ever before. We all know that the predictions of college enrollment are so staggering that they seem unreal; perhaps this is the reason that we find little concrete planning to meet this tremendous influx. In the smaller institutions, and particularly in the private colleges, there is a general feeling that the tide may affect other institutions, but not us, except by a carefully planned 10 per cent or 15 per cent, which is, after all, a whip to flog the budget horse but not a whip laid across our own backs.

The battle of the bulge is heaviest in the already massive institutions and in the publicly supported institutions of middle size. To the latter group, this may not be a disaster. The "short, happy life of the teachers' college" has led to the shift in a historically minute span of time from the normal school to the teachers' college to the arts college which also does much teacher preparation. Many of these institutions can and do accommodate more students, much to the profit of the students and the organization. But even they will feel the pinch when their enrollments suddenly pass the point of comfortable accommodation in classrooms, libraries, laboratories, dormitories, and curricula.

However, the large public institutions, which have traditionally had less control over admissions than have private institutions of all sizes, will probably get the brunt. Already there is a calculated dropout rate; dormitories are planned to accommodate fewer students than are admitted because the fall freshmen will be weeded out radically, and the houses will hold what is left.

To try to generalize about those institutions loosely classified as junior colleges is, as anyone who has tried knows, a very dangerous procedure. Their only point of comparability with others of their classification is that they do not offer the bachelor's degree. Some have day schools of college-age students—perhaps only in the hundreds—and evening schools of a very mixed student body and program involving thousands of students. Others have strictly liberal arts programs essentially designed as terminal in themselves or preparatory for senior college work. Some have programs purposely aimed at vocational preparation, though these tend more and more to require some nonvocational basic work.

Some are parts of federations or systems, as in New York and California, and some are seen as extensions of secondary education, while others are viewed as part of higher education. Some are in existence to serve a purely local population; others draw students from everywhere. Some have libraries of fewer than a thousand volumes, and a few have libraries of more than 60,000 volumes. Perhaps the only safe generalization to add to the one already made is that many, especially those with liberal arts or preprofessional programs, will stretch up and become four-year, degree-granting colleges. Sometimes this situation will be forced upon the institution by its constituency, and sometimes it will be the outcome of a planned development much wanted by the institution.

Everywhere one turns he hears of faculty shortages. In a publication read more by librarians than by others, it is useless to point out the even greater shortage of librarians, and the dim prospects that this situation is going to improve in the next decade or two.

Library school enrollment has been nearly static for years, despite

rising figures for college-graduate population, library salaries, pro-
liferation of attractive library positions, and such. In the literature
on new ways to meet the teacher shortage, there is constant emphasis
upon relieving those teachers a college does have of paper work,
upon new methods of using teacher/student time, upon devices and
gadgets and do-it-yourself learning, and most of all upon independent
study. One comes upon innumerable references to "turning the student loose in the library to do more for himself," but almost no references to the implications in hard fact of what all this may mean to
academic libraries. In the National Defense Education Act the word
"library" does not, I think, appear: it is quite easy to secure money
to advise students to go to college or to support programs heavily
dependent upon library resources (sciences and foreign languages,
for instance), but it is close to impossible for small libraries, unless
there is a lawyer *manqué* on the team, to wangle money for materials
to support any part of any program. It can be done, but the cost of
doing it, in terms of time and pother, is beyond the reach of librarians in smaller institutions.

The median number of professional staff, size of collections, and
total library operating expenditures by type for four-year institutions
is given in Table I, by enrollment size for four-year institutions in
Table II, and by enrollment for two-year institutions in Table III.[5]
This level of support does not secure many man hours, and the pros-
pect of serving even the median number of students as independent
scholars, plus trying to acquire and to organize collections adequate
for such study, is patently staggering. Compared with the A.L.A.
Standards as illustrated in the Introduction to the July 1961 issue of
Library Trends (p. 7), the gap is indeed wide because 57 per cent of
privately controlled and 21 per cent of the publicly controlled four-
year institutions have professional staffs of fewer than three professional librarians; 78 per cent of private and 71 per cent of public
two-year institutions have fewer than two professional librarians on
their staff. In four-year institutions 60 per cent of those under private
and 33 per cent under public control have collections of fewer than
50,000 volumes. In two-year institutions the situation is even more
drastic because 90 per cent of the privately controlled and 84 per cent
of the publicly controlled institutions have collections of fewer than
20,000 volumes.

Already doubling in brass for every sort of service to their clientele—and the differences in demand upon the smaller libraries as

compared with those serving the massive institutions lie more in degree than in kind—it is difficult to see how present needs can be met, to say nothing of the new needs created by radically changed enrollments and experimental teaching methods which throw more of the educational load on the library.

The fact that astonishes is that out of these smaller institutions, and especially out of the four-year, liberal arts institutions, comes a higher proportion of eventual scholars and persons of other kinds of distinction than comes out of the large institutions. Findings on this proportion have varied with respect to years and to fields as well as to criteria of distinction, but the generalization still holds true. While this may be a source of comfort to the three librarians in Minimum College and perhaps of embarrassment to the 150 librarians of Maximum University, it should give all librarians pause. If an acknowledged outcome of higher education in smaller institutions (with small libraries) is a higher proportion in graduate study admission and performance, has it been the close teacher-student relationship which produced results? If that relationship is to be replaced in some measure by independent use of library resources, can small library collections and small library staffs meet the need?

Mrs. Knapp's [6] report on the meagerness of actual library use by students in an excellent small college, and the program she now directs at Monteith College [7, 8] of Wayne State University may first jolt and then rouse to action college librarians and faculties. The aim of the Monteith program is to stimulate and guide students in developing a sophisticated understanding of the library and an increasing competence in its use. There are times in the life of every college librarian when he feels that the curriculum goes along one track and the library a parallel track, and that there is no way to break this geometric dilemma. More studies of the actualities of library relevance to educational programs and teaching methods must be made.

Occasionally shrewd and informed guesses can short-cut research. One expert advises that

The plant of experimental colleges and programs be developed around a large library-student union building. . . . While the library is typically described as the heart of the campus it is often more like the liver for it is often a large structure whose significance lies in the potential it may not be called on to release. What is proposed here is that the library be made the heart of the academic enterprise, in fact, and that it be made to deliver something like its full potential.

The student union may seem to be an unlikely place for scholarship. To the extent that this is true it has departed from an ancient university tradition.[9]

Foreign study, often for a full college year, will become more and more important. The study of foreign languages will become more thorough and widespread, the students' interest will lie not in the language as that of a literature alone, but in the language as a key to a total culture. Implications of these facts for libraries could be serious. Provision of library services abroad, either by cooperation or contract with foreign libraries, or by direct supply of materials and services, will become a real problem as study abroad becomes a more and more important part of undergraduate life.

In his article, Branscomb stresses the urgency of making the public aware of the need to invest in higher education. Within the academic world, it is urgent that college officers and trustees be made aware of the library's share in this need. While the diversity and depth of curricula may have more to do with the cost of materials than has sheer size of enrollment, the shift from classroom work to greater emphasis upon independent study will put a greater burden upon college libraries and librarians. Almost none of the literature which blithely advocates greater student dependence upon the library mentions the fact that this inevitably must mean better libraries and more and better librarians. It is up to librarians to see that this fact of academic life is made known where it matters.

The A.C.R.L. Standards for College Libraries and for Junior College Libraries aim to state minimal satisfactory conditions of finance, staffing, stock, quarters, and service. For many existing college libraries, the standards are low; for many, the suggested minimum library budget figure of 5 per cent of the total Educational and General Expenditure figure is the wild blue yonder. It is nearly impossible to generalize about the Junior College standards, thoughtful as they are, because for lack of well defined sub-categories, such a wide variety of institutions must be lumped together. If, however, such a minimum could be set for all those institutions not now spending 5 per cent of the Educational and General budget on their libraries, the dollars let loose for library purposes would revolutionize holdings, staffs, and services.

It is necessary that studies be made to discover the relative value of greater investment in libraries and librarians as opposed to greater investment in new institutions, in faculty costs, in general physical facilities, and in other elements of institutional costs so constantly taken for granted as of enormous importance. It is also up to librarians to work closely with those entrusted with formal education for librarianship in developing programs beyond the first professional degree. The aim to share in educational responsibility and faculty status can be more readily achieved if librarians will expect more of themselves in the way of scholarly study and published research. At a time when preparation for college teaching is under scrutiny and perhaps ready for some changes, it would be wise to see if we should demand more preparation for college librarianship.

Miss Reagan's study showed that the most telling force for and against joining the library profession is the effect or other persons upon the individual.[10] College librarians might ponder their role in recruiting with this fact in mind. Certainly from the thousands of students still undecided upon post-college careers, we might identify and interest those who would be welcome additions to the profession. We might discover those already determined to become librarians and have them help in recruiting others. The shortage of well prepared librarians is now acute and probably will continue to be so. If, from each of the thousand or more higher institutions offering liberal arts undergraduate degrees, one candidate for library school might be sent each year, the improvement in the personnel situation would be startling. In addition, every effort should be made to urge trained persons, especially women with growing children, to return to the fold. Unless librarians themselves take a larger share in recruiting, the situation will be extremely difficult. Even with a systematic and broad attack on this problem, it is not likely that the market will be glutted; so no present librarian of any competence need fear for his job.

We already have some clear-cut examples of effective cooperation among smaller libraries, but we have a distressing number of instances where cooperative ventures have failed to work out or have consumed inordinate amounts of time and energy for the benefits derived. Many academic libraries are currently caught on rather choppy seas of cooperative ideas. Sometimes it is a group of colleges which have joined forces at some level such as the Great Lakes College Association, with twelve colleges from four contiguous states, or the Associated Colleges of the Midwest, with ten colleges from contiguous states. In these cases, the cooperative enterprise did not rise out of interests in library cooperation but for total institutional purposes. In other instances, some of these same institutions are involved in purely library cooperative planning, but planning that does not coincide with the geographic concepts of the two associations mentioned above and that does include libraries in other institutions and in other states.

Interlibrary cooperation based upon the examples of M.I.L.C., H.I.L.C., the Farmington Plan, the New England Deposit Library, and other well known formal arrangements may come to be far more common than it is today. To arrive at formal schemes, however, will take a real investment in time and money, and above all some larger leadership than can be expected to come from the librarians of the smaller institutions. That there is need for overall planning and action is becoming more obvious every day.

Smaller institutions cannot hope to provide all the research materials their faculties need. If more and more faculty members are to join teaching staffs before the completion of their doctorates, and if there is to be increasing emphasis upon independent undergraduate work, the scope of each college collection will have to be widened. It cannot be widened by developing each library to meet all needs. The needs must be met through communal ownership, through lending and borrowing, through copying, through sending scholars to materials, and through other methods, some of them yet to be devised.

Little libraries are reluctant to continue borrowing primarily from large libraries; yet the problems of developing both coverage and depth through cooperative schemes seem close to hopeless. The crux of the matter, of course, is the ever-widening sea of print and the problems of selection of materials. With barely enough money to buy and process the daily essentials, the really small libraries cannot undertake to supply the larger needs of scholarship through a division of fields of responsibility, through joint purchase of research publications, and through elaborate systems of loans to each other. It looks as though the strong research libraries will still be called upon to support the research needs of faculties everywhere, and, to some extent, the specialized needs of the thousands of students who are to be put on their own to educate themselves via libraries. Perhaps this problem could be at least partly overcome by the creation of a national research library to lend lavishly to this particular group of higher institutions.

In smaller colleges, interest in effective book selection media continues to be a vital question. Even though it must be admitted that librarians and faculties probably do not make full use of reviewing media already at hand, the need for more systematic, speedy, and appropriate analysis of new publications persists as does the need for evaluative guides to older literature. The dangers of undiscriminating use of published lists will not be belabored here. The Council on Library Resources is supporting exploratory studies pertaining to tools of selection for the college library. In the next few years there should be practical help in this area. The matter of judicious elimination—selection in reverse—is a grave problem for all kinds of scholarly libraries. It is hoped that studies now going on at Yale and Chicago on selective retirement will serve as guides to lesser libraries.

Indeed, in many aspects of librarianship in smaller academic institutions, librarians will have to depend upon the findings of major agencies and large libraries for the solution to problems and for improvement of services. Almost every problem that is faced by the great research library is faced by the small library. In some ways the problems are more complex for smaller libraries, where every staff member must be versatile rather than a specialist, and where each book purchased may cost one-hundreth rather than one-ten-thousandth of the book budget.

College libraries feel the pressure from the general public, and public libraries feel the pressure from school and college students. If all libraries are to try to serve all publics, those with academic commitments and few dollars will constantly be torn between direct obligations to their special constituency and the public relations requirement to be kind to outsiders. Many see this failure to define the roles of various kinds of libraries as a false democracy. The next twenty years must resolve this confusion in the interests of the users of libraries. It is they, rather than the libraries as institutions, who will lose if not. Here again the relations among demography, bibliographic control, and manageable objectives must be sorted out without passion. Only when we have a clearer idea of who needs what, and where, and when, and what library unit can respond to these needs can we offer library service of the richness and diversity we really need for the national good.

Librarians are deluged with advertisements that make it clear that anything can be reproduced in any form, at the speed of light, and at an astonishing variety of prices. Copyright law is bound to change, and some changes could greatly benefit libraries. With enormous increases in enrollments in programs from the cradle to the grave, alert publishers will compete for the market. In collegiate work, if the predicted swing away from texts and toward individualized study materializes, both the individual buyer and the library buyer will be impressive, commercially speaking. According to Booher, the printed object itself could be produced by new processes and in satisfactory form at a fraction of present cost.[11] If this is so, the college library book dollar may, for once in its history, go farther than in the past.

At the heart of the situation for the smaller institutions lies this need for fundamental research. Isolated librarians, administrators, and small faculties can look closely at the situation at home, but are helpless when it comes to organized, objective, adequately financed studies so necessary in all of higher education and librarianship. Close behind organized research comes the pressing need for systematic reporting and synthesis of research findings.

In the meantime there is much that college librarians can do to help themselves. They can work with their faculty colleagues in guiding more young people into the profession of librarianship; they can make clear to their administrators the implications for libraries of growing enrollments and of changing teaching methods and of the response libraries should make to these changes. They can take a close look at the actual relationship, course by course, teacher by teacher, student by student, between libraries and learning. While a massive research effort on a national scale is called for, there is also profound need for smaller studies, and these smaller studies will have to be done, in many cases, where the library and the student and the teacher meet. Librarians in smaller institutions should not be too modest about their roles. They should help pinpoint areas where research is needed, and out of their experience and imagination should suggest ways of meeting library problems. If the increase in numbers of students will have, as one effect, greater student dependence upon libraries, librarians should recognize this as a chance to prove what libraries can really do. They should not be content with anything less than major planning to meet a major opportunity.

In brief, these are the prospects we face: there will be a doubling of the number of students in higher education; the load will fall unevenly to various kinds of institutions; there will be many new institutions and some mortality among old, small institutions; there will have to be planning on a national scale if appropriate institutions, educational programs, and placement of students are to be achieved; teachers and librarians will be in short supply; changing methods of

[203]

TABLE I

Median Number of Professional Staff, Size of Collections
and Total Library Operating Expenditure
in 4-Year Institutions (by Type) 1959-60

Type of Institution	PUBLIC CONTROL				PRIVATE CONTROL			
	No. of Instit.	Personnel in FTE	Collection in Vols.	Expend. in Dollars	No. of Instit.	Personnel in FTE	Collection in Vols.	Expend. in Dollars
Universities..........	89	19.7	405,500	360,800	59	20.0	450,900	308,900
Lib. Arts Colleges.......	87	5.0	67,300	81,900	668	2.0	42,900	29,900
Teachers Colleges.......	167	4.0	51,700	51,900	29	1.0	20,000	18,800
Technological Schools......	27	3.0	34,500	49,400	25	2.5	41,000	57,200
Theological Schools.	—	—	—	—	165	1.0	32,300	14,600
Other Prof. Schools........	11	3.0	43,200	50,700	109	1.0	9,800	10,000

SOURCE: U. S. Office of Education. Library Services Branch: *Library Statistics of Colleges and Universities, 1959–60. Advance Analytic Report.* J. C. Rather and Doris C. Holladay, comp. Washington, D. C., July 1961. OE–15030.

TABLE II

Median Number of Professional Staff, Size of Collections and Total Library Operating Expenditure (in $) in 4-Year Institutions by Size of Enrollment 1959-60

Enrollment Size (No. of Students)	PUBLIC CONTROL				PRIVATE CONTROL			
	No. of Instit.	Personnel in FTE	Collection in Vols.	Expend. in Dollars	No. of Instit.	Personnel in FTE	Collection in Vols.	Expend. in Dollars
Fewer than 500	29	1.0	22,700	17,800	482	1.0	23,300	12,800
500 – 999	57	2.0	32,700	28,000	271	2.0	42,500	28,500
1000 – 2499	125	4.0	56,200	57,600	203	3.5	63,500	45,600
2500 – 4999	81	8.0	103,400	117,800	38	6.0	114,000	93,300
5000 – 9999	43	15.0	277,800	337,400	39	11.7	208,700	373,600
10,000 or more	46	33.0	623,500	559,000	22	37.2	516,500	536,600

Source: See Table I.

TABLE III

Median Number of Professional Staff, Size of Collections and Total Library Operating Expenditure in 2-Year Institutions by Size of Enrollment 1959-60

Enrollment Size (No. of Students)	PUBLIC CONTROL				PRIVATE CONTROL			
	No. of Instit.	Personnel in FTE	Collection in Vols.	Expend. in Dollars	No. of Instit.	Personnel in FTE	Collection in Vols.	Expend. in Dollars
Fewer than 500..........	164	1.0	5,900	7,100	170	1.0	10,600	7,200
500 – 999.............	62	1.0	8,500	13,100	23	1.0	12,600	12,200
1000 – 2499...........	52	1.9	13,400	22,800	5	2.0	30,000	22,500
2500 or more...........	39	3.0	24,600	53,500	—	—	—	—

SOURCE: See Table I.

instruction will challenge libraries in every aspect of their operations. A host of studies must be made in both higher education and in college librarianship.

D. H. Burnham, architect and early planner of cities, formulated a motto for his own guidance. That motto might serve us today, in higher education and in library service to higher education: "Make no little plans; they have no magic to stir men's blood and probably themselves will not be realized. Make big plans; aim high in hope and work, remembering that a noble, logical diagram once recorded will never die, but long after we are gone will be a living thing, asserting itself with ever-growing insistency. Remember that our sons and grandsons are going to do things that would stagger us. Let your watchword be order and your beacon beauty." [12]

References

1. Freedman, M. B.: Impact of College. *In* U.S. Office of Education *New Dimensions in Higher Education, No. 4.* Washington, D.C., U.S. Government Printing Office, 1960.

2. Ruml, Beardsley: *Memo to a College Trustee; a Report on Financial and Structural Problems of the Liberal College.* New York, McGraw-Hill, 1959.

3. Little, J. K.: Trends Affecting Contemporary Educational Planning; the Program in Higher Education. *Journal of Higher Education,* 32:192-198, April 1961.

4. U.S. 85th Congress: Scholarship and Loan Program: Part 2. *In Hearings before Subcommittee of the Committee on Education and Labor.* Washington, D.C., U.S. Government Printing Office, Feb. 19, 1958, p. 906.

5. U.S. Office of Education: *Library Statistics of Colleges and Universities, 1959-60. Advance Analytic Report.* Washington, D.C., U.S. Government Printing Office, July 1961.

6. Knapp, Patricia B.: College Teaching and the College Library. A.C.R.L. *Monograph No. 23.* Chicago, American Library Association, 1959.

7. Wayne State University, Detroit. Monteith College: *The Monteith Library Program: Experimental Project in Library-Instructional Coordination.* Proposal approved by the Cooperative Research Branch, U.S. Office of Education, March 1, 1960. Patricia B. Knapp, Project Director (Mimeographed).

8. Wayne State University, Detroit. Monteith College: *Project No. 874: An Experiment in Coordination Between Teaching and Library Staff for Changing Student Use of a University Library.* Report No. 2, July 1, 1960-Jan. 30, 1961 (Mimeographed).

9. Hatch, W. R.: The Experimental College. *In* U.S. Office of Education *New Dimensions in Higher Education, No. 3.* Washington, D.C., U.S. Government Printing Office, 1960.

10. Reagan, Agnes L.: A Study of Factors Influencing College Students To Become Librarians. A.C.R.L. *Monograph No. 21.* Chicago, Association of College and Research Libraries, 1958.

[207]

11. Booher, E. E.: Books and Their Market. *Publishers' Weekly*, 179:20-24, March 6, 1961.

12. Moore, C.: *Daniel H. Burnham, Architect, Planner of Cities*. Boston, Houghton Mifflin Company, 1921, Vol. 2, p. 146.

Special Libraries

EUGENE B. JACKSON

A SPECIAL LIBRARY is engaged in activities serving the technical information needs of a special clientele which departs from standard library procedures and uses nonconventional sources and methods as necessary to fill those needs. Like documentation, it is an active not a passive service. In 1961 it differs from documentation by requiring a lesser level of subject matter competence and by a tendency to use existing literature and sources. The trends detailed in the article will show that by 1980 it will be impossible to distinguish between a special library and a documentation service.

Eight years have passed since special libraries were scrutinized in depth in this journal's October 1952 issue under the editorship of H. H. Henkle.[1] It is well worth rereading today. In fact, that issue forms a second prerequisite with the Hauser-Taitel article on the implications of the 1960 Census for evaluating the present projection of the special library to 1980.[2] The concurrent stories on the large public library, the university library, documentation and serials form the most obvious overlaps, but the very real difficulty of precisely defining "special clientele" and "special library" could mean the presence of implications and portents in the others that await the reader's discovery.

Among the postwar national developments affecting special libraries are the expanding national economy illustrated by the increase in the gross national product, the increase in per cent of gross national product devoted to research and development, the increase in the number of scientists and other professionals, the swelling of graduate school enrollments, the splintering of research fields, the splintering of the literature reporting the advances in those fields, the emergence of the research report and government-backed information dissemination

Mr. Jackson is Librarian, Research Laboratories, General Motors Corporation, Warren, Michigan.

TABLE I

Research and Development
Per Cent of Sales Made Up of New Products
(Products not made four years earlier)

Industry	1960 Actual	1964 Expected
Transportation Equipment (Aircraft, Ships, Railroad)......	35%	29%
Machinery..	14	23
Chemicals..	16	20
Electrical Machinery...................................	12	16
Fabricated Metals (Including Instruments)................	17	13
Stone, Clay and Glass.................................	9	13
Food and Beverages...................................	6	12
Paper and Pulp.......................................	9	12
Autos, Trucks and Parts...............................	10	11
Nonferrous Metals....................................	8	11
Miscellaneous Manufacturing...........................	6	11
Textiles..	9	10
Iron and Steel..	5	7
Rubber..	2	7
Petroleum and Coal Products..........................	2	5
All Manufacturing....................................	10%	14%

Source: McGraw-Hill Department of Economics.

TABLE II

Research and Development Spending: 1961

	Military Products	Commercial Products
Paper and Allied Products.........................	0%	100%
Food and Kindred Products........................	0	100
Textile and Apparel..............................	1	99
Chemicals.......................................	3	97
Stone, Clay and Glass............................	3	97
Petroleum Products..............................	4	96
Machinery......................................	6	94
Rubber Products................................	9	91
Primary Metals..................................	11	89
Other Manufacturing.............................	17	83
Electrical Equipment............................	30	70
Instruments (Professional and Scientific)...........	32	68
Aircraft and Parts...............................	91	9
All Manufacturing...............................	43%	57%

Source: McGraw-Hill Department of Economics.

services to facilitate their use, the diversification of industry, the emergence of nonprofit research institutes and university-oriented industrial parks, the introduction of computers and machine methods to information problems, the renewed emphasis upon definitive subject analysis, the massive increases in copying methods and quantities, and the tendency of population and economy to group in metropolitan areas.

Based upon output per man hour, employment, and weekly hours worked, the total growth has increased at the average rate of 3.6 per cent a year (.or from some 300 billions of 1959 dollars in the immediate postwar period to some 475 billions of 1959 dollars in 1959). Of great significance is the rise in research and development spending from one per cent of the gross national product in 1947 ($2 billion) to 2.5 per cent currently (around $12 billion).[8]

The government is providing about half the funds for research and development and expending about 15 per cent of the total. Industry is spending about three-fourths of the total and providing three-eighths of the funds. Some of the results of these expenditures are shown in Table I. The split between commercial and military products of research and development spending follows in Table II.

FIGURE I

EXTENT AND TYPES
OF SCIENTIFIC CONTRIBUTIONS

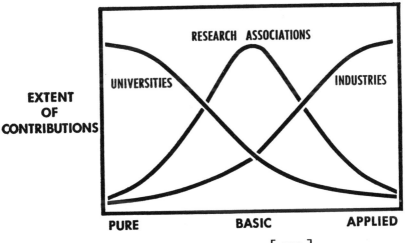

EXTENT OF CONTRIBUTIONS

RESEARCH ASSOCIATIONS

UNIVERSITIES

INDUSTRIES

PURE   BASIC   APPLIED

FIGURE II

RESEARCH CONTRIBUTION

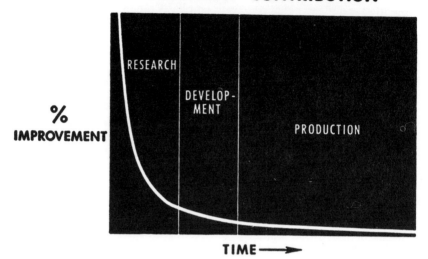

On a per technical man basis, the expenditure is in the neighborhood of $30,000–$40,000 per year. The range of size of agencies doing the research and development will vary from as few as 5 or 6 professionals to several hundreds in the larger organizations. The quickening tempo at which this work is being carried out is illustrated by the contrast between the 112 years necessary for photography to graduate from scientific discovery to a commercial product and the five years necessary for the transistor to make the same journey. Pure, basic, and applied contributions are coming in varying proportions from essentially all types of research activities (see Figure I).

In New York State alone, research and development is a billion dollar "business" (having doubled since 1954), including over 1,000 commercial and private research and testing laboratories that require the services of 30,000 professional scientists and engineers, 19,000 technicians, and 22,000 supporting personnel.[4] The efforts of these individuals could be diagrammed for research as shown in Figure II and for development as shown in Figure III.

Another illustration of the explosive growth of research and development is that the mailing lists for research reports of the U.S. National Aeronautics and Space Agency increased 35 per cent between the autumn of 1959 and that of 1960. On September 1, 1960, it had 3,174 addresses, of which 30 per cent were such important contributors as to merit the receipt of material with a military security classification of "confidential."

The U.S. Bureau of Labor Statistics reported that the civilian labor force grew by 2.6 million from October 1957 to an October 1960 total of 71.1 million. The increase for business and professional persons was from 6.6 million to 7.7 million. The U.S. National Science Foundation has identified 69,919 of the 1958 figure as scientists and engineers engaged in research and development in colleges and universities. In that same year 4,840 doctor's degrees, 16,500 master's and 77,800 bachelor's were granted in science and engineering.

Just how many special libraries there are supporting the national research and development effort and other parts of the national economy is a very good question. The first serious attempt, and one using a very broad definition of a special library, is currently underway by A. Kruzas. A part of the study is the listing of names and titles of professional persons involved in those activities, a fair indication of the number of persons presently engaged in special librar-

FIGURE III

DEVELOPMENT CONTRIBUTION

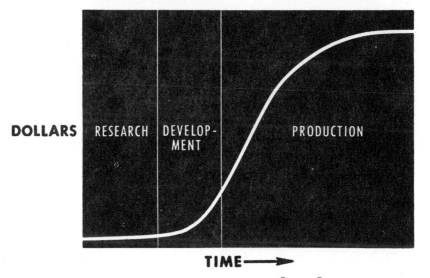

ianship. The best current estimate of 10,000 persons so engaged is lent credence by a tabulation of some 9,300 persons enrolled in library associations exclusive of elements of the A.L.A. and state associations.

The prevailing interdisciplinary team approach to the solution of research problems permitted a congressional committee to chart the interrelationships of forty-five areas of physical sciences and forty-one of life sciences.

At the same time that synthesizing has been going on, specialization of the "flea on eyelid of the elephant" type has continued apace. Both of these tendencies have been the excuse for new journals and uncounted monographs as well. Meetings ranging from casual huddles to international symposia have been recorded, and in some cases re-recorded. The research report mentioned earlier has been a favorite vehicle for this. Advances in reproduction equipment and processes have so freed these reports from the limitations of conventional publication that an essentially anarchistic state of formats exists.

A simple listing of the agencies set-up to cope with the dissemination and utilization of these materials would fill pages. (In the course of preparation of such a list for the N.A.T.O. Science Advisor this spring, over 75 defense-funded documentation agencies were uncovered.)

An announcement in the daily press by an American airplane auto-pilot manufacturer that he will enter the prefabricated housing field in Europe shows the tendency for industrial firms in the 1960's to diversify, to set sales records including narrowed profit margins, to obtain raw materials on a global basis, and to market throughout the free world. At the same time on another subject front, governmental relationships and international alliances are of a scope and complexity as to be almost beyond comprehension, where the urgent need for masses of accurate information located speedily has led to the development of an information retrieval system that can store 99 million micro-reduced documents in its memory and find any one in moments.[5]

It is even possible to be on friendly terms with computers today. In fact, publicity on a set of mathematical tables issued recently by a university press included the note that the author considered the university's computer to be his full co-author of the tables.

The trends looking toward 1980 that will affect special libraries include the following: a doubling of the gross national product; a geometric increase in research and development; an increase in the proportion of special librarians to research workers; the entrance of more technical persons into special librarianship; a broader and deeper spectrum of education for the field; an increasing tendency of the population, governmental units, and industry toward accumulation into metropolitan aggregates; major increases in college and university enrollments; the inauguration of university library service to nearby "research parks"; the differentiation of public library service to individuals from that rendered to organizations; continued growth of government-related informational agencies with pioneering responsibilities. Then will follow a picture of the major functions—acquisition, processing, dissemination, and utilization—of the special library as they will exist in 1980.

Hauser and Taitel state that the gross national product will be doubled by 1980, a projection which implies that the people will be able to afford the kind of library service they need. This projection would mean that the 1980 gross national product would approximate 1,000 billions of 1959 dollars, as compared with 1970 projections of other authorities varying from $724 billion to $837 billion. Hauser and Taitel see a 37 per cent increase of the population in these 20 years to 246 million persons. N.I.C.B. points out that these millions will include a significant increase in the number of young men—and more jobs will require higher skills. They project the capital required by 1970 to be between 892 and 1,023 billions of 1959 dollars, averaging out between $11,600 and $13,300 per worker. It is predicted by Resources for the Future, Inc., that all energy needed for the 1975 gross national product of $857 billion can be produced domestically and at essentially today's costs (in constant dollars).[6] This estimate excludes any production by atomic-energy means.

It is seen that by 1969 four per cent of the gross national product will be devoted to research and development, or about $28 billion (N.I.C.B.), of which the U.S. National Science Foundation recently said that $8.2 billion would be needed for the development of scientific brain power. At the same rates of increase to 1980, the respective totals would be $40 billion for research and development and $12 billion for scientific education (equal to the total for all research and development in 1959).

There is ample evidence in such works as Bogue [7] and the New York Metropolitan Region Study [8] to support the Hauser-Taitel predictions on the tendency toward "Metropolitanization" by 1980 of the population, governmental units, and industry. Looking still further ahead, J. P. Pickard has predicted that by the year 2000, 85 per cent of the country's 320 million people will live in urban areas. This is the most important phenomenon for special libraries, both because of their identification with companies (as pointed out by Henkle in the issue mentioned earlier), and because of the high correlation between metropolitan areas and Special Libraries Association membership addresses. Further, that the New York Metropolitan Region ("one-tenth of a nation") is uniquely important to S.L.A. is shown by the fact that it has consistently been the residence of 25-29 per cent of the membership in the last decade, and no major change in this proportion is to be seen.

In her presentations, Miss Winifred Sewell, S.L.A. President 1960–61, used the figure of 30,000 special librarians being needed for 1970. This seems a most reasonable prediction in view of the increase in the proportion of special librarians to research workers that will be dictated by the greatly increased volume of technical literature, the progressive need for more detailed information, and the compressed time cycles faced by research programs.

The greater compilations of information work will increase its stature and will bring more subject matter people into the field. The new study by Cohan and Craven [9] advances the proposition that there will be a profession of science information specialists. An advisory panel to the study lists twelve duties of the specialists as administering; locating materials; selecting materials; acquiring materials; descriptive cataloging; subject analyzing, which includes classifying/subject headings and indexing; abstracting and/or annotating; performing reference work; literature searching/bibliography; transmitting and copying; translating; and converting into machinable form. Other newer elements include developing of information systems, investigating of machine applications, information interpreting, researching with information, and information scouting.

This study recommends a liberal education with a major in science and a development of language competence. It outlines a new curriculum for a graduate school of science information specialists, special librarians, linguists, and the administrators who evolve from one of the three preceding. The curriculum which it recommends looks very similar to the heart of today's library school curriculum with a strong emphasis upon subject bibliography, inadequate attention to abstracting and cataloging, rather less emphasis upon administration, plus more work in machine methods than the usual library school offers. An additional element is reports preparation and publication.

Cohan and Craven see the possibility of two doctoral programs, one in "systems development," which could be rephrased as the application of operations research principles to information problems, and one in "literature science," which appears similar to present library school programs with emphasis upon reference.

It should be pointed out that many of the assertions of this study would fit into the framework of a complete technical information service. Such an activity would utilize records of *past* findings to indi-

FIGURE IV

A TECHNICAL INFORMATION SERVICE

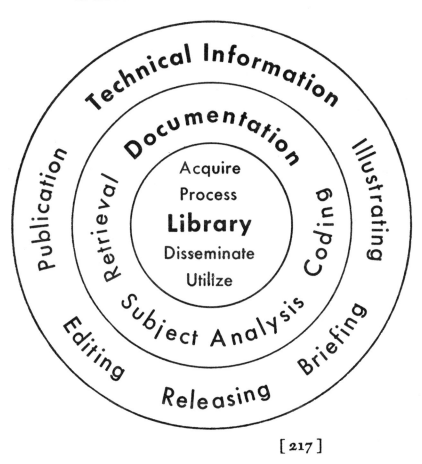

cate *present* situation and likely routes toward *future* goals. The elements of such a service could be diagrammed as in Figure IV.

It seems clear that there will be a spectrum of individuals attracted to the special library field with all gradiations between

pure librarian→pure documentalist→pure subject specialist

and that in addition to formal programs such as described in the Cohan-Craven study, there will need to be short courses on campus and intensive courses off campus for indoctrination in depth and on site.

This plan would necessitate task forces of instructors and here the educational experience of computer manufacturers could well be drawn upon. Their programs cover all levels of sophistication from the one-day session through two-week residences at their home office for customers through managing of international symposia. The task force mentioned above could follow a circuit among the research activities carrying the "gospel" of efficient literature service and assisting in its realization. One educational function of the task force would be to assist community colleges in preparing technicians for entry into the subprofessional level of special librarianship. They would also be able to earmark individuals with such capability that should be encouraged to undertake formal residence study in special librarianship, perhaps on leave from the employing organization. The feedback of these task forces to their home university should insure the vitality and pertinence of the residence instruction.

If the 30,000 special librarians of 1970 have swollen to 60,000 by 1980, that total would equal the number of scientists and engineers in research and development in colleges and universities in 1958. It does give one pause. Even if this figure is rejected as unrealistic, it does dramatize the urgent need for a quantum step forward in library education.

D. B. Baker's predictions on the growth of chemical literature [10] point out that it is unrealistic to expect continuous exponential growth indefinitely. He notes that "With existing tools improved and new information services, documentation workers will have relatively little difficulty in handling effectively the increasing scientific information over this decade [1970], provided the support in manpower and finances is adequate." [10] It might be pointed out that the last phrase is particularly unhelpful because the same statement could have been made by the supervising architect of the pyramids in a memorandum to the reigning Pharaoh.

Critically important in the next decade is the expansion of effort in the application of computers to information retrieval problems.[10] This increase will result in the need for a greater number of special librarians rather than fewer. Widespread experience with data processing installations is that, as the complexity of the equipment secured increases, more and more highly skilled persons are required to effectively utilize the capacity. In view of the preceding, the assertion is made that there will not be fewer than 40,000 special librarians in 1980 and not more than 60,000.

Special librarianship can expect that the next two decades will see the rise of many distinguished special librarians in the college and university field. Of necessity there will be more departmental libraries and those of higher caliber because of the enrollments mentioned elsewhere and the introduction of research earlier in the academic life and its continuation past the doctoral level.

In 1980 there will be university-managed and industry-sponsored special libraries that are arising and will arise in the vicinity of the principal universities. Their advanced use of new methods of bibliographic control, information retrieval, and data exchange will make their operations indistinguishable from those of special libraries of outstanding profit-making organizations in the same subject fields.

As all research relies increasingly upon the literature, if only because of skyrocketing costs of physical equipment, then the library service available to the research park must be fully equivalent to all other advantages of locating in the university community, or the total purpose for locating in that environment will not be realized.

Significant assessments will be made on the participating organization in research parks not only for the financing of day-to-day operations of facilities, especially set up for their benefit, but also for the total enrichment of the university library resources. Research report collections and materials information centers can no longer be orphans, but must be integrated into the overall university library program. While the accepted participation by university libraries in union list of serials type projects and similar *external* cooperative ventures are commendable, equally urgent is the *internal* union list of all informational materials, research reports or whatever, that are physically located in the university environment. Practices developed by special librarians at the universities must be seriously examined by the library administration as to their applicability to the total information inventory of the university.

Public library service to individuals will be strongly affected by the metropolitanization factors mentioned repeatedly in this issue. There will be a steadily diminishing influx of readers into subject departments. Yet here is the heart of the vital special librarianship segment of public librarianship. Services to organizations, however, are going to increase exponentially.

A telling survey made in the subject department of the Detroit Public Library between November 22 and December 22, 1960, showed that 1,288 telephone calls were received from organizations and special librarians during which 701 reference questions were asked and the loan of 1,458 items requested. During the same period only 122 requests were made by personal visits of representatives of organizations. During this survey a total of 241 organizations used the library, 22 per cent of which were from outside the city limits. Further, 129 of these organizations were not included on the standing list of 400 entities having company card privileges.[11]

A proposal is currently being considered by a fund-granting organization for a demonstration project on total information service to an industrialized metropolitan area. It seems so typical of what will be in existence in 1970–80 that it is considered here in some detail. The specific aim of the project would be to create a metropolitan intelligence facility which would (1) provide the ultimate in the location, evaluation, and dissemination of factual materials, (2) foster the maximum utilization of this facility by present and potential users, (3) prove by demonstration the overall value of this facility to the individual, to his organization, and to the community, (4) determine the actual costs of establishing and maintaining such a facility and formulate an equitable financial basis for its continuation by its participating parts, and (5) secure continuing and active support from its participants and beneficiaries.

Within the framework of the metropolitan library there would be a special staff of highly selected, competent reference and literature specialists including a project director, a field specialist, experienced reference librarians, and clerical assistance. They would make total use of existing resources of the public library. That is, they would identify and locate all possible research tools within the library and in the area so that they may be utilized in reference and interloan work; establish lines of communication with major reference facilities outside the immediate area as a source of loan and photocopies; develop specialized informational files and union lists to augment or to bridge gaps in existing sources; create a current file of individual specialists, both within the area and out, who because of their knowledge and/or experience are able to provide information which because of currency or rarity is not readily available; issue a periodic list of library and area acquisitions and/or a bulletin which would function to keep all participants informed of current developments; and investigate and develop newer techniques of information retrieval so as to speed reference requests.

This special staff would augment area resources by the identification of specific needs and by the initiation of remedial procurement and would identify specific and general needs of the library and of the area by constant monitoring and analysis of incoming requests and of their disposition; establish a search and selection procedure for acquisitions which will supplement that of the library and which will endeavor to anticipate area requirements; and would create a joint acquisition procedure whereby unnecessary duplication of expensive or little-used materials might be avoided but which would assure full use of these materials to the total area.

Determining by consultation with experts reasonable and realistic costs for all levels and types of service and developing patterns for adequately and equitably assessing these costs, this staff would establish by approved actuarial methods realistic cost data which would permit the project to be self-sustaining.

By continuous interaction with users, the special staff would survey in depth their real and potential needs and motivate partial- or non-users to full participation. An experienced Field Specialist would determine by survey techniques the necessary and potential service required by individual participants and would establish other useful lines of contact. The value and use of the project to create larger area participation would be demonstrated to the partial- or non-using organizations.

In support of the project would be a public library with one million volumes in ten subject departments, another one million volumes in two university libraries, untold open literature in 55 special libraries, and a grand total of 181 professional librarians. Such a project would do a total information job for small organizations and cooperate with and support special libraries of the largest organizations by the effective marshalling of the total metropolitan-area information sources. In view of this study and related competence, it is clear that by 1980 services to organizations which are "nucleated" about central research project offices of metropolitan area public libraries, while tax supported, will be supplemented by reimbursement for services rendered.

Pioneering in machine systems and formats beyond the financial resources of others will be the prime contribution of government-related information agencies to special librarianship to 1980.

The acquisition function in 1980 will feature cooperative procurement of materials on an industry-wide basis and metropolitan-area basis, and will include purchase of machine tapes, raw data tables, card decks, and massive numbers of photocopies.

Cooperative efforts on the metropolitan-area, industry-wide, and subject-wide basis of conventional materials will characterize the processing function in 1980 with considerable increase in at-source processing including even some proprietary materials on a reimbursable basis.

Utilization of "prepackaged" mats and tapes with readily-inserted local modifications will characterize the dissemination function in 1980. Additional steps will be taken assisting the dissemination medium in approaching that ideal in effectiveness—"man-to-man." [12]

The utilization function of 1980 will include remote consultation of central metropolitan-area or industry-wide information sources. There will be utilization of more transitory and marginal information and exploitation of unique local resources.

By 1980, special librarianship will be in its 71st year as a profession (or 82nd if based upon the founding of the Medical Library Association). It will have absorbed many elements from documentation. A merger will have taken place, but the surviving member will not need a broader charter than the S.L.A. objective of "Putting Knowledge to Work." It can look back proudly on a past filled with accomplishment, innovations, and leadership and forward to a full partnership on the team conquering ignorance, and misunderstanding.

References

1. Henkle, H. H., ed.: Current Trends in Special Libraries. *Library Trends,* 1:169-255, Oct. 1952.

2. Hauser, P. M., and Taitel, M.: Population Trends—Prologue to Library Development. *Library Trends,* 10:10-67, July 1961.

3. National Industrial Conference Board, Inc.: *Economic Growth in the 1960's; Prerequisites, Potentials, Problems* . . . New York, The National Industrial Conference Board [c1960]. 33 p.

4. New York (State): *Directory of Industrial Research Laboratories in New York State, 1960.* Albany, 1960. 280 p.

5. *Wall Street Journal,* July 12, 1961, p. 28.

6. Resources for the Future, Inc.: *Energy in the American Economy, 1850-1975, an Economic Study of its History and Prospects.* Baltimore, The Johns Hopkins Press, [1960], pp. 6-7.

7. Bogue, D. J.: *The Population of the United States.* . . . Glencoe, Ill., Free Press, c1959. 873 p.

8. Vernon, R.: *Metropolis, 1985, an Interpretation of the Findings of the New York Metropolitan Region Study.* Cambridge, Mass., Harvard University Press, 1960. 252 p.

9. Cohan, L., and Craven, K.: *Science Information Personnel.* New York, Science Information, 1961. 74 p.

10. Baker, D. B.: Growth of Chemical Literature Past, Present, and Future. *Chemical & Engineering News,* 39:78-81, July 17, 1961.

11. Information Retrieval. *Chemical & Engineering News,* 39:102-114, July 17, 1961.

12. Conferences with Katherine G. Harris, Director of Reference Services, and R. E. Runser, Chief, Technology Department of the Detroit Public Library, Detroit, Michigan, in January 1961.

Documentation

ALLEN KENT

IT HAS BEEN SAID that *documentation* can be defined as *librarianship in high gear*. The processes, or unit operations, of documentation may be considered to coincide completely or partially with those of librarianship, depending upon how narrowly or broadly a particular documentalist or librarian views his field.

A 1956 definition of documentation certainly reflects this viewpoint: "the group of techniques necessary for the ordered presentation, organization, and communication of recorded specialized knowledge, in order to give maximum accessibility and utility to the information contained." [1]

But despite evidence to the contrary, the author is convinced that the gap between documentation and library practice is narrowing and that the definition that in 1956 clearly distinguished *documentation* from *librarianship* no longer serves as well as it was once thought to. The narrowing of the gap is being caused by many forces. Two of the major ones seem to be these: (1) Many librarians have been awakening to the almost lost opportunity to serve the dynamic information requirements that they spurned for more than a decade. The ability of the documentalists to attract financial support and respectable salaries has caused many librarians to re-examine their stand and to begin to exploit in their day-to-day activities the fruits of documentation research. (2) The maturing of the documentation field has started to purge itself of the intemperates who, although recognizing the need for more dynamic information services, did not always take into account the well-learned lessons of librarianship in designing and operating systems for exploiting recorded knowledge. The more successful documentation systems have sound basic principles that are in common with those of sound library operations.

The author is Professor of Library Science, and Associate Director, Center for Documentation and Communication Research, School of Library Science, Western Reserve University, Cleveland, Ohio.

[224]

Of significant interest has been the increase in the periodical and report literature, to the point where, in the sciences alone, it is estimated that between 500,000 and 1,300,000 items are to be published in 1961. This number has been increasing dramatically with no sign of letup. The problems of selection and acquisition [2] of this massive outpouring of literature are impressive.

Libraries acquire materials by communicating with a supplier who either maintains a stock of documents or is willing to prepare copies of them. The techniques of ordering, follow-up, payment of invoices, and checking in of materials received are functions that parallel those conducted in the handling of any commodity in the business community. As would be expected, various types of data processing machines have been applied usefully to facilitate the burden of record keeping in connection with the acquisition function.[3]

More dramatic and more numerous developments [4] have taken place in documentation with regard to the subject analysis of materials—some appropriate and useful, others inappropriate, naive, and not useful. These developments may be categorized under indexing, classifying, abstracting, and processing of full texts.

Traditionally, the subject indexing operation has involved the selection of words or ideas from a graphic record on the basis of well-defined rules; indexing has been carried out in order to facilitate the identification or selection of desired documents after they have been stored. As in any form of content analysis, some value judgments are made in the selection of aspects of subject matter as important for inclusion in an index (or in omitting aspects of subject matter as unimportant).

The availability of computers and computer-like devices which can perform repetitive tasks effectively and economically has led to the application of machines for subject indexing purposes. Examples of machine applications are as follows:

(1) The concordance is an alphabetic index of *words* in a book in exact context. No discrimination is exercised in preparing this type of index. Each word that is present in the text is an index entry. Therefore, the decisions that must be made in conducting such an indexing operation are not very difficult and can be performed very well by machines.[5]

(2) The Key Word in Context (KWIC) Index (or Permutation Index) similarly requires little in the way of subject matter knowl-

edge and therefore is amenable to mechanization.[6, 7] The KWIC index is prepared by cyclic permutations of words in which each "substantive" term is brought to a predetermined position and alphabetized. This type of index is very much akin to the concordance; however, its applications have been limited to the preparation of KWIC indexes based on titles of papers only.

It should be obvious that the mere machine manipulation of words in this way does not increase the usefulness of the words as reference points in search. Therefore, if a conventional index which uses as entries only the substantive words in a title would not be considered useful, the use of computers to prepare the KWIC index will not result in a more useful product.

(3) Uniterm indexing, as described a number of years ago, involves the analysis of contents of graphic records in terms of key words which represent the content of the record that is being indexed.[8] These key words include not only single common English words, but also serial numbers and other symbols, if they are found in the text, and if, in the judgment of the indexer, they represent the content of the record.

In pursuing rules of "word" indexing, as in other word indexing procedures described earlier, one should recognize that certain assumptions are being made, primarily that the *user* of such an index is sufficiently familiar with the subject matter of his search that he can provide the control over the words used in the Uniterm index that the indexer has been instructed to overlook (or was not instructed to take into account).

(4) Controlled indexing, as opposed to "word" indexing, implies a careful selection of terminology used in indexes in order to avoid, to the extent possible, the scattering of related subjects under different headings.

Although proponents of indexing approaches to exploiting the literature believe that the most attractive feature of the index is its ability to identify specific aspects of information that may be discussed in a document, there is likewise a desire to combine some of the advantages of classification approaches, i.e., to group related subjects.

Another method for controlling the subjects chosen during analysis is based upon the frequency of occurrence of key words in running text—those occurring most frequently being considered, prima facie, to be most significant for analysis of the texts. This type of analysis may be conducted by keypunching the entire text of a document so that it may be scanned by machine, and compiling statistics as to the frequency of occurrence of various key words.

An independent variable in controlled indexing is the language used to record the results of analysis of graphic records. In many ways this variable is completely analogous to the control of subjects chosen. In the latter, various means are used to limit the subject matter that is made explicit during indexing. This may be considered analogous to providing an index with a special "point of view."

Independent of the control of subjects chosen, or "point of view" of the indexer, it is considered helpful to regularize the manner in which index entries are expressed. Some of these methods are identical with those used to control choice of subjects (the subject authority list).

Another control technique that has been used in modern documentation systems is the "role indicator," or "role factors" or "role directors." These techniques have been used in various machine systems and are quite analogous to the "modifications" used with index entries in conventional retrieval systems. These indicators are useful for limiting the area of meaning of the index entry, according to the "role" that this entry plays in a particular context.[9-11]

The major developments in the area of *classification* during the past decade or so have been concerned with the multidimensional classification. This type of classification involves the characterization of each graphic record from more than one point of view. This classification can be accomplished for the physical placement of records only when more than one copy is available for filing in more than one location in the classification system.

However, many classification systems are employed as guides to a physical collection of records, as in a classified catalog, where copies of catalog cards, each one representing a graphic record, are filed within the classification system. This system makes it convenient to have as many cards per record available as there are "dimensions" to the classification.

Although this type of classification has been very popular in Europe, there have been few applications of multidimensional classifications, such as the Universal Decimal Classification, in the United States. One of the multidimensional classification systems that have been proposed recently has been in the field of education media.[12]

Perhaps the documentation activity that has spread most extensively in the past two decades has been abstracting. Traditionally, an abstract has been considered "that which comprises or concentrates in itself the essential qualities of a larger thing, or of several things"—a summary of a publication or article accompanied by an adequate bibliographical description to enable the publication or article to be traced. In recent documentation literature, it is possible to identify three types of abstracts: (1) traditional abstracts, (2) extracts, and (3) telegraphic abstracts.

The *traditional abstracts* are of two general types: descriptive and informative. The *descriptive abstract* embodies a general statement of the nature and scope of a document; it is not pretended that this type of abstract can serve as a substitute for reading the original document; it merely presents several clues as to whether or not the information being sought might be contained in the original record. The *informative abstract,* on the other hand, has the purpose of presenting (concisely) information of probable high significance contained in the original record and in the ideal case to obviate the necessity of referring to the original.

The three functions that traditional abstracts have served are (a) *current awareness*: to aid a reader in keeping informed concerning new developments and in acquiring new technical information; (b) *reference*: to provide a back file of accumulated information which may be consulted as required; and (c) *indexing* (or *classifying*): to serve as a basis for indexing a record; the abstract is prepared after a decision has been made regarding the important aspects of a record. This same analysis can be used to provide those important aspects that should be incorporated into an index or other searching tool.

An *extract* is analogous to an abstract in that it represents what is considered the important subject matter of a graphic record that has been selected for quotation. It is felt by some that the use of direct quotations or extracts from a record provides more effective service to a reader than does an abstract.

Extracts may be selected by human analysts or by the application of machine techniques. When machines have been used for extracting, the resulting product has been called an "auto-abstract."[18]

The techniques used by humans to prepare extracts are subjective and involve the exercising of judgment by an analyst in order to determine which portion(s) of a document is of sufficient potential significance to warrant recording. When a machine is used for extracting, the entire text of a record is converted to machine-readable form and is scanned by a digital computer. When these methods are applied, it is assumed that the frequency and distribution of key words in the text can be used as the basis for determining the relative significance of sentences in text. In accord with this assumption, the sentences which are highest in "significance" (as determined by their containing the greatest frequency of key words) are printed out to produce an extract (or "auto-abstract").

A *telegraphic abstract* is a detailed index to a graphic record.[9-11] It is composed of (1) significant words selected from the articles; (2) code symbols called "role indicators" which fit the selected words into context; and (3) punctuation symbols which separate and group the words and role indicators into various units in somewhat the same fashion as conventional punctuation does.

The telegraphic abstract differs from a regular index in that: (a) it contains more words; (b) it has a prescribed arrangement along quite different lines; (c) it is, when abstracters have finished it, still only a semi-finished product. The finished product is a reel of tape with the information, which the abstracters have partly furnished, translated into a computer code ready for searching by machine.

Telegraphic abstracting, then, is a method for recording important characteristics of information contained in documents so that the information may be further processed for machine input where it will serve the function of an index enabling the document to be identified by machine in answer to requests for information. The design of the telegraphic abstract is part of an overall logic which also dictates the design of the code into which the words are encoded and the design of the strategy and program by which the information is searched. The telegraphic abstract, the encoded terms, and the search program taken together comprise a machine information retrieval system. The purpose of the telegraphic abstract is to provide "input" to the machine in a consistent and predictable form so that the machine can be programmed to search for certain predictable forms of information within this input.

Another "analysis" technique involves the "processing" of a full text for retrieval purposes. In general, this type of processing implies that certain subjects and points of view have been selected from the text by human or machine analysis in order to record decisions as to what in the text of a document is of greatest probable importance for retrieval purposes.

However, some research is now in progress which has as its aim to record for retrieval purposes essentially everything that is available in the full text of a source document. The rationale behind this approach is that the indexing policies required to serve all potential needs are so diverse that essentially only the recording of an entire document would provide adequate services.

It should be recognized that the approaches to recording of all texts for retrieval purposes make certain assumptions that should be made explicit:

(1) That the text will be "read" by machine, or that the text will be made available by publishers in machine-readable form (e.g., monotype tape). It is not yet evident that the full range of type fonts, styles, and reproduction techniques will permit effective and economical programs for machine recognition of text. Otherwise, it is necessary to "keyboard" all text into machine-readable form in order to make it amenable for further processing.

(2) That it will be economical to search by machines the tremendous full texts of documents produced even in restricted fields, without attempts to "compress" the available material by a "probabilistic" approach to analysis of the document.

(3) That most questions can be analyzed with sufficient precision, that a precise selection of matching information in the full text of a document will provide useful results. It is anticipated that the major problem to be faced is that "normalization" or syntactical analysis of running text by machine may well yield answers to questions from trivial mentions of a "subject" as well as to those which are more significant.

Also, it is tacitly assumed that requests for searches will be based upon *recognition memory* rather than *recall memory*. In the former, a request for a search is based upon the way in which the text has been recorded in the remembered record. In the latter, a request for a search is based upon recalling some subject that is of interest, whether or not it may have been seen before. In this latter case, the resources of natural language are sufficiently great that the alternate clues which would have to be provided are sometimes staggering.[14]

Another area of documentation development has been with regard to the storage of documents. This area has benefited from the wide availability of inexpensive office copying machines, which has resulted in the ability to store single copies of documents, with extra copies for demand distribution being prepared as required.

The larger centers either have used similar approaches or have converted the document collections to microform, with a variety of techniques being available for the preparation of disposable copies or of additional generations of microform for perusal at distant locations with suitable reading devices.

Another documentation operation that has been the subject of a considerable amount of activity in the documentation field is the identification of documents from collections and delivery of documents.[15]

The basic developments have resulted from the following considerations. Retrieval systems—especially machine systems—have been developed or are under consideration because it is "impractical," inconvenient, or too expensive to locate desired records from a file by other means. Usually the "size" of the file (as measured by the number of records, depth of analysis of each record, and complexity of subject matter covered) has reached the point where an existing retrieval system is not expected to provide adequate service in response to the average inquiries. When such a situation exists, it may be assumed that the number of records being incorporated into the file exceeds the ability of a potential user of the information it contains to read and to remember the contents of every record that is incorporated. When this situation has been reached, then for any record that is to be analyzed for retrieval purposes, it cannot be assumed that a person who may later want to see the record will have read it previously or even have seen it before. In these cases, requests for records containing desired information will be based upon clues, subjects, or verbalization of subjects which are probably drawn from the *requester's* background and *not necessarily from the text of records stored in the file.*

Now, when graphic records are to be stored away for potential retrieval at a later time, two decisions must be made by the analyst of the record:

1. Which aspects of the record are of probable importance to potential users?

2. How should these aspects be expressed in the retrieval system so that there will be a good probability of matching the way potential users will think of and express their requests?

The first decision is discussed earlier. The second decision is a particularly difficult one to make because an analyst reading a document is tempted to use words found in that document to record the results of his analysis. However, as was pointed out in previous discussion, these words are not necessarily those which are most likely to be used in information requests. So the analyst (or designer of codes, or subject authority lists) is faced with the task of providing a number of clues with regard to the subject matter of the document in an attempt anticipate *any* way in which a searcher's point of view might be expressed.

Now, how is the analyst to predict which words will come to a searcher's mind when he desires information on some subject?

The following approaches may be considered:

1. If the decision is made to operate the retrieval activity as a "closed" system, this relieves the analyst of the responsibility of predicting which words will be used by "outsiders" in searching the file. All searches must then be performed by operating personnel of the retrieval system who are in a position to interpret requests in terms of the language used by analysts.

2. If the decision is made to operate the retrieval activity as an "open" system, attempts must be made to control the use of terminology in one of two ways: (a) Analysts and systems designers may feel that they are in sufficiently good intellectual contact with their potential clientele to permit them to predict terminology that will likewise be chosen by their clientele in formulating questions. (b) It is possible to submit a potential clientele to association tests, which would provide some basis for using terminology according to its probable significance to information systems users.

The associations of words to other words, whether predicted by systems designers or derived from empirical or experimental data, are based partially upon personal points of view with regard to the significance of words and partially upon the inherent meaning of words.

The developments with regard to the identification of documents from collections have involved the use of subject authority lists, glossaries, classifications, thesauri, and semantic and other code dictionaries. In their development these various tools for controlling the scatter in meaning of terminology during searching operations have much in common. The first steps involve the collection and definition of the terminology expected to be encountered in the searching system. The resultant "language" may differ with regard to symbolization but may have many features in common—particularly the concepts covered by the "language."

Various devices have been used for identifying relevant documents in response to questions. When a question is asked of an information retrieval system the language of the original inquirer must be interpreted in terms of the language of the system. With the newer retrieval systems involving the recording of more and more detail relating to the contents of documents, there appears to be more advantage to systematizing the methods of exploiting the system—the strategy of searching—so that consistent results may be assured even when different users attempt to operate the system.

It is suggested that some of the principles of selecting a strategy of searching may be common to various retrieval systems. The steps to be taken are (1) analysis of the question with regard to aspects of importance and desired relationships among the aspects; (2) analysis of the alternate logical configurations of the question which would lead to optimum results.

The results of a search, regardless of retrieval systems, are being presented in the form of sets of (1) pertinent bibliographic references, (2) abstracts, or (3) full documents, which are presumed to be pertinent to the question. The means used to deliver responses are dependent upon the means used for storage of documents, as discussed earlier.

And now to review documentation activities of the past decade. The various literature searching and documentation developments, although masquerading under differing labels, have at least a single common purpose—to facilitate the communication of knowledge across barriers of time, space, and language. A subsidiary common purpose involves the desire to conduct in the most economical and effective manner the various unit operations involved in achieving this communication.

In attempting to achieve a balance between economy and effectiveness, one must weigh the importance of "custom" processing of the literature to take into account the peculiar point of view of a particular requirement, as against the economy of using a "standard" processing which is performed by a "centralized" organization. The more complete the standard processing, the less is the advantage for a "custom" processing to be performed.

For searching systems, there are usually required an analysis of the document and the selection of various aspects of probable interest and their recording in the form of abstracts, index entries, subject headings, and classification headings. It has not been considered feasible during the selection process to take into account most of the potential special points of view from which the document might be of interest during retrieval operations. However, some of the machine searching systems show promise of taking into account a sufficiently wide spectrum of potential needs that agreements on a common language, or the establishment of standards for interconvertibility among various machine languages, appear to be in order.[16] The potential savings in time, effort, and money in avoiding the unnecessary reprocessing of documents, or in avoiding the effort involved in the development of minor alterations of already existing systems, appear to warrant a determined effort to achieve agreements.

The possibilities of developing a common language for machine searching offer attractive economies if automatic abstracting or indexing should prove to yield sufficiently promising results for certain requirements. The use of a common language would then permit the translation and also the indexing of the same text with only a single scanning.

Now let us consider documentation in relation to demography. The study of demographic trends reveals many cross currents that may influence documentation developments. As would be expected, these trends reveal the concentration of documentation centers, public libraries, and special information centers in areas of high population concentration, where they can serve the largest numbers of individuals and organizations. However, individuals and organizations, although tending to concentrate in certain areas, also decentralize in many cases.

In order for one to discern meaningful patterns, one way in which the documentation situation may be viewed is to consider the postures of large and small organizations and individuals in areas of high and low population concentration.[17]

The large organizations tend toward broader, interdisciplinary interests. Their requirements are rather broad and encompass various subject specialties, from specific as well as from interdisciplinary points of view. Almost no organization, regardless of size, has the economic resources to acquire and to process the total available literature that will be of possible interest. However, it can establish a special library to acquire and process the core literature in the subjects of probable interest and rely upon the resources of public libraries, universities, and other special libraries which are generally available in areas of high population concentration.

In low population areas, there is less of a tendency for large public and university libraries to be readily available; nor are there many special libraries that can serve to backstop the considerable requirements for literature. Therefore, these organizations are faced with the alternative of building up literature resources in anticipation of possible needs, or of relying upon distant special information centers for demand service in response to specific questions. Examples of reliance upon both of these alternatives may be found.

Another matter to be studied is the posture of small organizations in areas of high population concentration. Although the smaller organizations tend to have more restricted subject interests, their documentation needs are not more restricted. This is the case because they are confronted with the same massive number of publications, and they cannot afford to devote effort to the perusal of this material and the selection of material of possible or probable interest. Since the resources of these organizations are limited, they usually cannot establish an effective special library and *must* rely upon the local resources available in their area, backstopped by the special documentation centers throughout the country.

If we now consider the situation of small organizations in areas of low population concentration, we can discern that these organizations are faced with especially difficult problems, since their documentation needs usually cannot be satisfied by resources and services in their immediate vicinity. And since their resources do not permit the buildup of sizable collections, they are generally forced to obtain service from distantly located documentation centers and libraries. Although their requirements for service may not be frequent, their need for effective and rapid aid is nonetheless critical.

Another situation to consider is the posture of individuals in areas of high population concentration. The problem of the individual who approaches the mounting literature is perhaps the most devastating. He is faced with the dilemma of (1) finding the total literature of potential interest, (2) being unable to acquire and process for his own use only a small fraction of the available literature, or (3) being unable to afford the fees of those special documentation centers when requiring service.

The public and university libraries are the sole source of sizable collections for the individual. However, the individual usually does not have sufficient time available to devote to the task of attempting to exploit these collections. Therefore, he must usually be content with a superficial penetration of the available literature.

Last, let us look at the posture of individuals in areas of low population concentration. Here the situation is almost hopeless. The absence of adequate library resources in his vicinity and the lack of sufficient financial resources to permit travel to distant centers or to pay the fees of special documentation centers usually force the individual investigator into organizational situations or into an urban area.

Summary

It may be evident from the foregoing that the trends in the documentation field are these: (1) for the published literature to increase in quantity and complexity as a consequence of the expected continuous expansion of research activity; (2) for the need for effective exploitation of the literature to increase because of the increasing pressures for avoidance of repetition of research effort; [18-21] (3) for the demands on documentation centers to increase because of the decreasing ability of individuals and organizations to cope with the literature on an individual basis; (4) for the continuing breakdown of all but mechanized methods of information retrieval.

The ability to record information on magnetic tape, punched cards, and punched tape, and to produce copies of these media automatically and at low cost represents a revolution in the documentation field as significant and with as far-reaching consequences as those of the invention of printing.[22] Thus is provided the opportunity to establish a new type of library, or a new aspect of traditional librarianship, which will make possible the collection and storage of analyzed and encoded published literature in a form ready for mechanized exploitation. The new types of libraries will be the customers of, or subscribers to, the centralized processing of this "machine feed." This centralized processing agency will acquire, analyze, and encode the scientific literature received from the entire world.[23]

The processor of "machine feed" can operate under the direct control of a central agency, or independently, with permissive cooperation, through a coordinating agency. The same would be true for libraries of other information centers. In any case, the character of the new information retrieval system should be analogous to that of the Bell Telephone System, which provides a communication network for the entire country, without a central office through which all communications must pass; rather, each point of the network is a potential substitute for a central office in that all the facilities of the entire system are available upon demand at any one point.

The analogy for a mechanized analysis-encoding-searching system for science is depicted in Figure 1. This configuration of activities provides the economic and technical advantages of centralization, but also permits any degree of decentralization that may be desirable in a particular locality or for a particular subject field.

It is the conclusion here that this type of central and coordinating agency will be in the future and will provide the next major alleviation of documentation problems.

The main function of this agency will be to conduct a continuing program of thorough acquisition and analysis of the world's literature and to make the resulting material available in many forms to a wide variety of users.

Some of the major services contemplated are charted in Figure 2. Specifically, these services involve (1) searching the accumulating machine record to provide at regular intervals current information on specific questions that are of continuing interest to subscribers; (2) searching the store of machine record retrospectively to provide information on a specific problem or make available the raw material for a review of the literature or other compendia; (3) copying of the machine record and transmittal to a local installation for search and other exploitation; (4) providing copies of abstracts and source documents for special subject fields in order to "stock" special libraries with the materials required to serve their clientele; (5) serving as a proving ground for the testing of new documentation and bibliographic methods, and promoting in other appropriate ways the improvement of the exploitation of recorded information through research.

In order to provide and utilize the machine record required for the information facility of the future, the following processing steps will be required:

(1) Acquisition of materials: selection and acquisition of source documents, or informative abstracts suitable for reprocessing.

(2) Analysis: review, by subject specialties, of the source documents or abstracts, for the preparation of stylized abstracts. (Alter-

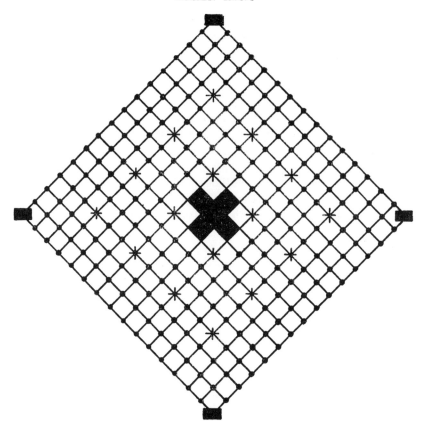

FIGURE 1

MECHANIZED INFORMATION SERVICE NETWORK

◇   geographic area to be served

•   area service and processing stations

+   regional repositories and service centers

▬   regional processing centers by subject fields

✖   headquarters coordinating operation

FIGURE 2
SPECIFIC SERVICES OFFERED BY
MECHANIZED INFORMATION
SYSTEM

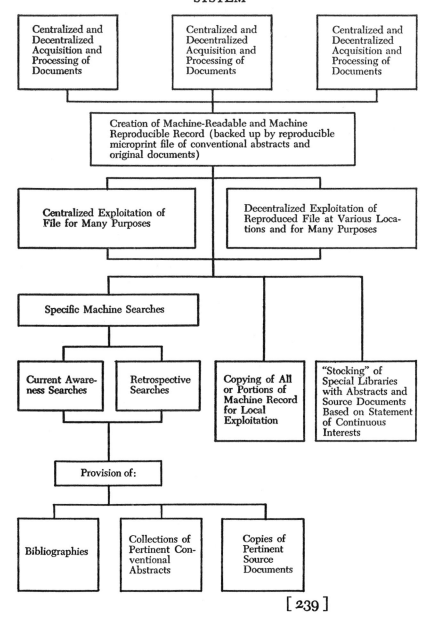

nate, compatible methods of analysis, possibly based upon machine processing of source text, could be substituted if this proved to be an economical and technically feasible procedure.)

(3) Encoding: transformation of the stylized abstract into code, using automatic procedures. This code must provide a ready means for controlling synonyms and partial synonyms, and for identifying the inherent meaning of terms used in the system.

(4) Recording: transfer of encoded abstracts (or other form of compatible document analysis) to a machine record (e.g., magnetic tape, punched tape, punched cards).

(5) Storing: microstorage of conventional abstracts and source documents for each item processed.

(6) Reference services:
  (a) receipt and analysis of questions;
  (b) programming and operation of searching device;
  (c) selecting and copying of abstract or source document to subscriber.

(7) Auxiliary services:
  (a) copying of machine records or searchable file for delivery to subscriber;
  (b) copying or reproducing of all or portions of microfile of abstracts and documents for delivery to subscriber;
  (c) copying or reproducing of machine record of code books for up-dating or initial delivery to subscriber who is conducting analysis of confidential documents for private use.

Several forms of cooperative activity are desirable, and one is essential to provide the fullest and most flexible service. The desirable cooperative activities are (1) the provision of appropriately informative abstracts already being prepared in various subject fields in order that duplication of analysis of source documents may be avoided; and (2) the coordination of machine languages for storage of the machine record, in order that similar work undertaken by other groups may be used in the proposed mechanized system.

The one essential area of cooperation relates to the acquisition of rights to reproduce copies of copyrighted informative abstracts and source documents. To permit copying and delivery of such material to subscribers, the payment of a royalty or other equitable reimbursement would be necessary.

The volume of such service that could be absorbed by the American economy has been estimated from a market survey of representative organizations in government, industry, and other agencies. The market survey assumed the existence of a comprehensive information system at various cost levels—service to be offered either from a central organization or within an individual organization. The market sample numbered 3,000, with a response of 20 per cent. Without extrapolation from the sample to the entire population, the replies to the questionnaire suggested that more than 2,000,000 questions, either retrospective or continuing, would be asked each year (either centrally or through a decentralized activity), and that the annual worth of such a service would be slightly more than $2,900,000,000.

The "product mix" of services described in the foregoing will be necessary to satisfy the needs of various types of individuals and organizations in a changing demographic picture.

References

1. Mack, J. D., and Taylor, R. S.: A System of Documentation Terminology. *In* J. H. Shera, A. Kent, and J. W. Perry, eds., *Documentation in Action.* New York, Reinhold Publishing Corporation, 1956, p. 20.

2. Adkinson, B. W.: International Utilization of Recorded Knowledge. *In* J. H. Shera, A. Kent, and J. W. Perry, eds., *op. cit.,* pp. 163-175.

3. Berry, M. M.: Application of Punched Cards to Library Routines. *In* R. S. Casey, *et al.,* eds., *Punched Cards.* 2nd ed. New York, Reinhold Publishing Corporation, 1958, pp. 279-302.

4. Kent, A.: *Textbook on Machine Literature Searching.* New York, Interscience Publishers, Inc., 1961 (in press).

5. Busa, R.: The Use of Punched Cards in Linguistic Analysis. *In* R. S. Casey, *et al.,* eds., *op. cit.,* pp. 357-373.

6. Citron, J., Hart, L., and Ohlman, H.: A Permutation Index to the Preprints of the International Conference on Scientific Information. *Report Sp44.* Santa Monica, Calif., System Development Corporation.

7. Luhn, H. P.: Keyword-in-Context Index for Technical Literature (KWIC Index). *A.S.D.D. Report, RC-127.* Yorktown Heights, N.Y., International Business Machines Corporation, Aug. 31, 1959, p. 6.

8. Taube, M., and Associates: *Studies in Coordinate Indexing.* Washington, D.C., Vols. I-V.

9. Melton, Jessica: Procedures for Preparation of Abstracts for Encoding. *In* J. W. Perry and A. Kent, *Tools for Machine Literature Searching.* New York, Interscience Publishers, Inc., 1958, pp. 69-150.

10. Kent, A., and Perry, J. W.: Telegraphic Abstracts in the Field of Ordnance, *op. cit.,* pp. 151-172.

11. Rees, T. H., Jr.: Standardized Telegraphic Abstracts from Articles in *New York Times. In* J. W. Perry and A. Kent, *op. cit.,* pp. 173-195.

12. Tauber, M. F., and Lilley, O. L.: *Feasibility Study Regarding the Estab-*

lishment of an Educational Media Research Information Service. A study performed pursuant to a contract with the United States Office of Education, Department of Health, Education, and Welfare (SAE 8328). New York, School of Library Service, Columbia University, 1960.

13. Luhn, H. P.: The Automatic Creation of Literature Abstracts. *IBM Journal of Research and Development,* 2:159-165, April 1958.

14. Swanson, D. R.: Searching Natural Language by Computer. *Science,* 132: 1099-1104, Oct. 21, 1960.

15. Kent, A., ed.: *Information Retrieval and Machine Translation.* New York, Interscience Publishers, Inc., 1960-1961, Vol. I, Ch. 1.

16. *Ibid.,* Ch. 61.

17. Kent, A., and Perry, J. W.: *Centralized Information Services.* New York, Interscience Publishers, Inc., 1958.

18. U.S. 85th Congress, 2nd Session. Senate Committee on Government Operations: *Science and Technology Act of 1958, Senate Document No. 90. S.3126.* Washington, D.C., U.S. Government Printing Office, 1958.

19. U.S. 85th Congress, 2nd Session. U.S. Senate: *Science and Technology Act of 1958.* Hearings before a subcommittee of the Committee on Government Operations, on S.3126, May 2, 6, and 7, 1958, Part 1, and on S.3126 and S.4039, June 25 and 26, 1958, Part 2. Washington, D.C., U.S. Government Printing Office, 1958.

20. U.S. 86th Congress, 1st Session. U.S. Senate: *Science Program—86th Congress.* Senate Report No. 120, Committee on Government Operations. Washington, D.C., U.S. Government Printing Office, 1959.

21. U.S. 86th Congress, 1st Session. U.S. Senate: *Create a Department of Science and Technology.* Hearings before the Subcommittee on Reorganization and International Organizations of the Committee on Government Operations, on S. 676, S.586, S. 1851, May 28, 1959, Part 2. Washington, D.C., U.S. Government Printing Office, 1959.

22. U.S. 86th Congress, 2nd Session. U.S. Senate: *Documentation, Indexing, and Retrieval of Scientific Information.* Committee on Government Operations, Document No. 113. Washington, D.C., U.S. Government Printing Office, 1960.

23. Shera, J. H., Kent, A., Perry, J. W.: *Information Resources—A Challenge to American Science and Industry.* New York, Interscience Publishers, Inc., 1958.

Library Resources: An Overview

RALPH M. DUNBAR

LIBRARY RESOURCES ARE VERY DIVERSE in character and enormous in quantity. For the most part, each type has had a different development and is likely to be affected in varying degrees by demographic and other factors.

In order to facilitate treatment, the field of resources has been divided into three parts, each handled by a separate author. *Books:* Trade books, textbooks, reference books, pamphlets, monographs (nonserial), paperbacks, and out-of-print books. *Serials:* Periodicals, government publications, technical research reports, monographic series, and newspapers. *Audio-visual materials:* Maps, recordings (music), nonmusical recordings, microreproduction, motion pictures, and other media.

The preceding list does not cover all categories, because some (such as "manuscripts") have been omitted, mainly for lack of space. Furthermore, the types, in some cases, are not mutually exclusive, but they do represent the commonly accepted groupings.

The impact of projected population changes upon library resources is illustrated here by three examples. Hauser and Taitel indicate in the preceding *Library Trends* issue that the number of senior citizens will increase from 1960 to 1980 by close to 50 per cent and will form a 10 per cent segment of the total population.[1] This gain will result undoubtedly in a marked increase in the demand for library materials. The actual amount and kind of this increase will depend upon a number of factors involving the older population, such as educational attainment, mental and physical health, housing conditions, economic status, use of leisure time, mobility, and will to migrate to various parts of the country. Predictions about the number and use of resources by the senior citizens must be weighed and adapted with these elements in mind.

The author was formerly Director, Library Services Branch, U.S. Office of Education.

Another projection for 1960 to 1980 relates to the changes in the educational characteristics of the population, such as growth in school population, decreasing illiteracy, and the increases in the proportions of high school graduates and of college graduates in the total population. It seems obvious that these gains in educational accomplishments will also affect the number and kind of library materials required to meet the needs during the next two decades.

The changes in the occupational structure will likewise have an effect upon library materials and their use. In the case of one segment, for instance, Hauser and Taitel note an increase during the 1950's of almost two-thirds in the number of professional, technical, and kindred workers. Accordingly, a similar increase may be expected in the 1960's, although not necessarily of the same magnitude as that of the past decade. The growth of this particular part of the occupational structure again has clear implications for library resources. Similar analyses for other population segments would reveal significant facts.

Besides population changes, there are other factors which may affect library resources. The necessity of having physical and bibliographical access to them has been pointed out by the specific examples listed by V. W. Clapp,[2] and the following general factors are suggested in his paper as of significance: (1) full and improved cooperation among libraries in the acquisition, processing, storing, and servicing of resources; (2) complete coordination of the various types of materials in order that the best possible service can be rendered; (3) technological advances, especially in the field of cataloging, copying processes, microforms, sound recordings, and interlibrary electronic communications; (4) improvement and perfecting of mechanical and electronic devices for the retrieval of stored data; (5) rising costs of library materials upon the maintenance of adequate collections.

Cooperation, the first mentioned factor, is a much discussed subject in library circles. *Library Trends* devoted an entire issue to it in January 1958.[3] Its proponents maintain that cooperation is an absolute necessity if the handicaps inherent within the acquisition, processing, storing, and servicing of resources by individual libraries are ever to be overcome. Limited and inadequate budgets also add a note of urgency to the pleas for cooperation. Despite the best efforts and great accomplishments of single libraries, serious gaps still remain in library facilities and services when these accommodations are considered on a nationwide basis.

Among the recent writers who have treated library cooperation are Esterquest,[4] Carlson,[5] Metcalf,[6] and Stanford.[7] They have pointed out the necessity for and the beneficial results of cooperation, the high costs frequently involved, and the practical difficulties. It might also be mentioned that Eastlick,[8] after a study of four hundred public documents and questionnaires to state library agencies, has concluded recently that cooperation is often a matter of lip service.

Cooperation among libraries has taken forms such as acquisitions, cataloging, storage, bibliographical centers, reference centers, interlibrary loans, joint surveys of resources, and interlibrary councils for various purposes. Only a few references will be cited as examples of this rich literature.

The current status of successful cooperative cataloging, for example, is covered by Bendix,[9] Eckford,[10] and Kenney.[11] The effort to expedite cataloging by having printed cards available at the time the book is received from the publisher or dealer is described in the "Cataloging-in-Source" article.[12] After the Library of Congress decided not to continue this experiment because of cost and other difficulties, the persisting attempt to achieve the end is brought up-to-date in a *Library Journal* article of April 1, 1961.[13] Vosper, although covering only a small part of the acquisition problem, discusses Farmington Plan difficulties, which have much significance for cooperation in general.[14]

Cooperation has had a long history. It has progressed steadily, although perhaps slowly and at times with much discouragement. It seems certain that cooperation will take place on an ever-increasing scale. Growing cost of materials, the scarcity of many resources, and the demands for efficient service make cooperation a required factor in the years ahead.

Books, serials, maps, newspapers, technical reports, sound recordings, and motion pictures all seem to go their own ways insofar as bibliographic control or coordinated use is concerned. Writers sometimes question why catalogers generally have restricted themselves to books and monographs and left the making of periodical indexes to the commercial interests such as the Wilson Company, *Chemical Abstracts*, and others. Researchers and other seekers of information ask why the indexing of data does not go even further and cover all types of resources with some sort of unified control.

In view of pending developments, and with the help of individual initiative, cooperative endeavors, subsidies, and grants, it seems safe to predict that the goal of complete indexing may be achieved. Coordination of all or nearly all resource items should be a reality before the end of the next two decades.

Technological advances will be felt especially in cataloging, low-cost copying of resources, microforms, sound recordings, and inter-library communication. In the case of cataloging, the automatic type-writer [15] and various processes for card reproduction will reduce the cost and time element.[16] The Council on Library Resources just made a grant to the Library Technology Project of the American Library Association for a thorough study of catalog card reproduction and the development of a satisfactory machine for this purpose.[17]

Interlibrary communication, including such processes as teletype, facsimile, and televised transmission of information about resources, should make advances, especially if the need for facts is urgent, im-mediate, and sufficient in volume, and if costs of the operation can be kept reasonably low.[18, 19] These devices and others yet to be de-veloped will facilitate access to all library materials. It may be ex-pected also that business and industry will perfect many machines which libraries can adapt profitably to the servicing of their resources.

Retrieval of information stored in resources is a vital factor.[20] Com-mon devices in the past have been the catalog in printed form, the card catalog, and the periodical index. Under the efforts of scientists and others, machines have been and are now being developed to store, search for, and report back at high speed the desired coded data. The subject has been discussed in many books, articles, and talks. It is also treated elsewhere in this issue. The machines presently available may be too expensive, specialized, and complicated for most libraries. It is probable, however, that technological develop-ments will improve these machines during the next two decades so that the rapid recovery of stored data will be realized on a scale be-yond that now envisioned.

Rising costs of resources are of grave concern to the library ad-ministrator involved in the maintenance of adequate and balanced collections. This subject of costs is well covered in a publication by Schick and Kurth.[21]

The authors note, with a supporting table of price indexes, that since 1947–49 (a base period of relatively stable prices) the cost in 1960 of general books, periodicals, and serials services increased more than that of other commodities. Their figures show also that the aver-age retail price of general books in 1960 was $5.24, 46 per cent more than the average price in 1947–49, and the average retail subscription price of all periodicals was $5.32 in 1960, compared with $3.62 in 1947–49, an increase of 47 per cent.[22]

No projections of price trends are presented for the next two decades, but the information given in the publication clearly shows what has happened during the last 12 years. It indicates what the problem of acquiring adequate resources will be, if prices of these materials continue their upward trend and library budgets remain comparatively fixed.

This overview of resources is intended to be an introduction to the individual papers on books, serials, and audio-visual materials. As indicated in it, there are factors which will affect both the number and the kind of library materials in the future. Population changes, full cooperation, improved coordination, technological advances, perfected retrieval systems, and rising costs of materials will help to determine the future of library resources in the next two decades.

References

1. Hauser, P. M., and Taitel, M.: Population Trends—Prologue to Library Development. *Library Trends,* 10:28 July 1961.

2. Clapp, V. W.: Library Resources—the Professional Responsibility. *Library Resources and Technical Services,* 3:3-11, Winter 1959.

3. Esterquest, R. T., ed.: Building Library Resources Through Cooperation. *Library Trends,* 6:257-383, Jan. 1958.

4. Esterquest, R. T.: Cooperation in Library Services. *Library Quarterly,* 31: 71-89, Jan. 1961.

5. Carlson, W. H.: Mobilization of Existing Library Resources. *Library Trends,* 6:272-295, Jan. 1958.

6. Metcalf, K. D.: General Problems [of Library Cooperation]. *Library Trends,* 6:260-271, Jan. 1958.

7. Stanford, E. B.: Increasing Library Resources Through Cooperation. *Library Trends,* 6:296-308, Jan. 1958.

8. Eastlick, J. T.: The Sixties and After. *ALA Bulletin,* 55:556, June, 1961.

9. Bendix, D.: Regional Processing for Public Libraries: A Survey. *Library Resources and Technical Services,* 2:155-170, Summer 1958.

10. Eckford, M. L.: Library Service Center of Eastern Ohio; An Experiment in Centralized Processing. *Library Resources and Technical Services,* 5:5-40, Winter 1961.

11. Kenney, Brigitte L.: *Cooperative Centralized Processing: A Report of the Establishment and First Year of Operation of the Southwest Missouri Library Service.* Chicago, American Library Association, c1959.

12. Cataloging-in-Source—A Symposium. *Library Resources and Technical Services,* 4:269-284, Fall 1960.

13. LC Explores Scheme to Provide Catalog Cards with New Book. *Library Journal,* 86:1428, April 1, 1961.

14. Vosper, R.: International Book Procurement; or Farmington Extended. *College and Research Libraries,* 21:117-124, March 1960.

15. Johnson, N. W.: Automatic Catalog Card Reproduction. *Library Journal,* 85:725-726, Feb. 15, 1960.

16. Treyz, J. H.: Xerox Process and its Application at Yale. *Library Resources and Technical Services,* 3:223-229, Summer 1959.

17. Council on Library Resources, Inc.: *Recent Developments,* No. 59, May 21, 1961.

18. Adams, S.: Library Communication Systems. *Library Trends,* 5:206-215, Oct. 1956.

19. Mack, J. D.: Teletype Speeds Interlibrary Loans and References. *Library Journal,* 83:1325-1329, May 1, 1958.

20. Taube, M.: Documentation, Information Retrieval, and Other New Techniques. *Library Quarterly,* 31:90-103, Jan. 1961.

21. Schick, F. L., and Kurth, W. H.: *Cost of Library Materials: Price Trends of Publications.* Washington, D.C., U.S. Office of Education, 1961.

22. *Ibid.,* pp. 12, 16.

Book Publishing

ROBERT W. FRASE

PLANNING AHEAD FOR LIBRARY SERVICE in the next two decàdes requires the assessment of three factors—the number and nature of readers to be served, the volume and kinds of materials to be made available to those readers, and the price of the various component costs of library service. The following analysis of book publication concentrates upon the possible future volume of book title production and to a lesser extent upon book prices. Size of population and rate of population growth or decline probably have some effect upon the number of book titles published in individual countries, but the relationship is not a direct one and is virtually impossible to measure.

Of all the types of library materials, books seem to lend themselves best to an attempt to project the future on the basis of past trends. In this field consistent and comprehensive statistics compiled on United States title production by *Publishers' Weekly* extend over a period of many years. The international title production statistics assembled by UNESCO for a large number of countries are less complete and less consistent, but they are adequate for indicating general trends.

The *Publishers' Weekly* count of U.S. title production includes books of all types containing 49 pages or more. Prior to 1958 the lower page limit was 65, but it was reduced at that time to conform to the international standard suggested by UNESCO. Textbooks, reference books, monographs, and other kinds of nonperiodical publications are included in addition to trade books, regardless of whether the publisher is a regular commercial firm, a university press, or an institution entirely outside the publishing field. There are, however, certain major exclusions from the count, usually materials which do not ordinarily flow through the customary distribution channels of the book trade. Most important of the excluded materials are most

Mr. Frase is Associate Managing Director, American Book Publishers Council.

publications of federal, state, and local governments, books produced under author subsidy by a "vanity press," and dissertations.[1]

Table I, which follows, shows the actual volume of book titles (new books plus new and revised editions) reported by *Publishers' Weekly* for the years 1951 and 1960 and a projection of the trend line during this period to the year 1980.

TABLE I

U.S. Book Title Production
1951, 1960 and Projected to 1980

Classification	1951 Actual	1960 Actual	1980 Projected
Agriculture, Gardening.................	150	156	180
Biography...........................	639	879	1,400
Business............................	260	305	650
Education...........................	273	348	530
Fiction.............................	2,135	2,440	4,000
Fine Arts...........................	307	470	1,150
Games, Sports.......................	174	286	500
General Literature and Criticism........	531	736	1,600
Geography, Travel....................	286	466	1,000
History.............................	523	865	2,500
Home Economics.....................	227	197	200
Juvenile............................	1,072	1,725	4,000
Law................................	282	394	550
Medicine, Hygiene...................	478	520	690
Music..............................	96	98	130
Philology...........................	190	228	250
Philosophy, Ethics...................	338	480	1,000
Poetry, Drama......................	487	492	500
Religion............................	731	1,104	2,400
Science.............................	722	1,089	3,500
Sociology, Economics.................	506	754	1,500
Technical and Military Books..........	411	698	1,200
Miscellaneous.......................	437	282	400
Totals..............................	11,255	15,012	29,830
Projection of Totals..................			26,000

SOURCE: Actual figures for 1951 and 1960 are as reported by *Publishers' Weekly* and do not include most federal, state, and local government publications. Projections for 1980 are by the author, based upon the 1951-1960 trends. The 29,830 figure in 1980 is the sum of projections of the extended series. The 26,000 figure is the projection of the trend of the total.

As indicated in Table I, if the 1951–60 steady upward trend is continued, there will be somewhere between 26,000 and 30,000 book titles published in the United States in 1980, an increase of between 66 per cent and 100 per cent over 1960. An increase in title production of this magnitude is based upon the assumption that the current trend will continue. It would be reasonable, therefore, to assume a projection of this rate of increase as a basis for library planning until the trend line changes significantly. Libraries do not buy all titles which are published, but it may be assumed that they purchase a fairly constant proportion of new and revised editions in the fields in which they maintain collections. For individual libraries and types of libraries, a more refined method of planning for the future would be to use the trends of title production for individual classifications of books in proportion to their importance in the collection rather than using total title production.

Especially for university and research libraries, foreign materials are as important as domestic. The following Table II, compiled from UNESCO sources, gives a rough indication of the trends of book and pamphlet title production in a large group of foreign countries:

TABLE II

Book and Pamphlet Title Production in 31 Foreign Countries
1950, 1959 and Projected to 1980

Country	1950	1959	Projected to 1980
European Countries (19)	76,464	96,403	——
Asian Countries (5)	33,609	39,423	——
U. S. S. R.	43,100	69,072	——
Other Countries (6)	5,821	6,064	——
Total (31)	158,994	210,962	369,000

Source: UNESCO, *Basic Facts and Figures* (1960), and *Book Production 1937-1954*, 1957.

The 31 countries in Table II were chosen because both 1950 and 1959 figures were available in UNESCO reports. Although the sample of countries is sufficiently large for statistical purposes, it may not include enough Asian, African, and Latin American countries for projections because future increases in title production will be larger in these areas than in the established book publishing countries of Europe. The data presented in Table II are not as comparable as the *Publishers' Weekly* figures for the United States because the definitions from which these statistics were compiled may have changed during the last decade. It should also be noted that the figures are not directly comparable with those of the United States because books, pamphlets, and government documents are included in most of these countries in some undefined proportion, while in the U.S.

neither pamphlets nor most federal, state, and local documents are counted.

However, with these caveats, the data are indicative of the trend outside the United States. From 1950 to 1959 the increase for these 31 countries is 33 per cent. A projected increase from 1959 to 1980 comes to about 75 per cent. These figures are remarkably similar to those shown in Table I for United States book title production.

In planning for the future, libraries must consider the physical volume and cost of materials which they need to acquire. Pioneering work based upon the conceptions of W. H. Kurth of the National Library of Medicine has been done on the trend of American book and periodical prices since 1947 by the Committee on Cost of Library Materials Index of the American Library Association. The basic date for both books and periodicals is available in various published sources, including the *American Library and Book Trade Annual*,[2] and the 1961 edition of *Health, Education, and Welfare Trends*.[3] In addition, the U.S. Office of Education published a monograph on this subject by F. L. Schick and W. H. Kurth.[4] The A.L.A. committee is also endeavoring to encourage other countries to compile similar indexes of book and periodical prices, but to date only Mexican and Danish book price figures are avialable.

The A.L.A. book price index showed a change in the average prices of book titles included from 100 in the base period of 1947–49 to 146.2 in 1960. The books included in the index are generally hard-cover books of the types purchased by libraries and do not include paperbounds, reprint editions, encyclopaedias, and most textbooks. These exclusions make the index rise more rapidly than were it based upon all books published in the United States. The increasing proportion of paperbound books in the total title production (and even more in the total number of copies sold) has a tendency to lower average prices. Nevertheless, for library budgeting purposes, the index is properly designed and extremely useful.

The projection of the 1947–1960 trend of the book price index or any of its component parts to the year 1980 would be of questionable validity and dubious value. Book prices, like salaries and other library costs, tend to keep pace with the general price level and if the inflationary trend of the postwar period continues, book prices will undoubtedly also rise. Of more importance in library planning are the basic physical quantities involved—the number of people to be served and the volume of materials needed to provide this service. Once these are determined, budget planning for acquisition can take place on an annual or a biennial basis in terms of the most recent information on price trends.

In the past there existed special problems relating to the acquisition of out-of-print books—those which can no longer be obtained from their publishers. The price of these books has varied according to the original published price, available supply and demand, and related factors. It seems likely that if authorized by their publisher, American titles not in heavy demand but still under copyright will be made available through xerox copies or similar processes. This source of supply may result in fewer price variations than previously encountered. Out-of-print titles in heavier demand may appear as new or revised editions in cloth or as paperbacks. In this format they are included in the general projections of title production in Table I.

Summary

The number of individual book titles has been increasing steadily in the postwar period both in the United States and in other countries. If this trend continues, something on the order of 66 to 100 per cent more book titles will be published in 1980 than in 1960. Book prices have also been rising in the past decade in accordance with the slow inflationary trend of the entire economy. In the planning of library service over the next two decades, these factors need to be taken into account along with demographic trends.

References

1. Wright, W. E., ed.: Book Production in 64 Countries. *American Library and Book Trade Annual, 1960 Edition,* New York, R. R. Bowker, 1961, p. 47.
2. *Ibid.,* p. 52.
3. U.S. Department of Health, Education, and Welfare: *Health, Education, and Welfare Trends.* 1961 ed. Washington, D.C., U.S. Government Printing Office, 1961, pp. 58-59.
4. Schick, F. L., and Kurth, W. H.: *Cost of Library Materials: Price Trends of Publications.* Washington, D.C., U.S. Office of Education, 1961.

Serial Publications

PAUL L. BERRY

WITHIN LIBRARY TECHNOLOGY, serial publications have been considered traditionally as a separately distinguishable library resource because there are differences in their contents, format, bibliographical relationships, and the methods of acquisition and service.

Definitions of the term "serial" vary from authority to authority and from library to library, as A. Osborn makes clear in his study.[1] For this article the term is used to include all those publications which are issued with varying frequency, with a title common to successive issues, but without a foreseeable ending. Within this definition fall periodicals, governmental serials, newspapers, series, annuals, proceedings, transactions, and other less easily delineated categories. This lack of clarity in definition is partly responsible for the absence of an authoritative quantitative analysis of the extent of serial publishing. UNESCO recently attempted a quantitative survey on a world-wide basis,[2] but admitted the difficulties in obtaining reliable data and in arriving at definitions which are generally acceptable. The UNESCO study reports nearly 100,000 newspaper and periodical titles in the world in the 1950's, but this figure is far from complete for the broad sweep of serials considered here. Osborn estimates that there are between half a million and a million serial titles published each year.[3] Figures for the number of separate issues published during a year and for the number of copies produced are too great for a reasonable estimate, but from what we know of serials, their number is staggering.

The future of serial publications can be considered under two aspects: (1) the future of the serial publications themselves, and (2) whether and how libraries will use them. Serial publications, which have been part of our library resources for hundreds of years,[4] will remain library resources for many years to come. It seems safe to

The author is Chief, Serial Division, Library of Congress.

predict that there will be no abrupt change in the pattern of publishing and reading which is favorable to the serial publication, dealing as it does with information too current, too transitory, or too fragmentary for conventional book treatment.

D. E. Carroll is making an intensive study of the world production of newspapers and periodicals [5] which appears to indicate that the rate of increase in the production of these materials since about 1800 has been doubling at intervals of approximately twenty-five years. While there will eventually be a decrease in the rate of growth, the developments in the newer and presently underdeveloped countries should tend to maintain the present rate for the immediate future.

The growth in population in the United States for the past fifteen years has been accompanied by a fairly consistent increase in the circulation figures for newspapers and periodicals. During the next twenty years, demographic factors will undoubtedly have an effect upon the production and circulation of serial publications throughout the world. These factors in themselves may have relatively small effect upon the number of serial titles, their character, or the development of bibliographic controls. Changes in population characteristics such as educational attainment will increase the demands upon educational institutions and will affect library service, including the use of serials. However, the character and degree of these changes cannot be judged accurately.

There is some evidence that economic factors have an impact upon the production of serial publications. The figures reported by the U.S. Bureau of the Census [6] for the period from the late 1920's into the 1950's show a downward trend in book publishing and serial circulation (newspapers and periodicals) during the first half of the 1930's, with a progressive upward trend since the end of World War II. The Census figures do not show a corresponding increase in the number of periodical titles since World War II, a fact which may imply that other trends in the economy, such as increased costs of materials and labor, have adversely affected certain segments of the serial publishing industry. A continued high rate of economic growth, such as we have experienced during the past fifteen years, seems favorable to publishing, while a prolonged period of economic distress may have an adverse influence.

Although technological changes during the past twenty years have been unprecedented, the effects of such changes are not easily measured. Most noticeable has been the impact of the increased interest

in scientific fields of study, resulting in the production of more literature, predominantly serial in nature.[7, 8] Developments in printing—
such as high speed presses, improved offset, and low-cost duplication
methods—have had a decided influence upon serial publications.[9]

Social and political factors can affect serial production. In recent
years the United States has seen the reappearance of a specialized
literary publication, the "little" magazine.[10] We have also seen the
emergence of such serial types as the comic book and the men's
magazine (of a character that would not have appeared openly
ten years ago). The creation of new nations is bringing forth their
new literature, which will include serials.

Research and special libraries have long recognized the importance of this type of material and have collected it extensively.[11]
Some categories of serials which are quite valuable for research—
newspapers and foreign government publications—are collected ad-
quately by only a relatively small number of libraries. There are
indications, however, that all types of libraries now recognize more
fully the importance of this type of publication and will collect them
more actively during the next twenty years.

A perennial problem with serials has been to develop means of obtaining access to their contents.[12] In the past, a small number of limited bibliographic tools have provided a degree of access to the
contents of the major serials, but no comprehensive attack has been
made. Recent technological advances in the field of information retrieval offer the hope of improvement in the future. Well known examples of the application of new techniques to the control of serial
contents are the American Chemical Society's *Chemical Titles*,[13] a list
in which machine methods are used to produce current author and
key-word indexes from 600 chemical journals, and the Listomatic
system being used in the preparation of the National Library of Medicine's *Index Medicus*.[14] It is not likely that machines will solve completely the control of serial contents within twenty years, but undoubtedly significant improvements will be made.

If it is possible to develop bibliographies which are broader in
scope than the present tools and at the same time not prohibitive in
cost, such tools would become part of the reference apparatus of a
great many libraries. The availability of such bibliographies would
impose greater pressures to make more serials available. As a result,
the fact that libraries would probably share these resources more
extensively could lead to increased use of the regional library ap-

proach, increased interlibrary loans, and further developments in the technology of quick and inexpensive copying methods. Allied with this cooperation is the need for better knowledge of the location of serials, which is already on the way toward improvement with the forthcoming third edition of the *Union List of Serials*.[15] Projects for the preparation of regional union lists and lists of specialized types of serials surely will continue.

Costs of periodicals are demonstrably on the increase, according to studies made for the American Library Association and reported in a recent publication of the U.S. Department of Health, Education, and Welfare.[8] Unless library budgets increase sufficiently, the higher costs of serials could result in greater selectivity in their acquisition. If economic pressures on the publishers become too great, restrictions upon reproducing copyrighted materials could become more severe.

One predictable change of a technological nature affecting the use of serials in libraries will be further developments in microforms,[16] which are accepted now to provide inexpensive means of acquiring complete collections of important serial materials, and of preserving bulky collections in a small space and in a durable form.

Among serial publications, periodicals are of most significance to libraries. While general interest periodicals which are most commonly found in various types of libraries are expected to grow, an even greater rate of growth can be predicted for specialized periodicals. Studies such as those of Brodman and Taine [17] for medical periodicals and those for medical, educational, and social science periodicals reported by UNESCO [2] are valuable, but they admit the lack of information upon which to base adequate world estimates. C. H. Brown predicted in his 1956 study on scientific serials a sizable increase within twenty years.[7] It appears from recent literature [18] that the lack of reliable statistical data on periodicals is now receiving attention.

Serial and nonserial publications of the agencies of national, state, and local governments will continue among the library resources of the future. All signs point to an increased place in our lives of governmental activities at all levels. With the extension of governmental activities will come more publishing, much of it of vital importance for library collections. Researchers, government personnel, and the general public are becoming increasingly aware of the effects of government and are seeking access to the published results of governmental activities.

It is not likely that domestic and foreign governments will provide a complete solution for the acquisition and control of government publications. Present efforts to improve the depository library system for the United States Government publications might decrease the problem. If efforts at the national level appear dim, they are even dimmer at the state and local levels. For foreign government publications, the problem is particularly acute. A recent survey for the Farmington Plan Committee of the Association of Research Libraries [19] indicated deficiencies in the resources of foreign government publications.

A resource of increasing significance particularly to libraries serving industrial laboratories, academic institutions, and government agencies is the technical research report, which is not a completely new type of serial, but its growth during the past twenty years has added a new dimension to scientific and technical literature. A National Science Foundation report [20] shows that during the past twenty-one years the amount being spent annually by the U.S. Federal Government for basic research and development in governmental, industrial, and university facilities has grown steadily from $0.74 billion to $8.1 billion. In addition, industrial organizations and universities are spending further billions on research and development.[21] Unless there is a radical change in the methods of recording and reporting the results of this research—and proposed [22] technological developments could bring such a change—specialized libraries can look forward to an increase in the number of these reports in the future.

The already mentioned UNESCO survey [2] shows a world total of newspapers of general interest of 30,000 in the mid-1950's. In the United States, several sources during the past forty years have indicated a gradual decline of newspaper titles.[6, 23] For world totals, however, such a decline may be offset by the emergence of a strong press in the newly developing areas.

Many libraries have not included newspapers among their collections to any great extent because of custodial problems. Since the use of microfilm in the late 1930's, newspaper holdings are more common in a larger number of libraries. This trend is likely to continue and to increase, with libraries collecting a greater number of local and national newspapers. The most significant development in recent years has been the Foreign Newspaper Microfilm Project sponsored by the Association of Research Libraries,[24] which has made accessible to libraries through loan or purchase the most important newspapers of foreign countries.

The demographic implications for future library service will bring an increase in the number of serials publications and increased demands upon libraries for this type of resource.

References

1. Osborn, A. D.: *Serial Publications, Their Place and Treatment in Libraries.* Chicago, American Library Association, 1955, pp. 12-20.

2. United Nations Educational, Scientific and Cultural Organization. Statistical Division: *Statistics of Newspapers and Other Periodicals.* [Paris, 1959].

3. Osborn, *op. cit.,* pp. 5-6.

4. *Ibid.,* pp. 1-8.

5. Carroll, D. E.: Personal communication, June 21, 1961.

6. U.S. Bureau of the Census: *Historical Statistics of the United States, Colonial Times to 1957.* Washington, D.C., U.S. Government Printing Office, 1960, pp. 499-500.

7. Brown, C. H.: *Scientific Serials.* Chicago, Association of College and Reference Libraries, 1956, p. 1.

8. U.S. Dept. of Health, Education, and Welfare: *Health, Education, and Welfare Trends.* 1961 ed. Washington, D.C., U.S. Government Printing Office, 1961, p. 59.

9. Wolseley, R. E.: *The Magazine World; an Introduction to Magazine Journalism.* New York, Prentice-Hall, 1951, pp. 190-191.

10. Hoffman, F. J., *et al.*: *The Little Magazine, a History and a Bibliography.* 2d ed. Princeton, N.J., Princeton University Press, 1947, pp. 1-10.

11. Osborn, *op. cit.,* pp. 7-11.

12. Clapp, V. W.: Indexing and Abstracting Services for Serial Literature. *Library Trends,* 2:509-521, April 1954.

13. *Chemical Titles.* Washington, D.C., American Chemical Society, 1960-

14. The National Library of Medicine Index Mechanization Project, July 1, 1958-June 30, 1960. *Bulletin of the Medical Library Association,* 49:1-96, Jan. 1961, part 2.

15. Field, F. Bernice: The Program of the Joint Committee on the Union List of Serials. *Library Resources and Technical Services,* 4:303-308, Fall 1960.

16. Skipper, J. E., ed.: Photoduplication in Libraries. *Library Trends,* 8:343-492, Jan. 1960.

17. Brodman, Estelle, and Taine, S. I.: Current Medical Literature: A Quantitative Survey of Articles and Journals. *In* International Conference on Scientific Information, Washington, D.C., 1958: *Proceedings.* Washington, D.C., National Academy of Sciences, National Research Council, 1959, Vol. 1, pp. 435-447.

18. National Lists of Scientific Periodicals. *UNESCO Bulletin for Libraries,* 15:91-94, March-April 1961.

19. Wisdom, D. F.: *Foreign Government Publications in American Research Libraries: A Survey Prepared for the Farmington Plan Committee of the Association of Research Libraries.* Washington, D.C., 1961.

20. U.S. National Science Foundation. Office of Special Studies: *Federal Funds for Science*. Washington, D.C., U.S. Government Printing Office, 1961, Vol. 9, p. 29.

21. U.S. Congress. Senate. Committee on Government Operations: *Coordination of Information on Current Scientific Research and Development Supported by the United States Government*. Washington, D.C., U.S. Government Printing Office, 1961, p. 25.

22. *Ibid.*, pp. 35+.

23. *N. W. Ayer & Sons Directory, Newspapers and Periodicals*. Philadelphia, N. W. Ayer & Son, Inc., 1920, 1940, 1961. Vols. 52, 72, and 93.

24. Association of Research Libraries. Foreign Newspaper Microfilm Project: *Circular Letter No. 1-* , Chicago, 1955- .

Audio-Visual Materials

JOHN L. NOLAN

A DISCUSSION OF THE FUTURE of audio-visual materials as library resources should include all audio-visual forms and equipment used for educational and recreational purposes. Space limitations, however, preclude full discussion or even passing reference to all forms of audio-visual materials now in use; that these have reached formidable proportions may be seen in the standard lists such as Kinder [1] provides.

Even adequate space would not make possible a complete forecast, for precise predictions are necessarily limited to the kinds of libraries and materials for which reliable data are available. Overall quantitative projections are likely to be invalid because information on current library expenditures for audio-visual materials is not complete, nor are data on holdings and production readily obtainable. Moreover, any specific predictions could be drastically modified or even nullified by technological advances that can only be guessed at today. Demographic changes will undoubtedly bring about economic and cultural pressures that will force the development of new audio-visual forms as well as the improvement and greater use of existing forms. A blueprint of these forms and uses and the price tag which they will carry cannot be attempted here. It is, however, possible to take a very general look at the next two decades in the light of past and current developments, and it may be helpful to examine the ways in which available data might be used for precise projections within certain limitations and local situations.

For the purposes of this discussion, it will be assumed that all audio-visual materials in educational institutions are parts of the institution's library resources regardless of where they may be housed or used. Certain audio-visual materials (such as educational motion

---

Mr. Nolan, who is Associate Director of the Reference Department, Library of Congress, prepared this section with the assistance of Messrs. Dubester, Gerlach, and Lowens, and other members of the Reference Department staff.

pictures) have not been universally considered as belonging in libraries in some institutions and are maintained as separate collections.

Looking back at the use of audio-visual materials, one finds evidence of reliance upon visual aids since the beginnings of history. Cave wall drawings, Babylonian maps (on clay tablets), Egyptian pictographs, medieval art works, Renaissance woodcuts, and early illustrated books show the importance of the visual medium throughout recorded history. In this country, centers for audio-visual materials grew up early in the century, at first in museums, then in schools. But it is only within the memory of librarians today that (except for highly specialized collections, such as maps) libraries began assuming responsibility for audio-visual materials,[2] and it was not until after World War II that public libraries started seriously to build up audio-visual collections.

In the early 1950's, it was found in an A.C.R.L. survey[3] that college and university libraries had not developed adequate audio-visual collections. This survey was disappointing but not discouraging, for considerable groundwork had been laid and libraries and other repositories were reaching the point at which audio-visual materials could more readily be put to use. The audio-visual pioneering efforts in St. Louis, Rochester, Buffalo, and elsewhere; the development of the film and recording industries with their side benefits to educational motion pictures, microphotography, and sound recordings in libraries; and the inauguration of indexes and catalog controls for motion pictures and sound recordings are a few of the indications of the trend toward the wide acceptance of audio-visual materials that we see today in the rapidly growing collections and in the attention given to audio-visual problems and planning by librarians, teachers, technicians, foundations, governmental bodies, and others.

We have reached a point at which we should try to determine generally the future of audio-visual materials in the context of problems created by demographic factors. As the Hauser-Taitel tables indicate,[4] the administrators of high schools, colleges, and professional schools are faced with rapidly expanding student bodies, and public librarians must expect increasing number of users with new and intensified demands brought about by greater longevity and leisure, population shifts, and other factors resulting from demographic changes. Special librarians will also be forced to cope with new requirements as population changes result in the stepping up of research and development programs and the expansion of governmental and industrial needs for library services beyond those existing today. In simplest (and oversimplified) terms, the question is what kinds of audio-visual aids will be needed and in what quantities to meet the demands of the next two decades. The answers, where they exist at all, are far from simple, as will be seen if one considers some (though not all) of the specific types of material now in use.

Maps are among the oldest of visual aids. Over the centuries, map production has gradually increased and changed in character with the advent of property taxation, the discovery of new lands, the growth of trade, the invention of printing and engraving, the development of national surveys, the planning of great wars, and the evolution of private cartography.

Current cartographic production may be estimated at well over 75,000 items (maps, globes, etc., both foreign and domestic) per year (based upon the annual intake of the Map Division at the Library of Congress for the past five years). Federal budgets for U.S. mapping agencies have increased more than 800 per cent, from $8,200,000 to more than $65,000,000, between 1940 and 1960. Commercial mapping has expanded at an even greater rate. Increased map production and use during the next twenty years is inevitable but unpredictable. Anticipated population increases with attendant changes in occupations and interests are related to many immeasurable factors now tending to increase map production and use. Among the more effective are increasing needs for both expendable and reference maps in classrooms; increased interest in the sciences and recognition of maps as basic tools for both the physical and social sciences; more time for travel and leisure which will bring about greater use of road maps, charts, and recreation maps; and a new awareness of map values, resulting from school and military training in map use.

What quantitative effects these factors will have upon map production can only be guessed at, but it is clear that to meet the resultant problems of storage, preservation, and service, libraries must improve cataloging methods, mechanize retrieval of maps from stack areas, perfect lamination and other preservation techniques, and prepare for broader service form the map collections. The latter would include recognition of many new classes of maps such as marketing maps, propaganda maps, civil defense maps, standardized city plans, telecommunication maps, etc.; the preparation of exhibits; compilation of bibliographies; and development of special reference aids and tools for new forms of cartographic publications such as three-dimensional models, inflatable globes, and special folding air charts for high-speed travel.

Unlike maps, recordings have only recently become accepted as standard resources in libraries. Consequently, anything resembling a detailed, accurate census of library utilization of music recordings does not yet exist. From the few studies available,[5, 6] it would appear that most American library systems of any consequence today either already have some sort of collection of recorded music or plan to build one in the future.

Fast-moving technological changes make projection of present trends in this area particularly hazardous. The librarian of 1961 is aware of just how many problems he is saddled with because of past chaos in the technology of recorded sound, and there is no sign that anything approaching stability is in the offing. One informed sector of the industry committed to the disc is of the opinion that the familiar vinyl long-play will be supplanted, probably within the next decade, by a paper or paper-thin plastic magnetic disc. With such a disc, use-wear, almost entirely a function of stylus friction, will be eliminated. Others who hold that the future is in magnetic tape, look for vastly improved multi-track tape and miniature tape-cartridges.[7] Others still feel that such revolutionary processes as General Electric's thermoplastic recording (TPR), again without frictional contact, will make all other methods obsolescent.

Librarians are on fairly solid ground in predicting a considerable increase in library use of music recordings within the next two decades if no guess as to specific form or extent is hazarded. Most expected demographic changes, such as the trend toward suburban living, the natural increase in population, the increasingly greater proportion of people over 65, the shrinking work day, and the attendant expanding leisure day, plainly tend to reinforce such a general conclusion. The circulating collection for the average public library patron may well become the central music service of the public library, and its acquisition of scores and books on music may be geared to the size and scope of the record collection. The reference collection for the student may well contain the complete works of all the great masters and many minor ones, perhaps in a multiplicity of readings. And archival collections for the serious scholar such as those now growing in the Archive of Folk Song and the other collections in the Music Division of the Library of Congress, the New York

Public Library, Indiana and Stanford Universities, and elsewhere,[8] may well be getting over their growing pains.

By and large, the twenty years to come should see a more rapid rate of accretion in recorded music than in more orthodox library materials, such as scores and books, a tendency reinforced by demographic changes. An increasingly complex servicing operation in reference and archival collections, together with greatly expanded size and use of circulating collections, will aggravate already difficult library problems in space, logistics, service, and especially budget.

Although nonmusical recordings have not ordinarily been singled out for separate attention within the broader field of audio-visual activities, it is quite likely that the developments of the next two decades will witness a considerable emphasis upon and expansion of the role of these materials in library collections and services.

The present character of nonmusical recordings is as varied as are books. Included are recordings of poets reading their own poems on tape and disc, the taped recordings of interviews with prominent contemporary personalities in the form of oral histories, the record discs of selections from more extensive collections of recorded speeches and historic events, the recordings of plays, small discs used in practicing shorthand, discs and tapes used in language instruction courses, the "talking books" for the blind which cover a wide range, and many other kinds of recordings of which the above-mentioned are perhaps the more significant or frequently encountered. These recordings possess a basic identity with book materials, evidenced by the ease of transformation of the one into the other, and the reversibility of this transformation, as in the case of books changed into "talking books."

The technological advances of the past few decades that gave us today's magnetic tape recorder, long-playing record, and related equipment are still going forward; e.g., 16⅔ r.p.m. recordings have become a reality (though on a limited scale) to blind readers, and 8⅓ r.p.m. possibilities are now under experimental study as are encapsulated tapes played at slow speeds, and the thermoplastic recordings mentioned above. These forms invite comparison with conventional books in respect to size, ease of handling, and cost.

Further technological advances in recording techniques, processes, equipment, and media may, therefore, be anticipated within the next two decades; these will undoubtedly introduce greater flexibility, expand the use of this medium, and reduce costs so as to make nonmusical recordings more attractive as well as more popular to libraries and library budgets. Whether these advances will keep pace with demand is a problem librarians must face. Greater leisure, increased longevity, and other factors seen in demographic tables will bring stronger pressures to bear upon libraries for these audio-visual materials as well as for conventional books.

In addition, the expansion in the availability and exploitation of nonmusical recordings, with a consequent increase in the role that these materials will play as an aspect of library collections, will create problems with respect to their custody and bibliographic organization. Many of these recordings represent unique information or material worthy of preservation as a reflection of our cultural heritage and a resource for future research. The mechanics of such preservation have only recently become the subject of proper investigation.[9] Bibliographic control has been extended to these materials either as an aspect of the larger audio-visual family, or in their guise as a "book," the vehicle for transmission and preservation of information; but much remains to be done to organize nonmusical recordings in terms of their intrinsic character and their own potential contribution to the library economy.

Microphotography, though long known as a technique, has come into use as a library tool only within the past 30 years. Extensive copying projects for preservation, for saving space, and for acquisitions purposes have been underway for the past decade, microcopying services and microfilm reading rooms have been installed in libraries, commercial photocopying services have been established, new miniaturization techniques have been used for sizable publishing programs, and the medium has been widely adopted by scholarly groups and libraries. There can be no question of its acceptance, although scholars still object to certain technical disadvantages and to the costs of reading equipment.

While even wider use can be safely predicted, the physical aspects, costs, and methods of use in the future are far from clear. Flat microfilm and other forms of miniaturization [10] and electrostatic enlargement processes are all developing so rapidly and are so closely linked to the future of information storage, retrieval, and transmission systems that predictions as to future forms of microreproduction are extremely hazardous. Coupled with these unpredictable technological changes, and somewhat dependent upon them, are the cooperative enterprises now in existence as well as those under study. The American Historical Association, the Association of Research Libraries, and other groups are busy surveying needs and possibilities which will result in even more ambitious copying programs. The growing needs of scholars, scientists, and other users of research libraries, the increasing urgency to preserve deteriorating materials and to reproduce scarce materials for wider use, and the necessity for conserving space are factors that will force librarians to allocate greater sums to microcopying activities although how to correlate expenditures with these factors is a problem that can be worked out only in local situations.

Motion pictures were being made for educational purposes in the early part of the century, and by 1920 there were over two dozen state universities with film services. The development of 16 mm. safety film in the early 1930's, the standardization and simplification of equipment for school use, the impetus given by World War II (when speeded-up methods of teaching fighting men and industrial workers were urgently needed), and the surveys by G. McDonald, Patricia Cory, and others all contributed to the widespread library use of this medium. Now we have educational film indexes, catalog cards prepared by the government with the cooperation of the motion picture industry, a number of professional associations and journals concerned with educational films, film workshops, film circuits, and libraries with their own collections which are now serving millions of people, specialized uses of films (such as the U.S. Office of Education's captioned films for the deaf), and even archival collections of films.

Some indication of the importance attached to educational motion pictures may be seen in the investment of over 2½ billion dollars in this medium (including filmstrips) in the United States since World War II and a current annual dollar investment in excess of ¼ billion. These staggering figures include many industrial and other films, of which an unknown number are acquired by libraries; they are not, therefore, very meaningful in themselves. A breakdown of these figures may be of some value to the planner for the future library film needs.[11] Also helpful is the projection made by the Film Council of America in considering 16 mm. films over a 60-year period.[12]

While the trend in films and filmstrips is unmistakably toward a greater use, because of the changing relationships between motion picture films, educational television, and radio, it is difficult to predict what form this use will take. With the growth of school and library facilities for viewing, projecting, and listening to live and taped programs, collections of motion pictures, kinescopes, and tapes, or whatever the future equivalent may be, will very probably be considered routine resources. Some public and special libraries have already developed collections. Educational television has been developing for over a decade, and with such experiments as that at Hagerstown, Maryland, and most recently the Midwest Program on Airborne Television Instruction at Purdue,[13] along with the extensive use of closed-circuit television in medical and other fields, this medium seems destined to play an even more important role. But the extent and nature of the role is still under examination, especially in schools.[14]

The future of these media is even more unpredictable because of technological changes that are raising unanswerable questions: whether or not video tape will replace kinescopes, what effect this will have upon present motion pictures and upon the possibilities of 8 mm. film, to what extent centralization of projection is possible, what the full impact of transistor development will be; these are the imponderables.

Certainly as school and college populations increase, and as teachers become more scarce, the pressure to utilize all possible media will become greater. Librarians will be left behind, as many were during the development of motion pictures, if they fail to cooperate with the specialists in taking full advantage of this new service. It is not inconceivable that television will become an integral part of library reference services not only in the facsimile transmission of information but also in the consultation of catalogs and other sources at remote points when and if certain economic and technical problems can be solved.

Other audio-visual materials could be discussed if space permitted. Teaching machines especially would lend themselves to interesting speculation,[15-17] but enough has been said to indicate that any precise predictions of the effect demographic change will have upon audio-visual materials would be no more than speculation. All that can be done is to apply demographic data to local situations where the trends are fairly obvious and where information on audio-visual expenditures is available. This technique has been used for certain materials in the past, and there is no reason that it could not be applied with projected demographic data to materials that are not likely to undergo radical transformations. A more general approach could be made with types of libraries. Figures for audio-visual stocks in public libraries and in libraries in institutions of higher learning are available for earlier years and presumably will be issued again by the Office of Education in its Biennial Survey. Correlations between audio-visual holdings in the libraries reporting to the Office of Education and the users now served by these libraries can be found and projections made in the light of the Hauser-Taitel tables. Figures for school libraries are also available,[18] and could be similarly projected in local situations. Additional advice on planning budgets for school libraries is found in Rufsvold's *Audio-Visual School Library Service* [19] and other professional writings.[20-22] Further surveys will be necessary to secure comparable and current figures for all types of libraries.

This procedure may be dangerous, however, if it assumes that present holdings are adequate. Standards for audio-visual materials in libraries, insofar as they exist, are far from optimum. One example may be seen in the recommendations by the Audio-Visual Commission on Public Information.[23] It is to be hoped that standards will improve and will be observed and that technological changes will make it possible to provide more material per user.

Although generalizations are not very helpful to planners, particularly in budgetary matters, some conclusions from the foregoing discussion and from other data that could not be included here may be useful as broad guidelines for the next two decades. During this period it seems likely that we will see the following developments and needs:

1. Greater production of audio-visual materials for educational and recreational use. The audio-visual industry has doubled in the 1950–1960 period; it is predicted [24] that there will have been another doubling by the end of 1962! Even though this dramatic increase does not materialize so rapidly, it is obvious that demographic changes will strongly influence production. In addition, there are social, legislative, and cultural influences at work that are bound to have a great impact in this field. The new Educational Media Program under the National Defense Education Act is one example of the stimulus now being given to audio-visual materials.

2. An even more urgent need for trained personnel to handle the greater volume and variety of audio-visual materials. Training in the technical aspects of handling audio-visual materials will be necessary, of course, but far more important will be the need for imagination, initiative, and practical planning in this field. Whether or not

librarians will take the leadership in meeting new demands will depend upon what the library schools accomplish in the next few years. There is much to be done in carrying out the recommendations Lieberman made six years ago,[25] and even more must be done to meet the challenges presented by new forms and new combinations of forms. This problem is vigorously stated in the mandates Stone issues to school librarians (and others) in his recent survey of the crisis in education.[26] It should not be assumed, however, that librarians are not active along this front. Current examples of their interest in the problem may be seen in the recent Conference on Audio-Visual Services and the School Library Program sponsored by the Columbia University School of Library Service and Teachers' College, as well as in the proposed Institute on the Future of Library Education described by H. Lancour in his Preface to this series of articles in the preceding issue of *Library Trends*.

3. More intensive studies of needs for audio-visual materials: their usefulness, effectiveness, and relationship to the requirements of teaching and library services.

4. Expansion of technological research and development to make possible greater centralization of service, greater simplicity in use, and lower costs; in other words, automation to permit a greater degree of use through self-service and through mass service.

5. Greater coordination of the various audio-visual forms with one another and with printed materials through more intensive programming and through expansion of "educational" (rather than textbook) publishing.[27]

6. Development of more systematic bibliographic coverage and methods of organizing audio-visual materials for use.[28]

While some of the foregoing predictions may be wishful thinking, it is more than likely that demographic pressures will force us to carry through on many of these hopes and finally bring us the amenities of the space age so inimitably set forth by the cartoonist Saul Steinberg in his "communicenter" and related sketches.[29]

References

1. Kinder, J. S.: *Audio-Visual Materials and Techniques*. 2d ed., New York, American Book Co., 1959, pp. 10-11.

2. Quinly, W. J.: Audio-Visual Materials in the Library. *Library Trends*, 5:294, Oct. 1956.

3. Bennett, F.: Audio-Visual Services in Colleges and Universities in the

United States. Report of a Survey by the ACRL Committee on Audio-Visual Work. *College and Research Libraries*, 16:11-19, Jan. 1955.

4. Hauser, P. M., and Taitel, M.: Population Trends—Prologue to Library Development. *Library Trends*, 10:58-59, July 1961.

5. Thompson, Elizabeth W.: A Report from 100 Libraries on Current Practices Regarding Records in Libraries. *Library Journal*, 85:4516-4517, Dec. 15, 1960.

6. Davis, C. K.: Record Collections, 1960; Lj's Survey of Fact and Opinion. *Library Journal*, 85:3375-3380, Oct. 1, 1960.

7. Hall, D.: Prospects in Taped Sound. *New York Times*, Sept. 4, 1960, Sec. 2, p. 13.

8. Colby, E. E.: Sound Recordings in the Music Library: With Special Reference to Record Archives. *Library Trends*, 8:556-565, April 1960.

9. Pickett, A. G., and Lemcoe, M. M.: *Preservation and Storage of Sound Recordings*. Washington, D.C., Library of Congress, 1959.

10. Davison, G. H.: Microcards and Microfiches; History and Possibilities. *Library Association Record*, 63:69-78, March 1961.

11. Flory, J., and Hope, T. W.: Scope and Nature of Nontheatrical Films in the United States. *Journal of the Society of Motion Picture and Television Engineers*, 68:387-392, June 1959.

12. Film Council of America: *Sixty Years of 16 mm. Film, 1923-1983*. Evanston, Ill., Film Council of America, 1954. See especially p. 13.

13. Fusco, G. C.: Technology in the Classroom. *School Life*, 42:20, March 1960.

14. Schramm, W. L. *et al.*: *Television in the Lives of Our Children*. Stanford, Calif., Stanford University Press, 1961.

15. Lumsdaine, A. A., and Glaser, R., eds.: *Teaching Machines and Programmed Learning; a Source Book*. Washington, D.C., National Education Association, 1960.

16. Waller, T.: Teaching Machines; Implications for the Librarian. *Library Journal*, 86: 1654-1656, April 15, 1961.

17. Stein, J. W.: Machines That Teach Better than Books? *College and Research Libraries*, 22:195-198, May 1961.

18. National Education Association: *Research Bulletin*, 33:102-108, 118-120, Oct. 1955. See especially p. 107.

19. Rufsvold, Margaret: *Audio-Visual School Library Service*. Chicago, American Library Association, 1949. See especially Chapter 5 for charts on different kinds of schools and for the bibliography.

20. For example: Strohbehn, E. F.: A Design for an Audio-Visual Budget. *Nation's Schools*, 53:94-102, March 1954.

21. Schooling, H. W.: The Audio-Visual Education Budget. *Elementary School Journal*, 57:244, Feb. 1957.

22. Erickson, C. W. H.: *Administering Audio-Visual Services*, New York, Macmillan, 1959, pp. 322-356.

23. Schuller, C. F.: Minimum Standards for A-V Budget. *Nation's Schools*, 59:100-104, April 1957.

24. Kirtley, W. G.: The Challenge of the Sixties. *Educational Screen and Audiovisual Guide*, pp. 409-410, Aug. 1960.

25. Lieberman, I. *Audio-Visual Instruction in Library Education.* New York, Columbia University School of Library Service, 1955, pp. 121-130.

26. Stone, C. W.: The Crisis in Education—a Mandate for Librarians. *ALA Bulletin,* 55:122-128, Feb. 1961. (This issue includes several other articles of great interest in the audio-visual field.)

27. Booher, E. E.: Books and Their Market Twenty-Five Years from Now. *Publishers' Weekly,* 179:20-24, March 6, 1961.

28. Rufsvold, Margaret, and Guss, Carolyn: *Proceedings of Work Conference on Bibliographic Control of Newer Educational Media Convened at Indiana University, October 5-7, 1960, under the Sponsorship of the U.S. Office of Education.* Bloomington, Ind., Indiana University, 1960.

29. Mitchell, M. B.: A Forward Look at Communications. *Britannica Book of the Year.* Chicago, Encyclopedia Britannica, Inc., 1958, pp. 49-64 (and especially p. 54) of the Feature Article Section.

◇◇

Governmental Action For Library Development

DAVID H. CLIFT
AND
GERMAINE KRETTEK

THE NATION'S LIBRARY SERVICE is clearly in need of bold and imaginative planning and action on an unprecedented scale. Two recurring themes run like a thread through all of the preceding papers in this issue—a thread that is often bright with the promise of opportunity and often somber with the realization of obstacles.

Experts in many areas of librarianship have, in this issue, examined the country's library service of today and predicted what it must be in 1980. They have looked at needs, problems, and opportunities and they have, in many instances, suggested ways in which the needs and problems can be met and the opportunities realized.

The matters they have dealt with require wide public and professional recognition if library service is to progress so that it can meet the demands of the society it will be serving in 1980.

Many roadblocks stand between our library service of today and the attainment of nationwide quality and quantity library service by 1980. The authors suggest a variety of areas for action. These include research within and outside the library profession—to identify problems and suggest solutions; a broad educational program to make the public aware of the advantages of superior library service; recruiting to the profession—to produce more librarians; improved library education—to produce better librarians; cooperation among libraries—to make resources go farther; development of the state library agency; metropolitan area library development; equalization of library service; the provision of more books and other library materials; the

David H. Clift is Executive Director, and Germaine Krettek is Director of the Washington Office, American Library Association.

development of a flexibility in library service equal to the requirements of a mobile population. Changes are inevitable, for without change there can be no progress.

As one looks at the country as a whole in terms of the changes which appear inevitable in the years ahead, it becomes obvious from the observations of the writers in this issue that the demands upon all libraries will be insistent, complex, and of such magnitude that library leadership must be positive, dynamic, and informed, and that comprehensive consultative assistance will be essential.

There is surely no single means open to librarians, educators, and citizens for the solution of the problems. The steps advocated by the authors in this issue cannot be taken singly and in comfortable and comforting order. Time—and need—will not allow this. History must be hurried up and the steps must be taken together on many fronts.

This paper will deal with one of those fronts to which many of the authors referred—federal and state legislation.

Howard points out that the federal government has been undergoing almost revolutionary changes in its role in the life of the American people. "The role of the federal government seems destined," he believes, "to be one of greater interest in the general welfare of the people, of great social programs and great scientific research." This evident greater interest is beginning to include a concern for library service, as witnessed by the enthusiasm with which Congress has followed the development and success of the program made possible by the Library Services Act.

Miss Thornton remarks upon the concern now being shown by the federal government, through federal aid, in higher education. Although the library has not yet had the kind of attention required by its importance to higher education, the developing trend of aid to these institutions seems certain to strengthen library service. Miss Graham sees federal support for public education aiding school libraries.

Henderson, after noting that library service meeting professional standards must be available to poor and wealthy communities alike, adds that "Equalization will have to be provided through state and federal aid in the interests of a high level, area-wide library service."

Greenaway states that "development of metropolitan and regional services will require the combined physical efforts of local, state, and federal government."

Brahm makes clear the strategic position of the state library agency and the heavier role it will play in the years ahead. He cites many reasons for this, including the important fact that the state's financial resources exceed those of local government.

Federal legislation in many areas thus will become increasingly important as national resources are required to help meet national requirements. As the country's need for libraries and their services gains recognition, more realistic financing will become imperative. Resources in depth, a wide range of more highly developed services, modern buildings and equipment, and sufficient personnel, both professional and nonprofessional, will be required to such a degree that funds must be provided in rapidly increasing amounts at every level of government.

Problems involved in financing education—and we consider libraries, public as well as school and college, as a basic part of the total education program—are closely related to the fact that our population has grown more rapidly than the tax base.

In the early days of our history, real property accounted for 75 per cent of our wealth; today, real property accounts for only 25 per cent.[1] Thus at the present time, property tax represents only a small part of our total wealth. Yet local governments still rely primarily upon real property for their tax base, especially for schools and public libraries. It thus becomes clear that in order to provide the funds needed for adequate library support, new sources of revenue must be found in addition to the property tax. Greater flexibility in means of support must be obtained to achieve fiscally sound units capable of providing an effective library program.

At the state level many changes will have to be made in existing library laws to give legal authority to the developments already projected in terms of larger units of service, coordination and cooperation, expanded programs, and numbers of professional and other personnel, all of which require substantially increased appropriations.

To obtain current information on recently enacted state legislation, on plans for the next legislative sessions, and on long-range legislative requirements for library development, a questionnaire was prepared in May 1961 and distributed to the 50 state library agencies. Thirty-seven replies were received, indicating that many of the problems of institutions of higher education, school libraries, and hospital and institution libraries do not necessarily require legislation for their solution, but are primarily matters of institution and agency policies which involve budgeting approval, appropriations, standards, and regulations.

In the sessions during the first half of 1961, fourteen states (Colorado, Massachusetts, Michigan, Minnesota, Montana, Nevada, New Mexico, Ohio, Oregon, Pennsylvania, Tennessee, Washington, West Virginia, and Wyoming) reported passage of laws to clarify, amend, or codify existing library laws; 4 states (Colorado, Florida, Massachusetts, and Pennsylvania) passed grants-in-aid legislation. Other successful state legislation in 15 states related to authorization for state library buildings, establishment or expansion of cooperative services, enabling legislation, services to state institutions, certification of librarians, scholarship and training programs, and increased appropriations to meet the standards. Similar kinds of legislation are planned to be introduced when state legislatures next meet, with emphasis continuing upon revision of laws (1) to permit the establishment, improvement or extension of library services into larger units (county, multi-county, regional, and interstate); (2) to encourage greater coordination and cooperation; (3) to establish or increase state grants to realistic levels or remove financing limitations of various kinds. At the present time a total of 27 states out of the 50 have cash grant-in-aid programs to public libraries and three additional states have state grant-in-aid programs other than cash. State aid programs in 23 states are badly needed.

There is general agreement that for the next 10 to 20 years this legislative trend will continue. Legislation to permit interstate agreements as well as larger units within a state is contemplated by five of the states reporting on future legislative plans. There is recognition by several states of the desirability of developing legislation to clarify state library functions and unify state library services into a single agency. A number of states stress the need to strengthen facilities and improve service in libraries at all levels and in all kinds by providing intercooperation of public, school, college and university, and special libraries and by coordination of reference and research facilities.

It is encouraging for the future of library service that in the majority of the states, librarians and trustees are facing up to the realities of library service as it is today, are assessing in depth the needs of the next decade, and are planning the necessary steps to achieve quality service for all of our citizens. Most of the state legislative planning is being done through state library associations which represent the various types of libraries in the state.

To assist the states and the multiplicity of libraries within them to attain their goals and provide the level of library service outlined in the foregoing chapters, federal legislation must also be developed. At the present time the nationwide gaps are shocking and, considering the dimensions of the inevitable demands of the future, will become increasingly greater unless within the next few years sizable national assistance is secured to back up local and state support.

A broad and far-reaching plan taking into account the fiscal responsibilities of all levels of government would seem a first step. The appointment by the President of the United States of a National Commission for Libraries should be sought to survey adequately the existing library situation, to study the needs of the future, and to outline possible solutions.

Until an authoritative study is made on a national scale, legislative plans will have to be based upon what information is available in relation to the standards developed to date. Study of "Libraries in the Sixties; ALA Goals for Action," presented in the introduction to the July 1961 issue, makes clear the current lack in personnel, books and other materials, and operating expenditures for school, college and university, and public libraries. Unfortunately adequate statistics and standards for state libraries, hospital and institution libraries, and the special libraries which also are part of the national library resources have not been developed at the present time although the needs of these libraries are equally great and must likewise be considered and met. Lack of these and other essential statistics emphasizes the need for the gathering and interpreting by the federal government of additional nationwide data on libraries. This gap in published data is a source of concern to many libraries as shown in a recent compilation of sources of library statistics.[2] A solution is being sought by the Statistics Coordinating Committee of the Library Administration Division of the American Library Association.[3]

The increased responsibilities of the Library Services Branch in assisting in the expanding library programs of the nation should also be recognized and additional staff and resources provided. Increased liaison between the Department of Health, Education, and Welfare, the Office of Education, and professional library associations would help to bring about this essential development. Sufficient information may be lacking in many areas, but there is unanimity of opinion among the contributors that the greatest single need now and in the foreseeable future is personnel. This is borne out by a recent statement of the Bureau of Labor Statistics that "By 1970, as many as 80,000 trained librarians may be needed." [4] This is almost twice the present number of full-time professional librarians, is well under the number called for by the standards for today's needs, and less than a third of the number that is estimated to be needed by 1980. And only once in 20 years have more than 2000 students graduated from our library schools in any one year.

Facing these figures and their implications realistically will take courage and untrammelled vision by every segment of the profession, but especially library administrators and their governing authorities, library educators, and all the national library associations. An aggressive, imaginative, and continuing recruitment program is essential, but it must be backed up by a number of elements. Professional responsibilities must be clearly defined and adhered to, status and working conditions of both professional and nonprofessional staff members improved, and salaries established and maintained at levels requisite to obtain and retain competent personnel. There must be a very considerable increase in scholarship, fellowship, and in-service training programs at all levels of government. At the present time 16 States are offering about 75 scholarships under the Library Services Act. Some graduate fellowships are available under the National Defense Education Act. Other grant and loan programs under various auspices are also available. The total number, however, is woefully inadequate in relation to the need. In an effort to supplement these opportunities, it is recommended that a federal scholarship, fellowship, and in-service training program be planned to provide the professional personnel needed to extend and develop library service across the nation. For example, a grant of $1 million per year to institutions of higher education for the training of master's degree students would provide 500 scholarships of $2000 each. Such a program should necessarily have two parts. Additional grants should also be available for fellowships to increase the number and improve the quality of the teaching staff in library schools. Fewer than 20 per cent of those currently teaching in library schools have doctorates in library science. Only 129 doctorates were awarded by library schools in the 25 years between 1939–1959. [5]

Introduced in the first session of the 87th Congress is the Academic Facilities and Scholarship Act (H.R.7215) which would authorize grants and loans for building academic facilities, including libraries, and provide an estimated 40,000 undergraduate scholarship grants. [6] Such grants will add to the pool of college graduates who may be recruited for professional library schools.

[278]

Governmental Action for Library Development

On July 31, 1961, the Senate Committee on Labor and Public Welfare reported out a bill, S.2345 (Report No. 652) to extend and improve the National Defense Education Act of 1958, which includes a new Title X authorizing $30,000,000 for school library resources and $7,500,000 for training ($5 million for fiscal 1962) and $10 million for college and university library materials annually for a four-year period. The text of S.2345 is appended. Part B of the proposed title would authorize contracts with institutions of higher education for the operation of library training institutes. The enactment of this legislation could do much to relieve the current critical shortage of trained school librarians and supervisory personnel.

Part A of the new Title X would make available to state educational agencies grants for the acquisition of library materials and equipment and would authorize the establishment and/or improvement of state and local school library supervisory services.

Part C is essentially the proposal developed by the Association of College and Research Libraries (A.L.A.) of matching grants-in-aid to college and university libraries for the purchase of books, periodicals and related materials, and the necessary binding.

This recognition by the Senate Committee on Labor and Public Welfare of the importance of libraries in education is heartening. It is unfortunate, however, that complicating and divisive issues have made the enactment of such a substantive educational measure unlikely this year.

Another bill introduced aimed at improving the quality of education is S.2063 "to establish a President's Advisory Council on Education." Steps should be taken to insure the appointment of a librarian of stature on this Council if it is created. The library profession has not always been adequately represented on such national commissions.

In the public library field a number of bills have been introduced this year which are significant because their adoption would indicate further understanding by Congress of the basic educational role of tax-supported libraries which serve the general public. These measures relate to federal surplus property distribution (S.2119)[7] and income tax regulations on charitable gifts (H.R.7481).[8]

None of these federal measures, however, will provide the assistance required to alleviate the many serious gaps and deficiencies which already exist in public library service and which will mount in light of projected demands.

A beginning has been made in relation to the library deficiencies in places with populations of 10,000 or less through the Library Services Act of 1956 (Public Law 84-597). The legislation has been so successful in showing how the federal government can cooperate with state and local governments in remedying a serious lack that Congress took steps for its continuance in 1960 (Public Law 86-679). Even so, twenty-five million Americans are still without direct access to local public library service and countless additional millions are receiving only token service. The increasing growth of the metropolitan and fringe areas is presenting urgent questions which go beyond city limits and overlap state borders. These problems must be resolved.

A possible solution might be found through an amendment to the present Library Services Act to eliminate the population ceiling. The authorization would need to be increased correspondingly.

Quality library service can be made available to all only if a fair share formula of financial assistance is effected. A formula suggested by past study calls for 60 per cent local, 25 per cent state, and 15 per cent federal funds for public library purposes. On a $3.50-$4.00 per capita basis as suggested for library systems, this would entail an annual expenditure of some $630 million instead of the present $260 million.

Special legislation may be needed to help solve the problems of large metropolitan regions, which often cross state lines. A bill designed to facilitate agreements between states was introduced in both House and Senate early in 1961. S.464, granting the consent of Congress to interstate compacts between two or more states "for the development or operation of library facilities and services," was passed by the Senate on June 29, 1961. The House Judiciary Committee, however, refuses to grant such consent in advance and insists that specific compacts or agreements be drafted and submitted for approval.

A bill providing for cooperation among libraries in a state or region in connection with government documents distributed through the depository system is also pending in the 87th Congress. H.R.8141, "to revise the laws relating to depository libraries," was passed by the House on August 22, 1961. A companion measure (S.2029) has been introduced in the Senate.

In the documentation field, which is going to have a heavy impact upon the whole American cultural scene as well as upon library development, it seems essential that there be closer planning and cooperation between librarians and documentalists.

The problems involved in the organization, processing, and retrieval of information in the fields of science and technology have been considered in a number of legislative proposals in recent years, and it is probable that specific legislation in this area will be developed in the future. In 1960 a study of federal and nonfederal scientific information processing and retrieval programs was prepared by the staff of the Senate Committee on Government Operations.[9]

Various aspects of library service are included in a number of other measures currently under consideration by the Congress; i.e. the use of federal funds for the construction of library buildings as well as other community facilities; special postal legislation; the project for acquisition of foreign library materials under Public Law 480; legislation to implement the so called "Florence Agreement." Many of the appropriations bills include substantial items for programs and projects of the federal libraries.

A further sharing of tax support at the federal level together with greatly increased state and local support seems inevitable if we are to attain the goal in this century of providing all our citizens with library service of quality in proportion to their needs.

It is perhaps significant of Congress' recognition of the role of the federal government in helping to support the library needs of the future that it recently appropriated $70,000 so that the U.S. Office of Education "may participate in the forthcoming Century 21 Exposition in Seattle, Wash., in order to exhibit modern library services and design."[10] Based upon the premise that the patron, the man of the future, will be longer lived, with more leisure time, higher income, better education, wider travel experience, more varied interests, a stronger orientation toward international developments, and a greater awareness of new techniques and scientific advancements, Library 21 will act as a guidepost to dynamic library planning. Future legislation can take its cue from this bold and at the same time realistic approach to the library of tomorrow.

References

1. U.S. Senate. 87th Congress, 1st Session. Committee on Labor and Public Welfare: Senate Document No. 41. *Proposed Federal Aid for Education.* Washington, U.S. Government Printing Office, 1961, p. 16.

2. U.S. Department of Health, Education, and Welfare: *Statistics of Libraries.* J. C. Rather and N. M. Cohen, comp. Washington, D.C., U.S. Government Printing Office, 1961.

3. Schick, F. L.: Research Statistics Program of the Library Services Branch. *ALA Bulletin,* 55:409-412, May 1961.

4. U.S. Department of Labor. Women's Bureau: *Employment Outlook for Librarians.* Washington, D.C., U.S. Government Printing Office, 1961, p. 6. Preliminary version of statement prepared by the Women's Bureau for the Bureau of Labor Statistics to be published in the 1961 edition of the *Occupational Outlook Handbook.*

5. Danton, J. P.: Doctoral Study in Librarianship in the United States. *College and Research Libraries,* 20:435-453, Nov. 1959.

6. U.S. 87th Congress, 1st Session: H.R.7215. A bill "to authorize assistance to public and other nonprofit institutions of higher education in financing the construction, rehabilitation, or improvement of needed academic facilities, and to authorize fellowship grants for undergraduate study in such institutions."

7. U.S. 87th Congress, 1st Session: S.2119. A bill "to amend the Federal Property and Administrative Services Act of 1949 so as to permit donations of surplus property to schools for the mentally retarded, schools for the physically handicapped, educational television stations, and public libraries."

8. U.S. 87th Congress, 1st Session: H.R.7481. A bill "to amend Section 170 (b)(1) of the Internal Revenue Code."

9. U.S. 86th Congress, 2nd Session: Senate Document No. 113. *Documentation, Indexing and Retrieval of Scientific Information.* Washington, D.C., U.S. Government Printing Office, 1960.

10. U.S. Senate, 87th Congress, 1st Session. Committee on Appropriations: Senate Report No. 618, p. 14. *Departments of Labor, and Health, Education, and Welfare, and Related Agencies Appropriations Bill,* 1962. Washington, D.C., U.S. Government Printing Office, 1961.

Appendix[1]

TITLE X—STRENGTHENING SCHOOL LIBRARY RESOURCES NEEDED FOR TEACHING AND LEARNING

Part A—Library Programs in Public Elementary and Secondary Schools

Appropriations Authorized

Sec. 101. *There are hereby authorized to be appropriated $30,000,000 for the fiscal year ending June 30, 1962, and for each of the three succeeding fiscal years, for making grants to State educational agencies under this part to assist them in establishing and maintaining programs of library service in public elementary and secondary schools, which will carry out the objectives of this Act as stated in section 101.*

Allotments to States

Sec. 1002. *From the sums appropriated pursuant to section 1001 for any fiscal year the Commissioner shall reserve such amount, but not in excess of 1.6 per centum thereof, as he may determine for allotment as provided in section 1108. From the remainder of such sums the Commissioner shall allot to each State an amount which bears the same ratio to the amount of such remainder as the school-age population of such State bears to the school-age population of all of the States. The amount allotted to any State under the preceding sentence for any fiscal year which is less than, $50,000 shall be increased to, $50,000, the total of increases thereby required being derived by proportionately reducing the amount allotted to each of the remaining States under the preceding sentence, but with such adjustments as may be necessary to prevent the allotment of any such remaining State from being thereby reduced to less than, $50,000.*

State Plans

Sec. 1003. *(a) Any State which desires to receive payments under*

---

[1] The text is reprinted verbatim from U.S. 87th Congress, 1st Session: *National Defense Education Act Amendment of 1961.* Senate Report No. 652. Washington, D.C., U.S. Government Printing Office, 1961, pp. 102-104.

this part shall submit to the Commissioner, through its State educational agency, a State plan which meets the requirements of section 1104(a) and—

(1) sets forth a program of library service in public elementary and secondary schools to meet the library needs of all students and to provide the facilities and resources for challenging education for superior students under which funds paid to the State from its allotment under section 1002 will be expended solely for projects approved by the State educational agency for (A) acquisition of library materials (printed and audiovisual) and library equipment which are suitable for use in providing resources for teaching and learning and which will carry out the objectives of this Act as stated in section 101, (B) the establishment or improvement of local school library supervisory services, (C) minor remodeling of existing space used for library quarters, (D) the establishment or improvement of library supervisory services within the State educational agency, and (E) administration of the State plan;

(2) provides for the establishment of State standards for public elementary and secondary school libraries;

(3) sets forth principles for determining the priority of such projects in the State for assistance under this part and provides for undertaking such projects, insofar as financial resources available therefor make possible, in the order determined by the application of such principles; and

(4) provides an opportunity for a hearing before the State educational agency to any applicant for a project under this part.

(b) The Commissioner shall approve any State plan and any modification thereof which complies with the provisions of subsection (a).

Payments to States

Sec. 1004. Payments under this part shall be made to those State educational agencies which administer plans approved under section 1003. For the fiscal year ending June 30, 1962, such payments shall equal the amount expended in carrying out the State plan, and for the fiscal year ending June 30, 1963, and for each of the two succeeding fiscal years, such payments shall equal one-half of the amount so expended; except that no State educational agency shall receive payment under this part for any fiscal year in excess of that State's allotment for that fiscal year as determined under section 1002.

Part B—Library Training Institutes
Appropriations Authorized

Sec. 1011. There are hereby authorized to be appropriated

Appendix

$5,000,000 for the fiscal year ending June 30, 1962, and $7,500,000 for each of the three succeeding fiscal years, to enable the Commissioner to arrange, by contracts with institutions of higher education, for the operation by them of short-term or regular session institutes for the provisions of training to improve the qualifications of school librarians, or individuals preparing to engage in school library work. Each individual, engaged, or preparing to engage in library work in a public or private nonprofit elementary or secondary school, who attends an institute operated under the provisions of this part shall be eligible (after application therefor) to receive a stipend at the rate of $75 per week for the period of his attendance at such institute, and each such individual with one or more dependents shall receive an additional stipend at the rate of $15 per week for each such dependent for the period of such attendance.

Part C—Library Grants to Institutions of Higher Education

Appropriations Authorized

Sec. 1021. There are hereby authorized to be appropriated $10,000,000 for the fiscal year ending June 30, 1962, and for each of the three succeeding fiscal years, to enable the Commissioner to make grants to institutions of higher education to assist and encourage such institutions in the acquisition for library purposes of books (not including textbooks, periodicals, documents, and other related materials (including necessary binding).

Grant Conditions

Sec. 1022. From the sums appropriated pursuant to section 1021 for any fiscal year, the Commissioner may, upon application therefor, make a grant for the purposes set forth in such section to any institution of higher education—

(1) in an amount not exceeding 25 per centum of the amount expended by such institution during the fiscal year ending June 30, 1961, for books, periodicals, documents, and other related materials (including necessary binding) for library purposes, or not less than—
    (A) $1,000 if it provides a two-year educational program which is acceptable for full credit toward a bachelor's degree;
    (B) $2,500 if it provides an educational program for which it awards a bachelor's degree or a more advanced degree; or
    (C) $5,000 if it provides an educational program for which it awards both bachelors' and advanced degrees; and

[285]

(2) if such institution furnishes proof satisfactory to the Commissioner—

(i) that it will expend, during the fiscal year for which the grant is requested, for all library purposes an amount not less than the amount it expended for such purposes during the fiscal year ending June 30, 1961,

(ii) that it will expend, during the fiscal year for which the grant is requested, for library purposes for books, periodicals, documents, and other related materials (including necessary binding) an amount not less than the amount it expended for such materials during the fiscal year ending June 30, 1961, and

(iii) that it will expend for library purposes during the fiscal year for which the grant is requested, in addition to the amount required under clauses (i) and (ii) above, an amount not less than the amount of such grant, and that at least 50 per centum of such expenditure will be for library purposes for books, periodicals, documents, and other related materials (including necessary binding).

Limitation

Sec. 1023. No grant shall be made under this part for books, periodicals, documents, or other related materials to be used primarily in connection with any part of the program of a divinity school, theological seminary, or other institution, or a department or branch of an institution, whose program is for the education of students to prepare them to become ministers of religion or to enter upon some other religious vocation.